From Timbuktu to Katrina:
Readings in
African American History

Volume II

QUINTARD TAYLOR

The Scott and Dorothy Bullitt Professor of American History
University of Washington

THOMSON

WADSWORTH

Australia • Brazil • Canada • Mexico • Singapore • Spain • United Kingdom • United States

From Timbuktu to Katrina: Readings in African American History, Volume II
Quintard Taylor

Publisher: *Clark Baxter*
Acquisitions Editor: *Ashley Dodge*
Assistant Editor: *Kristen Judy Tatroe*
Editorial Assistant: *Ashley Spicer*
Assoc. Development Project Manager: *Lee McCracken*
Marketing Manager: *Janise Fry*
Marketing Assistant: *Kathleen Tosiello*
Marketing Communications Manager: *Tami Strang*
Content Project Manager: *Sarah Sherman*
Sr. Art Director: *Cate Rickard Barr*

Sr. Print Buyer: *Judy Inouye*
Sr. Rights Acquisition Account Manager, Text:
   Margaret Chamberlain-Gaston
Sr. Permissions Account Manager, Images: *Sheri Blaney*
Production Service: *Integra Software Services Pvt. Ltd*
Printer: *West Group*
Cover Designer: *Lisa Devenish*
Cover Photos: Top: © Don Cravens/Time & Life
   Pictures/Getty Images; Bottom: © Francis Miller/
   Time & Life Pictures/Getty Images

Library of Congress Control Number: 2007920376

ISBN-10: 0-495-09278-9
ISBN-13: 978-0-495-09278-0

Thomson Higher Education
25 Thomson Place
Boston, MA 02210-1202
USA

For more information about our products,
contact us at:
Thomson Learning Academic Resource Center
1-800-423-0563

For permission to use material from this text or
product, submit a request online at
http://www.thomsonrights.com
Any additional questions about permissions can be
submitted by e-mail to
thomsonrights@thomson.com

Not to know what happened before one was born is to always remain a child.
–Cicero

*I am not ashamed of my grandparents for having been slaves. I am only
ashamed for having at one time been ashamed.*
–Ralph Ellison

*Awful as race prejudice, lawlessness and ignorance are, we can fight time if
we frankly face them and dare name them and tell the truth; but if we
continually dodge and cloud the issue, and say the half truth because the
whole stings and shames; if we do this, we invite catastrophe. Let us then in
all charity but unflinching firmness set our faces against all statesmanship
that looks in such directions.*
–W. E. B. DuBois

Contents

Preface

Documents tell a powerful story. They can assist, clarify, and enhance a narrative account that provides context for events that impact millions of people over centuries. This compilation of readings is designed with that purpose in mind. It is a glimpse into the African American community through the examination of historical documents over five centuries. These documents begin with the medieval West African city of Timbuktu. They suggest that the West African savannah and coastal societies from which the vast majority of fifteenth through nineteenth-century enslaved Africans came were numerous, varied, and complex, both powerful and weak, and that their own historical narratives reflect both the triumphs and tragedies that mark all societies. The second volume concludes with a discussion of the impact of Hurricane Katrina, reminding us that African American history continues to unfold in myriad ways into this twenty-first century.

The number of documents available to tell that story far exceeds the capacity of one or two volumes, of course. Indeed, unlike previous collections of documents that have focused on what historians considered the most significant texts—just determining what is significant often sparks intense debate—this collection includes documents and vignettes spanning the fourteen to twenty-first centuries, covering politics, culture, gender, social life, religion, racial identity, education, social class, sports, music, the environment, medicine, immigration, and even crime. These readings represent an unprecedented attempt to span what historians now recognize as the enormous breadth and range of documents that reflect on African American life in the United States. Many of the selections, such as Dr. Martin Luther King Jr.'s *Letter from a Birmingham Jail,* will be familiar to students of African American history. However, other documents, such as Lucy Parson's 1886 speech *"I Am an Anarchist"* or *African Americans and Environmental*

History: A Manifesto, are included precisely because they rarely gain exposure beyond the gaze of a handful of experts in a particular subfield of African American history. In a few rare instances, I have relied on excerpts from secondary sources that appear as vignettes such as Daniell F. Littlefield, Jr., and Mary Ann Littlefield's "The Beams Family: Free Blacks in Indian Territory," *Journal of Negro History* (January 1976) and Melvin L. Oliver and Thomas M. Shapiro's 1995 book, *Black Wealth/White Wealth: A New Perspective on Racial Inequality,* to provide context for understanding an entire era or series of episodes in a way that documents alone cannot accomplish. These volumes also include cartoons that convey much more than humor; they tellingly reveal tensions and anxieties in society that may not be expressed more directly through the texts. Collectively, however, these sources, primary and secondary, provide, I hope, a broad, rich, diverse, and yet composite portrait of the African American experience.

The readings are arranged chronologically into eight chapters each in volumes I and II. Each chapter has a brief historical introduction of the period and an explanation of the way in which the individual documents help tell the larger story of the chapter and the era. Each document, in turn, is introduced by a short description giving its specific historical context.

The documents were selected on the basis of their ability to explain a small part of the larger narrative of African American history. They are usually printed in this volume in their entirety. Some documents, including many of the speeches, are abridged because of publishing space limitations. However, through an arrangement between the publisher of these volumes, Thomson Wadsworth and TheBlackPast.org website (http://www.TheBlackPast.org), the entire documents can be accessed on the Web at the internet address listed in the document's introduction.

From Timbuktu to Katrina is the consequence of a number of dedicated people's efforts. I want to thank three research assistants, Turkiya Lowe, Susan Bragg, and especially Karla Kelling Sclater, each of whom spent countless hours in research libraries or online locating documents. Both Turkiya and Susan discovered documents that I might have overlooked, while Karla was particularly diligent and dedicated in the final months of volume preparation; in a real sense, this work owes a great deal to their efforts. I also express my appreciation to fellow historians Albert Broussard, *Texas A&M University*; Ronald Coleman, *University of Utah*; Willi Coleman, *University of Vermont*; Kimberley Phillips *College of William and Mary*; Shirley Ann Wilson Moore, *California State University, Sacramento*; Malik Simba, *Fresno State University*; Paul Spickard, *University of California*, Santa Barbara; Joe William Trotter, *Carnegie Mellon University*; Matthew Whitaker, *Arizona State University*; and Noralee Frankel of the American Historical Association.

I am grateful to the staff of various libraries and research facilities, including the Library of Congress; the Bancroft Library at the University of California, Berkeley; the University of California at San Diego Libraries; the Bowdoin College Library; the Lutheran Theological Seminary at Gettysburg Library; the University of Oregon Libraries; the Kansas Historical Society; the Schomburg Center for Research in Black Culture at the New York Public Library; and the

Moorland-Spingarn Research Center at Howard University. I am especially appreciative of the efforts of Robert Fikes, Reference Librarian at San Diego State University; Patrick Lemelle at the Institute of Texan Cultures at the University of Texas, San Antonio; Danielle Kovacs, Curator of Manuscripts, Special Collections, and University Archives at the W.E.B. DuBois Library, University of Massachusetts; Patricia Rodeman, Suzzallo Circulation, the University of Washington Libraries; and the supportive staff of the Interlibrary Loan Library at the University of Washington. Also, I gratefully acknowledge the crucial assistance of my department head, John Findlay, who always seemed to find resources to support this project.

I want to thank Ashley Dodge for recognizing this project as a potentially useful addition to the growing body of literature on African American history. Additionally, I want to acknowledge my gratitude to Sarah Sherman, Menaka Gupta and Margaret Chamberlain-Gaston for guiding the manuscripts through the publication process. I also acknowledge the considerable Internet research skills my daughter, Jamila Taylor, brought to this project.

Finally, I am grateful to the patience, support, and wise counsel of Catherine Dever Foster. You were a constant source of inspiration, encouragement, and love throughout this entire project.

About the Author

QUINTARD TAYLOR, the Scott and Dorothy Bullitt Professor of American History at the University of Washington, is the author of *The Forging of a Black Community: Seattle's Central District from 1870 through the Civil Rights Era* (Seattle: University of Washington Press, 1994) and *In Search of the Racial Frontier: African Americans in the American West, 1528–1990* (New York, W.W. Norton, 1998). He is the co-editor with Lawrence B. de Graaf and Kevin Mulroy of *Seeking El Dorado: African Americans in California* (Seattle: University of Washington Press, 2001) and with Shirley Ann Wilson Moore of *African American Women Confront the West, 1600–2000* (Norman: University of Oklahoma Press, 2003). Taylor is the author of over forty articles. His work on African American Western History, African American, African, Afro-Brazilian, and comparative ethnic history has appeared in the *Western Historical Quarterly*, *Pacific Historical Review*, *Oregon Historical Quarterly*, *The Annals of the American Academy of Political and Social Science*, *Journal of Negro History*, *Arizona and the West*, *Western Journal of Black Studies*, *Polish-American Studies*, and the *Journal of Ethnic Studies*, among other journals. Taylor has taught at universities in Washington, Oregon, California, and Nigeria over his thirty-five-year career in higher education.

For additional information, please see the Quintard Taylor website, http://faculty.washington.edu/qtaylor/

From Timbuktu to Katrina: Readings in African American History

Volume II

1

Race in a New Century

African Americans entered the twentieth century understandably concerned about their collective future and fate. The tide of segregationist legislation that began in the nineteenth century flowed over into the first decade of the new century. Antiblack violence in the form of lynchings and race riots actually peaked in number and intensity in the second decade of the twentieth century. Yet even in the first years of the century, developments emerged that would challenge this pessimistic view of the future. A small, dedicated minority of African American leaders vowed to continue to fight for full civil rights. As the various vignettes in this chapter will show, at the moment when racial oppression seemed greatest, changes were already underway that would challenge its ability to control black life.

The first vignette, **George H. White's Farewell Address to Congress**, makes that point when North Carolina Congressman White details the political manipulation and intimidation that made his the lone black voice in the U.S. Congress at the beginning of the twentieth century but who confidently and correctly predicted that twentieth-century African Americans would arise "phoenix like" and return representatives to the Halls of Congress. **Black Soldiers on the Filipino Insurrection, 1901** profiles some black military personnel's recognition of the irony of their fighting a war of conquest predicated on assumptions of racial superiority that were often used against them. The vignette **W. E. B. DuBois and the Talented Tenth** argues for responsible, committed race leadership among the best and brightest African Americans. The vignette **The Niagara Movement** describes the attempt to provide that leadership. In **W. E. B. DuBois Writes a Schoolgirl**, we see a poignant attempt to encourage a young girl on the verge of succumbing to despair and failure because of racial discrimination. **Brownsville, 1906** is the announcement of the discharge of an entire regiment of soldiers because of the unlawful actions of a few. **Early Housing Discrimination: A 1911 St. Louis Restrictive Covenant** describes an evolving practice that would arguably have the most pronounced effect on black economic fortunes through the century.

The Crisis: **The First Editorial, 1910** highlights the establishment of the National Association for the Advancement of Colored People (NAACP). The magazine simultaneously rivaled and enhanced its parent organization because of its inspired editing by W. E. B. DuBois and its biting cartoons. Two of those cartoons, **American Logic** and **Woman to the Rescue**, appear in this chapter. The vignette, **The National Urban League** describes the other civil rights organization founded during this period, one devoted to assisting African Americans in their adjustment to urban life.

George H. White's Farewell Address to Congress

In January 1901, at the beginning of a new century, George H. White was ending his term as a congressman from North Carolina's Second Congressional District. Realizing that he was bringing to a close a thirty-two-year period during which nearly forty Southern African Americans sat in Congress, White used the occasion of his farewell address to remind Congress and the nation of the reason for his defeat and the elimination of black representation in the nation's capital. He also predicted that African Americans would return to Congress. His prediction became a reality in 1928, when Oscar DePriest was elected to represent a Chicago congressional district. Part of White's address appears here. To read this speech in its entirety, please visit TheBlackPast.org at http://www.blackpast.org.

I want to enter a plea for the colored man, the colored woman, the colored boy, and the colored girl of this country. I would not thus digress from the question at issue and detain the House in a discussion of the interests of this particular people at this time but for the constant and the persistent efforts of certain gentlemen upon this floor to mold and rivet public sentiment against us as a people and to lose no opportunity to hold up the unfortunate few who commit crimes and depredations and lead lives of infamy and shame, as other races do, as fair specimens of representatives of the entire colored race . . .

In the catalogue of members of Congress in this House perhaps none have been more persistent in their determination to bring the black man into disrepute and . . . show that he was unworthy of the right of citizenship than my colleague from North Carolina, Mr. Kitchin. During the first session of this Congress . . . he labored long and hard to show that the white race was at all times and under all circumstances superior to the Negro by inheritance if not otherwise, and . . . that an illiterate Negro was unfit to participate in making the laws of a sovereign state and the administration and execution of them; but an illiterate white man living by his side, with no more or perhaps not as much property, with no more exalted character, no higher thoughts of civilization, no more knowledge of the handicraft of government, had by birth, because he was white, inherited some peculiar qualification . . .

In the town where this young gentleman was born, at the general election last August for . . . state and county officers, Scotland Neck had a registered white vote of 395, most of whom . . . were Democrats, and a registered colored vote of 534, virtually . . . all of whom were Republicans, and so voted. When the count was announced, however, there were 831 Democrats to 75 Republicans; but in the town of Halifax, same county, the result was much more pronounced. In that

SOURCE: <u>Congressional Record</u>, 56th Congress, 2d sess., vol. 34, pt. 2 (Washington, D.C.: Government Printing Office, 1901), 1635, 1636, 1638.

town the registered Republican vote was 345, and the total registered vote of the township was 539, but when the count was announced it stood 990 Democrats to 41 Republicans, or 492 more Democratic votes counted than were registered votes in the township. Comment here is unnecessary...

It would be unfair, however, for me to leave the inference upon the minds of those who hear me that all of the white people of the State of North Carolina hold views with Mr. Kitchin and think as he does. Thank God there are many noble exceptions to the example he sets, that, too, in the Democratic party; men who have never been afraid that one uneducated, poor, depressed Negro could put to flight and chase into degradation two educated, wealthy, thrifty white men. There never has been, nor ever will be, any Negro domination in that state, and no one knows it any better than the Democratic party. It is a convenient howl, however, often resorted to in order to consummate a diabolical purpose by scaring the weak and gullible whites into support of measures and men suitable to the demagogue...

I trust I will be pardoned for making a passing reference to one more gentleman – Mr. Wilson of South Carolina – who, in the early part of this month, made a speech, some parts of which did great credit to him.... But his purpose was incomplete until he dragged in the Reconstruction days and held up to scorn and ridicule the few ignorant, gullible...Negroes who served in the state legislature of South Carolina over thirty years ago.... These few ignorant men who chanced at that time to hold office are given as a reason why the black man should not be permitted to participate in the affairs of the government which he is forced to pay taxes to support...

If the gentleman to whom I have referred will pardon me, I would like to advance the statement that...what the Negro was thirty-two years ago, is not a proper standard by which the Negro living on the threshold of the twentieth century should be measured. Since that time we have reduced the illiteracy of the race at least 45 percent. We have written and published nearly 500 books. We have nearly 800 newspapers, three of which are dailies. We have now in practice over 2,000 lawyers, and a corresponding number of doctors. We have accumulated over $12,000,000 worth of school property and about $40,000,000 worth of church property. We have about 140,000 farms and homes, valued in the neighborhood of $750,000,000, and personal property valued about $170,000,000. We have raised about $11,000,000 for educational purposes, and the property per-capita for every colored man, woman and child in the United States is estimated at $75. We are operating successfully several banks, commercial enterprises among our people in the South land, including one silk mill and one cotton factory. We have 32,000 teachers in the schools of the country; we have built, with the aid of our friends, about 20,000 churches, and support 7 colleges, 17 academies, 50 high schools, 5 law schools, 5 medical schools and 25 theological seminaries. We have over 600,000 acres of land in the South alone. The cotton produced, mainly by black labor, has increased from 4,669,770 bales in 1860 to 11,235,000 in 1899. All this was done under the most adverse circumstances.

We have done it in the face of lynching, burning at the stake, with the humiliation of "Jim Crow" laws, the disfranchisement of our male citizens, slander and degradation of our women, with the factories closed against us, no Negro permitted to be conductor on the railway cars . . . no Negro permitted to run as engineer on a locomotive, most of the mines closed against us. Labor unions—carpenters, painters, brick masons, machinists, hackmen and those supplying nearly every conceivable avocation for livelihood—have banded themselves together to better their condition, but, with few exceptions, the black face has been left out. The Negroes are seldom employed in our mercantile stores. . . . With all these odds against us, we are forging our way ahead, slowly, perhaps, but surely. . . . You may use our labor for two and a half centuries and then taunt us for our poverty, but let me remind you we will not always remain poor! You may withhold even the knowledge of how to read God's word and . . . then taunt us for our ignorance, but we would remind you that there is plenty of room at the top, and we are climbing . . .!

Mr. Chairman, before concluding my remarks I want to submit a brief recipe for the solution of the so-called "American Negro problem." He asks no special favors, but simply demands that he be given the same chance for existence, for earning a livelihood, for raising himself in the scales of manhood and womanhood, that are accorded to kindred nationalities. Treat him as a man . . . open the doors of industry to him. . . . Help him to overcome his weaknesses, punish the crime-committing class by the courts of the land, measure the standard of the race by its best material, cease to mold prejudicial and unjust public sentiment against him, and . . . he will learn to support . . . and join in with that political party, that institution, whether secular or religious, in every community where he lives, which is destined to do the greatest good for the greatest number. Obliterate race hatred, party prejudice, and help us to achieve nobler ends, greater results and become satisfactory citizens to our brother in white.

This, Mr. Chairman, is perhaps the Negroes' temporary farewell to the American Congress; but . . . phoenix-like he will rise up some day and come again.

Black Soldiers on the Filipino Insurrection, 1901

The following letters are two of many that appeared in the Indianapolis Freeman, *the chief critic among black newspapers of the Spanish American War (1898) and the subsequent campaign against Emilio Aguinaldo and the Filipino insurrectionists (1899–1901). The first letter is from William Simms, who identified himself as a soldier in Bong-a-Bong, Philippines. The second letter is from Pvt. William R. Fulbright, 25*[th] *Infantry, and is dated June 10, 1901.*

SOURCE: Indianapolis Freeman, May 11, 1901, 4; Indianapolis Freeman, August 3, 1901, 1

Simms: I was struck by a question a little boy asked me, which ran about this way – "Why does the American Negro come from America to fight us when we are much friend to him and have not done anything to him? He is all the same as me, and me all the same as you. Why don't you fight those people in America that burn the Negroes, that made a beast of you, that took the child from its mother's side and sold it?"

Fulbright: This struggle on the islands has been naught but a gigantic scheme of robbery and oppression. Many soldiers who came here in poverty to battle for the "stars and stripes" have gone home with gold, diamonds, and other valuables while the natives here who were once good livers [*sic*], are hardly able to keep the wolf from the door. Graves have been entered and searches have been made for riches; churches and cathedrals have been entered and jewelry stolen. The commissary scandal is being thoroughly investigated. . . . The way some of our officers have conducted themselves is enough to cause the worst insurrecto to shudder with fear when he knows the American flag is to wave over his people and that they are to look to the American government for protection. The natives say we have good men for soldiers but drunkards for officers – my lips are closed. The natives equivocally denounce the attitude of our government and claim that its administration is unjust and humiliating. . . . If we are to unfurl our flag on these islands let us make these natives joint heirs in our citizenship. . . . The eyes of the civilized world are upon us and now is the time for action.

W. E. B. DuBois and the Talented Tenth

In response to the rising influence of Booker T. Washington's educational philosophy on black institutions and black thought, W. E. B. DuBois launched a call for the creation of a college-educated elite, a "talented tenth." His argument, reprinted here, appeared, ironically, in a book edited by Washington.

The Negro race, like all races, is going to be saved by its exceptional men. The problem of education, then, among Negroes must first of all deal with the Talented Tenth; it is the problem of developing the Best of this race that they may guide the Mass away from the contamination and death of the Worst, in their own and other races. . . . If we make money the object of man-training, we shall develop money-makers but not necessarily men. . . .

SOURCE: W. E. B. DuBois, "The Talented Tenth," in Booker T. Washington et al., The Negro Problem: A Series of Articles by Representative Negroes of To-Day (New York: J. Pott & Co., 1903), 33–34, 43–44, 45–47, 54, 62.

AMERICAN LOGIC.

THIS MAN is not responsible for THIS MAN even if they do belong to the same race.

THIS MAN is responsible for all that THIS MAN does because they belong to the same race.

SOURCE: The Crisis (New York) 6 (June 1913): 80.

The cartoon "American Logic" serves as a reminder of the impact of the double standard imposed on black people by racial bias.

From the very first it has been the educated and intelligent of the Negro people that have led and elevated the mass....

...Who are to-day guiding the work of the Negro people? The "exceptions" of course. And yet so sure as this Talented Tenth is pointed out, the blind worshippers of the Average cry out in alarm: "These are exceptions, look here at death, disease and crime – these are the happy rule." Of course they are the rule, because a silly nation made them the rule: Because for three long centuries this people lynched Negroes who dared to be brave, raped black women who dared to be virtuous, crushed dark–hued youth who dared to be ambitious, and encouraged and made to flourish servility and lewdness and apathy....

Can the masses of the Negro people be in any possible way more quickly raised than by the effort and example of this aristocracy of talent and character? Never; it is, ever was and ever will be from the top downward that culture filters. The Talented Tenth rises and pulls all that are worth the saving up to their vantage ground. This is the history of human progress....

How then shall the leaders of a struggling people be trained and the hands of the risen few strengthened? There can be but one answer: The best and most capable of their youth must be schooled in the colleges and universities of the land.... All men cannot go to college but some men must.... Out from the normal schools [created after the Civil War] went teachers, and around the normal teachers clustered other teachers to teach the public schools; the college trained in Greek and Latin and mathematics, 2,000 men; and these men trained full 50,000 others in morals and manners, and they in turn taught thrift and the alphabet to nine millions of men, who today hold $300,000,000 of property. . . .

These figures illustrate vividly the function of the college-bred Negro. He is, as he ought to be, the group leader, the man who sets the ideals of the community where he lives, directs its thoughts and heads its social movements. . . .

Can such culture training of group leaders be neglected? Can we afford to ignore it? . . . You have no choice; either you must help furnish this race from within its own ranks with thoughtful men of trained leadership, or you must suffer the evil consequences of a headless misguided rabble.

The Niagara Movement

The Niagara Movement's first general meeting was convened on the Canadian side of Niagara Falls to dramatize its protest against American inequities. Its first address to the nation in July 1905, is printed here.

We believe that (Negro) American citizens should protest emphatically and continually against the curtailment of their political rights. We believe in manhood suffrage: we believe that no man is so good, intelligent or wealthy as to be entrusted wholly with the welfare of his neighbor.

We believe also in protest against the curtailment of our civil rights. All American citizens have the right to equal treatment in places of public entertainment according to their behavior and deserts.

We especially complain against the denial of equal opportunities to us in economic life; in the rural districts of the south this amounts to peonage and virtual slavery; all over the south it tends to crush labor and small business enterprises: and everywhere American prejudice, helped often by iniquitous laws, is making it more difficult for Negro-Americans to earn a decent living.

Common school education should be free to all American children and compulsory. High school training should be adequately provided for all, and college training should be the monopoly of no class or race in any section of our common country. We believe that in defense of its own institutions, the United States should aid common school education, particularly in the south, and we especially recommend concerted agitation to this end. We urge an increase in public high school facilities in the south, where the Negro-Americans are almost wholly without such provisions. We favor well-equipped trade and technical schools for the training of artisans, and the need of adequate and liberal endowment for a few institutions of higher education. We refuse to allow the impression to remain that the Negro-American assents to inferiority,

SOURCE: Gazette (Cleveland), July 22, 1905, 1.

is submissive under oppression and apologetic before insults. Through help-lessness we may submit, but the voice of protest of ten million Americans must never cease to assail the ears of their fellows, so long as America is unjust. We regret that this nation has never seen fit adequately to reward the black soldiers who in its five wars, have defended their country with their blood, and yet have been systematically denied the promotions which their abilities deserve. And we regard as unjust, the exclusion of black boys from the military and navy training schools.

And while we are demanding, and ought to demand, and will continue to demand the rights enumerated above, God forbid that we should ever forget to urge corresponding duties upon our people.

The duty to vote.

The duty to respect the rights of others.

The duty to work.

The duty to obey the laws.

The duty to be clean and orderly.

The duty to send our children to school.

The duty to respect ourselves, even as we respect others.

W. E. B. DuBois Writes a Schoolgirl

William Edward Burghardt DuBois was unquestionably the most determined, persistent, and eloquent critic of racial injustice in the twentieth-century United States. Yet in 1905, he wrote to an African American schoolgirl who had begun to neglect her studies because she believed education provided no benefit for African Americans in a racist society. His letter to her appears here.

I wonder if you will let a stranger say a word to you about yourself? I have heard that you are a young woman of some ability but that you are neglecting your school work because you have become hopeless of trying to do anything in the world. I am very sorry for this. How any human being whose wonderful fortune it is to live in the 20th century should under ordinarily fair advantages despair of life is almost unbelievable. And if in addition to this that person is, as I am, of Negro lineage with all the hopes and yearnings of hundreds of millions of human souls dependent in some degree on her striving, then her bitterness amounts to crime.

There are in the U.S. today tens of thousands of colored girls who would be happy beyond measure to have the chance of educating themselves that you are neglecting. If you train yourself as you easily can, there are wonderful chances of

SOURCE: W. E. B. DuBois Papers, University of Massachusetts, Amherst Archives.

usefulness before you: you can join the ranks of 15,000 Negro women teachers, of hundreds of nurses and physicians, of the growing number of clerks and stenographers, and above all of the host of homemakers. Ignorance is a cure for nothing. Get the very best training possible & the doors of opportunity will fly open before you as they are flying before thousands of your fellows. On the other hand every time a colored person neglects an opportunity, it makes it more difficult for others of the race to get such an opportunity. Do you want to cut off the chances of the boys and girls of tomorrow?

Brownsville, 1906

On the night of August 13, 1906, approximately fifteen unidentified men gathered across the street from Fort Brown, on the edge of Brownsville, Texas, and began firing into buildings along the alley and adjacent 13th Street. Before the shooting stopped ten minutes later, Frank Natus, a bartender, was dead and the wounded included M. Ygnacio Dominguez, a police lieutenant, and Paulino S. Preciado, editor of the local Spanish-language newspaper El Porvenir. The Brownsville Raid, as the incident was soon called, was seen by many as retaliation for the harsh treatment African American soldiers of the 25th Infantry had suffered at the hands of townspeople. Soldiers from Fort Brown were assumed to be the culprits. When civilian and military authorities were unable to determine those responsible, President Theodore Roosevelt discharged 167 men in the regiment, arguing that his action would teach blacks that they should not "band together to shelter their own criminals." The brief article here that announced the discharge belies the firestorm of protest that would follow.

Washington, November 6 – By order of President Roosevelt, acting upon a report made to him by Brig-Gen. A. Garlington, Inspector-General of the Army, every man of companies B. C. and D of the Twenty-Fifth Infantry, the Afro-American regiment, will be discharged without honor from the army and forever debarred from reenlisting in the army or the navy, as well as from employment by the Government in any civil capacity.

The action is one of the most drastic ever taken by the President and is sure to cause a sensation throughout the service. The refusal of members of the battalion to give Gen. Garlington or to their immediate superiors the names of the men implicated in the shooting of citizens at Brownsville, Texas, near Fort Brown, on August 13, led the Inspector-General to recommend the discharge of all the men and the President concurred. . . .

SOURCE: Age (New York), November 8, 1906, 1.

This action of President Roosevelt is sure to arouse the bitterest surprise and anger everywhere among Afro-Americans. They believe that the Afro-American soldiers were heroic in refusing to betray their comrades to an unfair trial and certain death, and that they are merely another sacrifice offered by the President upon the altar of Southern race prejudice. It is said the soldiers have entered into a compact never to divulge the evidence.

The Crisis: The First Editorial, 1910

The newly founded NAACP established The Crisis *magazine to explain the organization's position on various issues and gather information from across the nation on the black plight. However, W. E. B. DuBois transformed the organ into the first national political, cultural, and literary journal for black America, and as such it became the most widely read black publication. The first editorial is reprinted here.*

The object of this publication is to set forth those facts and arguments which show the danger of race prejudice, particularly as manifested today toward colored people. It takes its name from the fact that the editors[*] believe that this is a critical time in the history of the advancement of men. Catholicity and tolerance, reason and forbearance can today make the world-old dream of human brotherhood approach realization while bigotry and prejudice, emphasized race consciousness and force can repeat the awful history of the contact of nations and groups in the past. We strive for this higher and broader vision of Peace and Good Will.

The policy of The Crisis will be simple and well defined:

It will first and foremost be a newspaper: it will record important happenings and movements in the world which bear on the great problem of inter-racial relations, and especially those which affect the Negro-American.

Secondly, it will be a review of opinion and literature, recording briefly books, articles, and important expressions of opinion in the white and colored press on the race problem.

Thirdly, it will publish a few short articles.

Finally, its editorial page will stand for the rights of men, irrespective of color or race, for the highest ideals of American democracy, and for reasonable but earnest and persistent attempt to gain these rights and realize these ideals. The magazine will be the organ of no clique or party and will avoid personal rancor of all sorts. In the absence of proof to the contrary it will assume honesty of purpose on the part of all men, North and South, white and black.

---

[*]Associated with Dr. DuBois on the editorial board were: O. G. Villard, J. M. Barber, Charles E. Russell, Kelly Miller, William S. Braithwaite and Mary D. MacLean.

SOURCE: The Crisis (New York), November, 1, 1910, 10–11.

Early Housing Discrimination: A 1911 St. Louis Restrictive Covenant

The following vignette is part of the 1911 restrictive covenant for a St. Louis neighborhood. In 1948, the U.S. Supreme Court ruled in Shelley v. Kraemer that such covenants were legally unenforceable by state action.

This contract of restrictions made and entered into by the undersigned, the owners of the property fronting on Labadie Avenue . . . between Cora Avenue on the west and Taylor Avenue on the East, Witnesseth: That for and in consideration of one dollar and other valuable considerations paid by the undersigned persons hereby contract and agree with the other and for the benefit of all to place . . . a restriction, which is to run with the title of said property . . . which should not be removed except by the consent of all of the property owners . . . the said property is hereby restricted to the use and occupancy for the term of Fifty (50) years from this date . . . that no part of said property or any portion thereof shall be occupied by any person not of the Caucasian race, it being intended hereby to restrict the use of said property for said period of time against the occupancy as owners or tenants of any portion of said property for resident or other purposes by people of the Negro or Mongolian Race. It is further contracted and agreed that upon a violation of this restriction either one or all of the parties to this agreement shall be permitted and authorized to bring suit or suits at law or in equity to enforce this restriction as to the use and occupancy of said property in any Court or Courts and to forfeit the title to any lot or portions or lot that may be used in violation of this restriction.

SOURCE: Shelley v. Kraemer, 335 U.S. 1 (1948).

The National Urban League

*The National League on Urban Conditions Among Negroes, soon to be known
as the National Urban League, was founded in New York City in 1910.
Although it was created to provide social services primarily for the African
American populations in Southern cities, by the end of its first decade the
organization would spend much of its time, resources, and energy in helping the
500,000 Southern migrants to Northern cities adjust to their new urban homes.
The following anonymously authored article, which describes those services in
New York City in 1914, anticipates the league's work in other Northern cities
for much of the twentieth century.*

When, during the spring of 1910, Mrs. William H. Baldwin, Jr., called
representatives of the many social-welfare organizations working among
Negroes to a conference at her New York City home, to consider means of
preventing duplication of effort and overlapping of work, of promoting cooperation among the agencies and of establishing new organizations to improve
neglected conditions, a new era was reached in the handling of the city problem
as it affected the Negroes.

From this meeting resulted the National League on Urban Conditions Among
Negroes, whose work of uplift is now being felt in ten cities, viz.: New York,
Philadelphia, Pa., Norfolk, Va., Richmond, Va., Nashville, Tenn., Louisville, Ky.,
St. Louis, Mo., Savannah, Ga., Augusta, Ga., and Atlanta, Ga., whose budget has
increased from $2,000 to $18,000 per year and whose staff of paid employees has
increased from one full-time and three part-time employees to sixteen salaried
persons in New York City, three in Nashville and two in Norfolk.

★ ★ ★

The problem of the city Negro is but the accentuated counterpart of the
problem of all urban inhabitants. Segregation and the consequence congestion,
the evils of bad housing conditions with their inevitable accompaniment of
dangerous sanitation and loose morals, the lack of facilities for wholesome
recreation and the ill regulated picture shows and dance halls combine to make
conditions which demand instant relief. Add to this a population constantly
augmented by Negroes from small towns or rural districts of the South, and the
problem of the league is before you.

★ ★ ★

SOURCE: The Crisis (New York), September 8, 1914, 243.

SOURCE: "Woman to the Rescue," The Crisis (New York) 12 (May 1916): 43.

The league has sought to establish agencies for uplift where needed. If no committee could be found ready to take over and conduct the particular undertaking, the league has handled the movement through its local office staff.

The Sojourner Truth house committee, with Mrs. George W. Seligman as chairman, has undertaken the task of establishing a home for delinquent colored girls under 16 years of age, because of the failure of the State and private institutions to care adequately for these unfortunates. The league made an investigation of this need and formed a temporary committee from which developed the present organization.

The league also inaugurated the movement for the training of colored nursery maids. A committee, of which Mr. Franck W. Barber is chairman, has worked out the details for courses of study in hospital training in care of infants, kindergarten training, child study and household arts.

During the summer of 1911 the league conducted, in Harlem, a playground for boys, for the purpose of demonstrating the need of recreational facilities for the children of Harlem. As a result of this movement, and a continuous agitation for more adequate play facilities, the city has practically committed itself to the operation of a model playground on any plot of ground in the Harlem district, the use of which is donated to the City Parks Department.

The travelers' aid work, in charge of Miss Eva G. Burleigh, has consisted principally in the meeting of the coastwise steamers meeting the competition of city life, and who are frequently sent to New York to be exploited by unreliable employment agents or questionable men. The league supports two travelers' aid workers in Norfolk, Va., which is the gateway to the North for hundreds of women and girls from Virginia and the Carolinas.

The preventive or protective work of the league consists of the visiting in the homes of school children who have become incorrigibles or truants, for the purpose of removing the causes of these irregularities. This work is in charge of Mrs. Hallie B. Craigwell and Mr. Leslie L. Pollard.

Probation work with adults from the court of general sessions is done by Mr. Chas. C. Allison, Jr. In connection with this work with delinquents the Big Brother and Big Sister movements are conducted. The league seeks to furnish to each boy or girl passing through the courts the helpful influence and guidance of a man or woman of high moral character.

The league conducts a housing bureau for the purpose of improving the moral and physical conditions among the tenement houses in Negro districts. It seeks principally to prevent the indiscriminate mixing of the good and bad by furnishing to the public a list of houses certified to be tenanted by respectable people. It also seeks to get prompt action of agents and owners or the city departments whenever there is need for correcting certain housing abuses.

Political Impotence

2

The Great Migration:

Blacks in the Urban North

World War I opened the first significant employment opportunities for black Americans in Northern cities and as a consequence 500,000 African Americans moved out of the South between 1916 and 1920, initiating a rural-to-urban black exodus that continued virtually uninterrupted until the 1970s. The vignettes in this chapter explain the Great Migration and its consequences for black and urban America.

The vignettes **Why They Leave the South** and **Black Southerners Explain the Exodus** suggest the various reasons for the "push" from the South. **Charles Denby Describes His Work** discusses the experiences of one man in a Detroit automobile factory. **East St. Louis, 1917: An American Pogrom** reminds us that competition for jobs exacerbated racial tension and in this instance led to a bloody race riot.

In July 1918, an optimistic W. E .B. DuBois penned an editorial in the NAACP publication, The *Crisis*, titled **"Close Ranks,"** in which he urged African Americans to put aside their racial grievances and support fully the nation's efforts in World War I. When that full support was greeted with continuing racial discrimination and an escalation of violence against African Americans in and out of uniform, DuBois responded with **"We Return Fighting."** Both vignettes appear in this volume.

The Chicago Race Riot of 1919 was the largest twentieth-century racial clash in the city. The vignette **Big Bill Thompson and the Black Vote** describes the growing political power of black Chicagoans, which some have argued exacerbated racial tensions leading to the riot. The vignette **The Chicago** *Defender* **Describes the Race Riot** details the violence as it unfolded in the city.

Sweet Home, Chicago discusses the ongoing discrimination in housing against the backdrop of the riot and suggests why such discrimination would ultimately fail. Finally, in **Mary McLeod Bethune on the Problems of the City Dweller,** we see a political activist and college founder and president describing the challenges awaiting those who migrate to the city.

Why They Leave the South

In the following brief article titled "Why They Leave the South: The Lynching Record for 1916," the Chicago Defender *reminded all that the migration was driven not only by increased economic opportunity in the North. Lynching and other forms of racially motivated violence that remained common well into the second decade of the twentieth century also persuaded African Americans to move to Northern cities.*

In view of the widespread discussion of the causes back of the migration of Negroes to the North it is timely to consider the lynchings for the year just closed. I find according to the records kept by Monroe N. Work, head of the Division of Records and Research of the Tuskegee Institute, that in 1916 there have been 54 lynchings. Of those lynched, 50 were Negroes and 4 were whites. This is 4 less Negroes and 9 less whites than were put to death in 1915 when the record was 54 Negroes and 13 whites. Included in the record are 3 women.

Fourteen (14) or more than one-fourth of the total lynchings occurred in the State of Georgia. Of those put to death 42, or 77 per cent of the total, were charged with offenses other than rape. The charges for which whites were lynched were murder, 3; suspected of cutting a woman, 1 (this a Mexican).

The charges for which Negroes were put to death were attempted rape, 9; killing officers of the law, 10; murder, 7; hog stealing and assisting another person to escape, 6; wounding officers of the law, 4; rape, 3; insult, 2; for each of the following offenses one person was put to death: Slapping boy; robbing store; brushing against girl on the street; assisting his son, accused of rape, to escape; entering a house for robbery or some other purpose; defending her son, who in defense of mother, killed man; fatally wounding a man with whom he had quarreled; speaking against mob in act of putting a man to death; attacking a man and wife with club.

Lynchings occurred in the following states: Alabama, 1; Arkansas, 4; Florida, 8; Georgia, 14; Kansas, 1; Kentucky, 2; Louisiana, 2; Mississippi, 1; Missouri, 1; North Carolina, 2; Oklahoma, 4; South Carolina, 2; Tennessee, 3; Texas, 9.

SOURCE: The Defender (Chicago), January 6, 1917, 2.

Black Southerners Explain the Exodus

Between 1916 and 1920, nearly 400,000 African Americans migrated from Southern farms to Northern cities. Before leaving, many of them wrote the Chicago Defender *and other Northern newspapers requesting support and assistance. Some of these letters are reprinted here.*

Pensacola, Fla., 4-21-17

Sir: You will please give us the names of the firms where we can secure employment. Also please explain the Great Northern Drive for May 15th. We will come by the thousands. Some of us like farm work. The colored people will leave if you will assist them.

Mobile, Ala., April 25, 1917

Dear Sir: I was reading in the paper about the Colored race and while reading it I seen in it where cars would be here for the 15th of May. . . . Will you be so kind as to let me know where they are coming to and I will be glad to know because I am a poor woman and have a husband and five children living and three dead . . . [M]y husband can hardly make bread for them in Mobile. This is my native home but it is not fit to live. . . . Will you please let me know when the cars is going to stop to so that he can come where he can take care of me and my children. . . . Hoping to hear from you soon, your needed and worried friend.

New Orleans, La., 4-23-17

Dear Editor: I am a reader of the Defender and I am askeso [*sic*] much about the great Northern drive on the 15th of May. We want more understanding about it for [when we ask] the depot agents never gives us any satisfaction . . . for they don't want us to leave here. I want to ask you to please publish in your next Saturdays paper just what the fair [*sic*] will be that day so we all will know & and can be ready. So many women here are wanting to go that day. They are all working women and we cant get work here so much now, the white women tell us we just want to make money to go North and we do so please kindly answer this in your next paper.

New Orleans, La., May 2, 1917

Dear Sir: Please sir, will you kindly tell me what is meant by the Great Northern Drive to take place May the 15th, on Tuesday. It is a rumor all over

SOURCE: Emmett J. Scott, "Letters of Negro Migrants of 1916–1918," <u>Journal of Negro History</u> 4, no. 3 (July 1919): 331–334.

town to be ready for the 15th of May to go in the drive. . . . Do please write me at once and say is there an excursion to leave the South. Nearly the whole of the South is ready for the drive. Or excursion as it is termed. Please write at once. We are sick to get out of the South.

Charles Denby Describes His Work

Alabama-born Charles Denby migrated to Detroit in 1924. In the following account, he described his first job at Graham Paige, an independent auto-manufacturing company.

My first job at Graham Paige was in the foundry shaking out the oil pan that fits under the motor.... I was very much surprised when I was hired. I asked the man if there were any jobs. He said, yes. I told him I preferred somewhere else when he told me to work in the foundry. I had worked in a foundry in Anniston [Alabama]. I knew what the work was like. He said there were no other jobs open. When white men came he told them about other jobs and hired them.... How could he say, to my face there were no other jobs when he told a white man ahead of me about polishing and put another in the carpentry shop.... They led us out to see where we would come to work the next morning.

As I looked around, all the men were dirty and greasy and smoked up. They were beyond recognition. There were only three or four whites. These were Polish. Negroes told me later they were the only ones able to stand the work. Their faces looked exactly like Negro faces. They were so matted and covered with oil and dirt that no skin showed. Hines [his friend] and I went home discussing how it was that they could say everyone was free with equal rights up North. There was no one in the foundry but Negroes....

At the end of the week they said we'd get no pay the first week. They held it in what they called abeyance. The job was very rugged. I had to work continuously, as fast as I could move. The heat from the cubulos, which were round furnaces for melting the iron, was so hot that in five minutes my clothes would stick with dirt and grease. We'd walk through on our lunch period to talk to a friend. We couldn't recognize him by his clothes or looks. The men working in his section would tell us where he was or we could tell a friend by his voice.

My job paid five dollars a day. The first foreman was quiet, he didn't do much raring or hollering like the other foremen. They would curse and holler. They would pay us off right there if we looked back or stopped working. Workers passed out from the heat. The foremen rushed a stretcher over and

SOURCE: Charles Denby, <u>Indignant Heart: The Journal of An Afro-American Automobile Worker</u>, 30, 33. South End Press, 1978. Copyright © 1978 by South End Press. All rights reserved. Reprinted with permission by South End Press.

two workers would take the man out, give him fifteen minutes to revive and then he would have to go back to work. When a man passed out, the foreman would be running out to see if the guy was conscious. He would be cursing all the time.... They never mentioned a wound serious enough to go to first aid. Workers would get a layer of iron from the cubulo, bring it to the iron pourers, fifteen to twenty men with long ladles. These would be filled with hot iron running like water. As their ladles filled up, the men had to straighten their arms out level and pour the iron down a little hole the size of a milk bottle. All the time they had to turn slow, like a machine. If they poured too fast, the iron would explode the mold and burn the other men. The iron would drop on a wet spot and hit the men like a bullet and go into the skin. The man getting hit still had to hold the ladling iron level to keep from burning the other men. They would wait their chance to pick out the balls of iron, and sometimes the foreman picked it out as the men went on working.

East St. Louis, 1917: An American Pogrom

Oscar Leonard, Superintendent of The Jewish Educational and Charitable Association of St. Louis, wrote about the East St. Louis Riot of 1917, calling it an American pogrom. His account appears here.

Two days before the nation was to celebrate the signing of the Declaration of Independence with its recognition that "all men are created free and equal" came the news that in East St. Louis Negroes were being slaughtered and their homes pillaged and burned by white Americans. East St. Louis . . . is an industrial town cross the Mississippi [from St. Louis]. It is part of the state which gave us Abraham Lincoln. This circumstance made the "pogrom" upon the Negroes more tragic. They were being murdered mercilessly in a state which had fought for their freedom from slavery. They were forced to seek refuge and safety across the river in Missouri, which was a slave state at one time.

I just called the riot a "pogrom," the name by which Russian massacres of Jews has become known. Yet when I went to East St. Louis to view the sections where the riots had taken place, I was informed that the makers of Russian pogroms could learn a great deal from the American rioters. I went there in the company of a young Russian Jew, a sculptor, who had witnessed and bears the marks of more than one anti-Jewish riot in his native land. He told me when he viewed the blocks of burned houses that the Russian "Black Hundreds" could take lessons in pogrom-making from the whites of East St. Louis. The Russians at least, he said, gave the Jews a chance to run while they were trying to murder

SOURCE: Oscar Leonard, "The East St. Louis Pogrom," <u>The Survey</u> 33 (July 14, 1917): 331–333.

them. The whites in East St. Louis fired the homes of black folk and either did not allow them to leave the burning houses or shot them the moment they dared attempt to escape the flames.

What is the reason for this terrible situation?

Fundamentally, the reason is purely economic. It is not rather the white people in Illinois, or rather in East St. Louis, have any terrible hatred for the Negro. The two races go to the same schools. The laws of Illinois even permit intermarriage between whites and blacks. Negroes hold state, county and municipal offices. They own a great deal of property in the state and in the city where the riots took place. But being the most disinherited of men, Negroes at times work for lower wages than do whites. Some of them will not join labor unions and most of them would not be admitted if they cared to join.

This condition is extremely objectionable to the white workers with whom they compete for jobs. But this very fact makes the Negro laborer more attractive, to employers who want labor at the cheapest possible terms. They favor any labor force that will not join unions, that will not strike, that will not make periodic demands for increased wages or shorter workdays. Such an element introduced into the community acts as a whip over the heads of the white workers. Employers know that. Laboring people are, painfully aware of it. This is the main reason for the race antipathy in East St. Louis, as I judge from talking to business men, laborers, professional men and labor leaders.

East St. Louis is what Graham Romeyn Taylor called a "satellite city." It is not a city of homes in the American acceptance of that term. It is a manufacturing town where industries locate because land is cheap, transportation facilities good, coal and water near and cheap. The many factories make the place unattractive for home-building. Capital goes there simply in search of dividends. It isn't interested in the welfare of the city or of the workers who help make those dividends. Only those who must, live there. Those who can live in St. Louis, while working in East St. Louis, do so.

The result is that the city is run to suit the lowest political elements. The foreign laborers who were imported by the industries in East St. Louis know nothing of American standards. There is practically no social work being done in that city which boasts a population of 100,000 souls. Saloons are numerous and gambling dens abound. They run wide open.... One can not visit East St. Louis without seeing at a glance that saloons are more numerous than the schools and churches. That in itself would indicate how much control the liquor interests have over the city.

This, too, has helped bring about the situation which resulted in the massacre of Negroes both May 28 and July. The undesirable Negro element, like the undesirable white element, was used by self-seeking politicians. In order to be able to control that element the politicians had to make concessions. Evil dives were permitted. Lawless Negroes were protected. All too frequently the St. Louis papers reported outrages committed upon white women by Negroes in East St. Louis. There were robberies and stabbings and shootings of white men at frequent intervals. Yet criminals were not punished. They were "taken care of." This helped stir the ill will of the better element among the white population.

The employers insist that they do not encourage immigration and absolutely deny that they import Negroes. They insist that there are not enough
white workers to take the jobs. They point to the fact that since the Negro left
East St. Louis, on July 2 and that entire week, four industries have entirely shut
down. When asked why it is that Negroes do come in such large numbers to
East St. Louis they say that the lure of better wages than the South pays attracts
them.

R. F. Rucker, superintendent of the aluminum ore says that the employers
were glad to employ Negroes when there were not enough white workers to fill
the jobs. According to him, many of the white workers went east to take
employment in munitions factories. . . . Some Negroes who had come voluntarily
from the South were given their places. These men wrote home of the fine
opportunities for employment at high wages and urged their friends to come to
East St. Louis.

. . . Feeling against the Negroes was stirred constantly. Here and there personal encounters between the two races took place. Sunday evening, July 1, a
rumor was spread that the Negroes had gathered in one of their churches to plan
revenge upon the white population. A number of policemen in charge of
Detective Sergeant Coopedge drove over to the church. As they approached
the place they were fired upon by Negroes and Coopedge was killed. The same
night a policeman and two other white men were shot by Negroes.

These deeds acted as a match applied to powder. Monday morning it was
apparent that there would be trouble. Mayor Mollman said he tried to prepare
for it. East St. Louis has just thirty-six policemen. The mayor says that he spoke
personally to them, urging them to do their duty. They were not inclined to
interfere because their comrades had been shot. The deputy sheriffs felt the
same way. Some militiamen were in town, but according to all accounts the
militia fraternized with the white population. The mayor was urged to call up
the governor and ask for reinforcements and for a declaration of martial law.
He refused to do so. His opponents say that he had political reasons for his
failure to act.

Be that as it may, the fact remains that through someone's negligence, black
men and women and children were murdered wantonly. In the seven Negro
districts of the city fires were started at the same time. Negroes were hanged and
stoned and shot and kicked. White women and boys as well as men took part.
A black skin was a death warrant on the streets of this Illinois city. How many
black persons were killed will never be known . . .

According to eye-witnesses, many Negroes must have been burned in their
homes so that no remains will be found. It is believed that one hundred
Negroes who took refuge in an old theater in one of their sections were burned
when the building was set on fire. I saw that building, of which only part of one
wall was left.

It was a distressing sight to see block after block where peaceful homes had
been located burned to the ground. The innocent suffered with the guilty.
Thrifty black folk, who were doing their bit by raising vegetables, were murdered. I saw the ruins of their homes, into which had gone the labor and savings

of years. The little thrift gardens had escaped the flames and the orderly rows where seeds had been planted gave the plots the appearance of miniature graveyards.

"Close Ranks"

In the following editorial, W. E. B. DuBois called for African Americans to support the United States in the World War I war effort despite denials of their civil rights at home. He was widely criticized for not using this opportunity to remind the nation of its injustice to demand the end of racial discrimination.

This is the crisis of the world. For all the long years to come men will point to the year 1918 as the great day of decision, the day when the world decided whether it would submit to military despotism and an endless armed peace – if peace it could be called – or whether they would put down the menace of German militarism and inaugurate the United States of the World.

We of the colored race have no ordinary interest in the outcome. That which the German power represents today spells death to the aspirations of Negroes and all darker races for equality, freedom, and democracy. Let us not hesitate. Let us, while this war lasts, forget our special grievances and close our ranks shoulder to shoulder with our own white fellow-citizens and the allied nations that are fighting for democracy. We make no ordinary sacrifice, but we make it gladly and willingly with our eyes lifted to the hills.

SOURCE: The Crisis (New York), 16, no. 3 (July 1918): 111.

"We Return Fighting"

W. E. B. DuBois recouped credibility and reestablished himself at the forefront of black protest with his editorial "Returning Soldiers." The editorial, however, was more than DuBois reeling from criticism of his earlier call to "Close Ranks," it was an admission that because of black participation in World War I, segregationists were more determined to keep the racial status quo as reflected by escalating violence, particularly against black soldiers in uniform.

We are returning from the war! The <u>Crisis</u> and tens of thousands of black men were drafted into a great struggle. For bleeding France and what she means and has meant and will mean to us and humanity and against the threat of German race arrogance, we fought gladly and to the last drop of blood; for America and her highest ideals, we fought in far-off hope; for the dominant southern oligarchy entrenched in Washington, we fought in bitter resignation.

For the America that represents and gloats in lynching, disfranchisement, caste, brutality and devilish insult—for this, in the hateful upturning and mixing of things, we were forced by vindictive fate to fight, also.

But today we return! We return from the slavery of uniform which the world's madness demanded us to don to the freedom of civil garb. We stand again to look America squarely in the face and call a spade a spade. We sing: This country of ours, despite all its better souls have done and dreamed, is yet a shameful land.

It lynches . . .

It disfranchises its own citizens . . .

It encourages ignorance . . .

It steals from us . . .

It insults us . . .

It organizes industry to cheat us. It cheats us out of our land; it cheats us out of our labor. It confiscates our savings. It reduces our wages. It raises our rent. It steals our profit. It taxes us without representation. It keeps us consistently and universally poor, and then feeds us on charity and derides our poverty . . .

This is the country to which we Soldiers of Democracy return. This is the fatherland for which we fought! But it is our fatherland. It was right for us to fight. The faults of our country are our faults. Under similar circumstances, we would fight again. But by the God of Heaven, we are cowards and jackasses if now that war is over, we do not marshal every ounce of our brain and brawn to fight a sterner, longer, more unbending battled against the forces of hell in our own land.

We return.

We return from fighting.

We return fighting.

Make way for Democracy! We saved it in France, and by the Great Jehovah, we will save it in the United States of America, or know the reason why.

SOURCE: The <u>Crisis</u> (New York), 18, no. 1 (May 1919): 13–14.

Big Bill Thompson and The Black Vote

The benefits of the great migration were usually felt first at the ballot box. Northern states allowed African Americans to vote, and soon some politicians, recognizing the potential in the votes of the Southern migrants, began to organize in black communities. Nowhere was that organization more successful than in Chicago. With the help of a Republican political machine headed by Chicago mayor William Hale "Big Bill" Thompson, blacks became, and remain, a political force in Illinois elections. The following vignette announces Thompson's election and the role the black vote played in it.

"Negroes Elect 'Big Bill'" Mayor is Winner in Hard Fight

Mayor Thompson was re-elected today by such a narrow margin that it was that big lead given him over his principal rivals, Robert M. Sweitzer and Maclay Hoyne, by the negroes in the Second ward gave him the victory. The German wards also helped to re-elect the mayor. Thompson's lead is between 9,000 and 12,000.

Returns from the Second ward were held back under orders to the police until it was seen how many votes the mayor needed. Then they were gradually permitted to sift through and the Thompson stock which had been going down as a result of bulletins from other wards, began to climb and cheer came to the city hall crowd.

The negroes were in a frenzy of delight when they learned that their votes had put "Big Bill" in the mayor's chair for another four years. South State street, South Wabash avenue and the other thoroughfares in the district witnessed a demonstration of hilarity seldom seen on an election night.

Because the early returns were held up by the police on the orders of Chief Garrity, the figures indicated the election of Sweitzer. Later returns, however, showed that the race was close and the figures from 1,500 precincts gave the lead to Thompson.

Thompson supporters staged a wild celebration all over the city when the result was made known. When a newspaper bulletin, predicting Thompson's election by 8,000 to 12,000 majority, was received, the mayor smiled picked up the telephone and called his wife. He read the bulletin to her and said, "They give it up." He declined to make a further statement at the time.

Mr. Sweitzer mowed down the pluralities given Mayor Thompson in the heavy republican strongholds four years ago, but did not reduce them enough to give him the lead he had expected. Sweitzer, the returns showed, also was aided by the vote given to Hoyne in the republican wards. Mr. Hoyne's vote in these wards was not surprising, however, as republican leaders were openly working for him. Hoyne failed to show any strength in the democratic wards and ran a poor third.

SOURCE: The <u>Daily Journal</u> (Chicago), April 1, 1919, 1.

Mayor Thompson's plurality in 2,005 precincts out of the 2,215 in the city was 12,921. When the mayor was informed of the vote which had been cast he issued the following statement: "Truth and justice have again prevailed. The voters have rendered the verdict. In spite of the malevolent attacks made upon me by the interests which seek to prey upon the people, my administration has been approved by the people. This republican victory in Chicago is also a proclamation to the nation that our people have turned unmistakably to the republican party for deliverance from the ills and burdens of national democratic misrule. This victory today should inspire the republicans of the nation to begin at once the work which will insuer [sic] the election of a republican president next year. It was a vote of confidence in the republican party and a spoken desire of this great industrial community to return to the sane and safe policies of our city, under which the nation has always been prosperous and happy. To those men and women who, have been so loyal in their support of my candidacy I wish to tender my grateful and appreciative thanks. I shall continue to conduct myself so they may always be proud of this expression of continued confidence."

The Chicago *Defender* Describes the Race Riot

Beginning on July 28, 1919, Chicago experienced the worst race riot in the twentieth century. For over three weeks, white mobs in the city attacked African American residents and their property. In the following account, the Chicago Defender *described the rioting.*

"For fully four days this old city has been rocked in a quake of racial antagonism, seared in a blaze of red hate flaming as fiercely as the heat of day – each hour ushering in new stories of slaying, looting, arson, rapine, sending the awful roll of casulties to a grim total of 40 dead and more than 500 wounded, many of them perhaps fatally. A certain madness distinctly indicated in reports of shootings, stabbings and burnings of buildings which literally pour in every minute. Women and children have not been spared. Traffic has been stopped. Phone wires have been cut.

Stores and Offices Shut

Victims lay in every street and vacant lot. Hospitals are filled; 4,000 troops rest in arms, among which are companies of the old Eighth regiment, while the inadequate force of police battle vainly to save the city's honor.

SOURCE: "Riot Sweeps Chicago: Ghastly Deeds of Rioters Told," The Defender (Chicago), August 2, 1919, 1.

Fear to Care for Bodies

Undertakers on the South Side refused to accept bodies of white victims. White undertakers refused to accept black victims. Both for the same reason. They feared the vengeance of the mobs without.

Every little while bodies were found in some street, alley or vacant lot – and no one sought to care for them. Patrols were unable to accommodate them because they were being used in rushing live victims to hospitals. Some victims were dragged to a mob's "No Man's Land" and dropped.

The telephone wires in the raging districts were cut in many places by the rioters as it became difficult to estimate the number of dead victims.

Hospitals Filled with Maimed

Provident hospital, 36th and Dearborn Streets, situated in the heart of the "black belt," as well as other hospitals in the surrounding districts, are filled with the maimed and dying. Every hour, every minute, every second finds patrols backed up and unloading the human freight branded with the red symbol of this orgy of hate. Many victims have reached the hospitals, only to die before kind hands could attend to them. So pressing as the situation become that schools, drug stores and private houses are being used. Trucks, drays and hearses are being used for ambulances.

Monday Sees "Reign of Terror"

Following the Sunday affray, the red tongues had blabbed their fill, and Monday morning found the thoroughfares in the white neighborhoods throated with a sea of humans – everywhere – some armed with guns, bricks, clubs, and an oath. The presence of a black face in their vicinity was the signal for a carnival of death, and before any aid could reach the poor, unfortunate one his body reposed in some kindly gutter, his brains spilled over a dirty pavement. Some of the victims were chased, caught and dragged into alleys and lots, where they were left for dead. In all parts of the city, white mobs dragged from surface cars, black passengers wholly ignorant of any trouble, and set upon them. An unidentified young woman and a 3 months old baby were found dead on the street at the intersection of 47th Street and Wentworth Avenue. She had attempted to board a car there when the mob seized her, beat her, slashed her body into ribbons and beat the baby's brains out against a telegraph pole. Not satisfied with this, one rioter severed her breasts, and a white youngster bore it aloft on a pole, triumphantly, while the crowd hooted gleefully. All the time this was happening, several policemen were in the crowd, but did not make any attempt to make rescue until too late.

Kill Scores Coming from Yards

Rioters operating in the vicinity of the stock yards, which lies in the heart of white residences west of Halsted street, attacked scores of workers – women and men alike returning from work. Stories of these outrages began to flutter into the black vicinities and hysterical men harangued their fellows to avenge the killings – and soon they, infected with the insanity of the mob, rushed through the streets, drove high powered motor cars or waited for street cars, which they attacked with gunfire and stones. Shortly after noon traffic south of 22nd Street and north of 55th Street, west of Cottage Grove Avenue and east of Wentworth Avenue, was stopped with the exception of trolley cars. Whites who entered this zone were set upon with unmeasurable fury.

Policemen employed in the disturbed sections were wholly unable to handle the situation. When one did attempt to carry out his duty he was beaten and his gun taken from him. The fury of the mob could not be abated. Mounted police were employed, but to no avail.

35th Vortex of Night's Rioting

With the approach of darkness the rioting gave prospects of being continued throughout the night. Whites boarded the platforms and shot through the windows of the trains at passengers. Some of the passengers alighting from cars were thrown from the elevated structure, suffering broken legs, fractured skulls, and death.

The block between State street and Wabash avenue on East 35th street was the scene of probably the most shooting and rioting of the evening and a pitched battle ensued between the police, whites and blacks.

The trouble climaxed when white occupants of the Angelus apartments began firing shots and throwing missiles from their windows. One man was shot through the head, but before his name could be secured he was spirited away. The attack developed a hysterical battling fervor and the mob charged the building and the battle was on.

Police were shot. Whites were seen to tumble out of automobiles, from doorways and other places, wounded or suffering from bruises inflicted by gun-shot, stones or bricks. A reign of terror literally ensued. Automobiles were stopped, occupants beaten and machines wrecked. Street cars operating in 35th street were wrecked, as well as north and south bound State street cars. Windows were shattered and white occupants beaten.

Trolley cars operating east and west on 35th street were stopped, since they always left the vicinity in a perforated state. Shortly after 8 o'clock all service was discontinued on 42d, 47th and 51st streets.

Stores Looted; Homes Burned

Tiring of street fights, rioters turned to burning and looting. This was truly a sleepless night, and a resume of the day's happenings nourished an inclination for renewed hostilities from another angle. The homes of blacks isolated in white neighborhoods were burned to the ground and the owners and occupants beaten and thrown unconscious in the smoldering embers. Meanwhile rioters in the "black belt" smashed windows and looted shops of white merchants on State Street.

Other rioters, manning high powered cars and armed, flitted up and down the darkened streets, chancing shots at fleeting whites on the street and those riding in street cars.

Toward midnight quiet reigned along State Street under the vigilance of 400 policemen and scores of uniformed men of the 8th Regiment.

Rioting Extends Into Loop

Tuesday dawned sorrowing with a death toll of 20 dead and 300 injured. In early morning a 13-year-old lad standing on his porch at 51st and Wabash avenue was shot to death by a white man who, in an attempt to get away, encountered a mob and his existence became history. A mounted policeman, unknown, fatally wounded a small boy in the 48th block on Dearborn street and was shot to death by some unknown rioter.

Workers thronging the loop district to their work were set upon by mobs of sailors and marines roving the streets and several fatal casualties have been reported. Infuriated white rioters attempted to storm the Palmer house and the post office, where there are a large number of employees, but an adequate police forced dispersed them and later the men were spirited away to their homes in closed government mail trucks and other conveyances. White clerks have replaced our clerks in the main post office temporarily and our men have been shifted to outlying post offices. The loop violence came as a surprise to the police. Police and reserves had been scattered over the South Side rioting districts, as no outbreaks had been expected in this quarter. Toward noon stations therein were overwhelmed with calls."

Sweet Home, Chicago

In an editorial dated August 1919, the Chicago Defender *assessed the role of housing competition in the Chicago Race Riot. However the* Defender *also argued that racial discrimination in housing, no matter how pronounced at the moment, would ultimately fail because of the law of supply and demand that impacted both white home sellers and black home buyers.*

THE RECENT RIOT in our city is attributed by some persons to the friction growing out of some of our group purchasing property in what is called white neighborhoods. In reality, that had very little if anything to do with it. Neither did the industrial questions cut much of a figure, because most of the laborers of our group have become unionized, thus doing away with the occasion for friction along those lines. For the riot there were two causes, an immediate and a primary cause.

SOURCE: Editorial, "Home, Sweet Home," <u>Defender</u> (Chicago), August 30, 1919, 4.

WITH REFERENCE to the housing proposition nothing has occurred that is extraordinary or unusual except in one particular. The accessions to the population, so far as our group is concerned, has been more rapid during the past four years than at any time prior thereto. This has necessitated the expansion of territory occupied by members of our group. The expansion has been going on in Chicago for the last half-century and nothing has been said or thought of it and done about it until recently. The rapidity of the expansion of the past few years has attracted more attention, has been more noticeable and therefore created a little friction which otherwise would have been overlooked.

TO THE OPINON of some this has created a problem which must be solved. The fact seems to be lost sight of that the rapid influx includes not only persons of our group but other races and nationalities as well, as for instance, the Poles, Italians, Greeks, Lithuanians, and Hebrews all have outgrown their original districts; any one of these groups presents as much of a problem as the group to which we belong.

NO LAW, ordinance, rule or regulation can be adopted or enforced which will have the effect of segregating any one of these groups to any particular territory. And yet it is very easy for people of a particular race, group or class to bar those not satisfactory to them from securing a home in that particular section or territory. All that is necessary for them to do is to agree among themselves not to sell, lease or rent any property within said territory to those of any other group or class whose presence may not be desired. In this they will be clearly within their rights, and no one will have any right to object, certainly no member of our group.

BUT THE UNDERSTANDING or agreement is one that could not be enforced by due process of law, hence if any one of the property owners in such territory should see fit to sell — which they very often do — to any member of a group to which objection should be made, he will also be within his rights. Since we cannot expand in any direction without occupying territory previously occupied by whites, and since the white man is exceedingly anxious to get the Colored man's dollar, he is usually willing to sell whenever the same can be done to his financial advantage.

IT IS SAFE TO ASSUME that in most of such instances the sale to a member of our group is not from choice but from necessity. In such cases the vendor cannot find a white person that is willing to make the purchase or will pay the price, and since he needs the money and must have it, if he finds a member of our group both willing and able to make the purchase the sale is consummated. This is the way expansion has heretofore taken place and under such circumstances no fault should be found and no objections should be made to such transactions. If left alone the housing question will regulate itself. It is simply a cause of supply and demand.

Mary McLeod Bethune on the Problems of the City Dweller

In a 1924 article in Opportunity, *the magazine of the National Urban League, Mary McLeod Bethune, President of Bethune-Cookman College in Florida, wrote about the challenges facing the growing numbers of urbanizing African Americans. Part of her article appears here.*

During the past 30 years there has been a great shift of population from the country to the town, and every class of towns, from village to great cities, has grown, whereas the country districts have actually decreased in population. The increase of the Negro urban population in the South in the decade 1910–1920 was 396,444 or 56,000 more than the increase for the same period in the number of Negroes in the North from the South – 340,260. More than one-third – 34% of the total Negro population is living in urban territory. The census reports show an actual decrease of 234,876 or 3.4% in the Negro rural population of the United States. In 1910 the number of Negroes reported as living in rural territory was 7,138,534. In 1920 the number thus living reported was 6,903,658.

A powerful contributory cause for recent legislation in the restriction of immigration was the alarming extent to which our future citizens were concentrating in the large seaport and manufacturing cities instead of seeking the extensive and unworked agricultural lands of the middle West and the West. . . . The causes back of this almost universal movement of population cityward are usually conceded to be economic, educational and social.

In spite of the manifold movements, plans and efforts to make farming and other rural pursuits pay, the country lad still turns his eye towards the city as his El Dorado. He wants a shorter working day; wages that will insure him good clothes and creature comforts; an opportunity to advance in earning power as he increases his ability to be of service in his calling; a fair chance to acquire wealth and become a leader in his community. To the country lad with plenty of time to dream while he plods thru days and days of monotonous routine, this is what the city means. To many an adult, weary of the grind and isolation of wresting a living from the soil, it offers an opening for a new chance, a realized vision. And so they come – young and old – beardless youth and gnarled old age all expecting that the road to wealth and power and influence lies down the great white way of the modern city.

The cry of the Soul to know has given another push to this modern move towards the city. Longer school terms; better-equipped school buildings; more capable teachers; the broadening influence of lectures; concerts, motion pictures,

SOURCE: Mary McLeod Bethune, "The Problems of the City Dweller," <u>Opportunity</u>, February 1924, 54–55.

libraries, parades and festive and holiday occasions have lured many a grizzled homesteader to abandon home and ancestral acres and move cityward. The widening out and diversification of the modern high school with its facilities for teaching the technique of skilled trades and business; home economics and agriculture as well as the arts and sciences. The extending of education at the public expense in some cities to include even a college education. The offering of night courses for underprivileged boys and girls, men and women. These are advantages which even the phonograph, the motion picture machine and the radio cannot compensate for in the country.

Then, again, in spite of automobiles, Fords, good roads, and the transmission of electric light current over long distances, the country is still a lonely place for thousands and thousands of dwellers. Weary of quilting parties, barn raisings and quarterly meeting, they are impelled cityward by the age-old urge towards companionship and recreation. . . .

The city's churches, its civic clubs, its parks, its easily accessible amusement resorts and centers, its playground, its bathhouses and skating rinks; its roof gardens theatres and cabarets exert a pull as mighty as the social push of the rural populations toward the metropolitan centers.

Though not so often mentioned as a cause, the desire for protection has impelled many a rural dweller to move into or nearer the city. This is especially true with Negro rural dwellers in nearly every part of the South, where the lack or indifference of constabulary or police agencies make the possession of property uncertain – often hazardous and the safeguarding of life uncertain. These people turn towards the cities for protection in the exercise of the rights guaranteed them under the constitution, and a half chance to defend themselves should these rights be infringed upon. They also seek the protection from fire and ravages of disease which the superior organization and supervision of city life afford . . .

To meet this problem is the social challenge of our generation! To assist the city dweller to make the adjustments necessary to a full possession and enjoyment of the manifold blessings and privileges of urban life is the business of the Church; the mission of the trained social worker; the raison d'etre of organized philanthropy and charity. To this task should be applied the earnest and intelligent aid of every group that makes up the population of our cities. It requires cooperation among racial groups widely differing in language, national customs, and color. It requires mutual racial respect and confidence. It requires tolerance and a courageous application to all sorts of unusual maladjustments, of the principle of the Golden rule. Whether the newcomer to the city is from Texas or South Carolina; whether he is from the Steppe of Russia or the sunny Plain of Italy; whether he is of Nordic hue, or wears the "shadowed livery of the burnished sun," his problem is to obtain for himself and family a living wage, and a place to invest it in cleanliness, fresh air, sanitary surroundings and wholesome recreation. Forcing individuals or groups into segregated ghettoes, with poor sanitation, unpaved streets, run-down houses, filthy alleys and surroundings conductive to depravity of both thought and action is neither a scientific nor altruistic approach to the problem of the city dweller. . . . The

work of...Americanizing the foreigner..., the breaking down of racial barriers and the conceding to every man his right to own and enjoy his property
wherever his means permit him to own it . . . must still be the foundation of the
programme of organizations like the Urban League and other great social
agencies whose militant efforts in these directions have made them national in
scope and purpose.

3

Prosperity and Depression

This chapter focuses on black life in the years between the World Wars, a period marked by continued migration and urbanization and particularly by the outpouring of art, literature, and music in Harlem and across the rest of urban America. The migration of African Americans to New York, Detroit, Chicago, Philadelphia, Boston, and other industrial and cultural centers in search of work also increased their national visibility and influence. The power of jazz, for example, is one manifestation of this new influence.

Northern African American urban women are profiled in **Betterment Organizations Among Harlem Women.** The growing influence of African Americans in professional sports is illustrated in **A League of Their Own: Founding the Negro Baseball League**. The problem of continuing Southern educational discrimination is highlighted in the table **White and Black Education in 1924: A Comparison**.

A number of vignettes depict the Harlem Renaissance, beginning with **Alain Locke Describes the "New Negro" in 1925. Harlem Renaissance Poetry: "If We Must Die"** and **"I Want to Die While You Love Me"** provide glimpses into the literature of the period. **The Debate over "Racial" Art** reminds us that the Renaissance had its African American critics. Finally, **Zora on "Being Colored"** gives one woman's view of racial dynamics during the Renaissance.

The interwar years were also marked by the rise of two radically different movements that promised full freedom and equality for African Americans. The first movement, led by Marcus Garvey, is illustrated in two vignettes. The first, **Marcus Garvey's Views on Race and Nation** provides a brief introduction to Garveyism, the political nationalism that proved exceedingly popular among people of African ancestry throughout the world. The second, the cartoon

At the Crossroads from <u>The Negro World</u>, the newspaper of Garvey's Universal Negro Improvement Association, offers one view of the reasons for the popularity of "Garveyism." **Marcus Garvey: A Seattle Woman Remembers** describes the reaction to Garveyism through the recollections of a child during that period. In **A Lunatic or a Traitor,** we see W. E. B. DuBois's critique of the Garvey Movement.

The other movement that proved appealing for some African Americans, particularly in the 1930s, was Marxism. The vignette **The Messenger: A Black Socialist Newspaper** offers a "left" alternative to the Communist Party. **Black "Pilgrims" in the Soviet Union** discusses the visits of black leaders to that country and the response of its political leadership.

The vignette **Negro Women in Steel** illustrates the growing support of organized labor in the 1930s, while **Franklin Roosevelt: Roy Wilkins Remembers** recalls the ambiguous impact FDR's policies had on African America. The final vignette, **Segregated Baseball, 1939,** describes both the continuing barriers in sports and the role of gifted athletes in undermining those barriers.

Betterment Organizations Among Harlem Women

Harlem writer Elise Johnson McDougald in a 1925 Survey Graphic *article, briefly discussed the various organizations middle-class Harlem women crafted to address problems and improve conditions among the masses of African Americans in that section of New York.*

Obsessed with difficulties that might well compel individualism, the Negro woman has engaged in a considerable amount of organized action to meet group needs. She has evolved a federation of her clubs, embracing between eight and ten thousand women, throughout the state of New York. Its chief function is to crystallize programs, prevent duplication of effort, and to sustain a member organization whose cause might otherwise fail. It is now firmly established, and is about to strive for conspicuous goals. In New York City, one association makes child welfare its name and special concern. Others, like the Utility Club, Utopia Neighborhood, Debutante's League, Sempre Fidelius, etc., raise money for old folks' homes, a shelter for delinquent girls and fresh air camps for children. The Colored Branch of the Y. W. C. A. and the women's organizations in the many churches, as well as in the beneficial lodges and associations, care for the needs of their members.

On the other hand, the educational welfare of the coming generation, has become the chief concern of the national sororities of Negro college women. The first to be organized in the country, Alpha Kappa Alpha, has a systematized and continuous program of educational and vocational guidance for students of the high schools and colleges. The work of Lambda Chapter, which covers New York City and its suburbs, is outstanding. Its recent campaign gathered together nearly one hundred and fifty such students at a meeting to gain inspiration from the life-stories of successful Negro women in eight fields of endeavor. From the trained nurse, who began in the same schools as they, these girls drank in the tale of her rise to the executive position in the Harlem Health Information Bureau. A commercial artist showed how real talent had overcome the color line. The graduate physician was a living example of the modern opportunities in the newer fields of medicine open to women. The vocations as outlets for the creative instinct became attractive under the persuasion of the musician, the dressmaker and the decorator. Similarly, Alpha Beta Chapter of the national Delta Sigma Theta Sorority recently devoted a week to work along similar lines. In such ways as these are the progressive and privileged groups of Negro women expressing, their community and race consciousness.

We find the Negro woman, figuratively, struck in the face daily by contempt from the world about her. Within her soul, she knows little of peace and

SOURCE: Elise Johnson McDougald, "The Double Task: The Struggle of Negro Women for Sex and Race Emancipation," The Survey Graphic LIII (March 1925): 691.

happiness. Through it all, she is courageously standing erect, developing within herself the moral strength to rise above and conquer false attitudes. She is maintaining her natural beauty and charm and improving her mind and opportunity. She is measuring up to the needs and demands of her family, community and race, and radiating from Harlem a hope that is cherished by her sisters in less propitious circumstances throughout the land. The wind of the race's destiny stirs more briskly because of her striving.

A League of Their Own: Founding Negro Baseball

In the following account, Edwin Bancroft Henderson describes the origin of the Negro Baseball League.

The first Negro team composed of paid members is recorded as a playing aggregation that at first was a team of waiters of the Argyle Hotel at Babylon, New York. This club of hotel waiters and bellhops was organized in 1885 by Frank Thompson, head waiter of the hotel. During that summer the team played nine games with the best of the white semi-pro clubs around New York and Long Island, winning six and losing four. In September, Thompson called them the "Cuban Giants," and started them on a professional career.

Knowing the growing prejudices that had infiltrated into the social structure of the North and East, the management realized that to pass off the boys as Cubans or Spaniards would enable them to play in places where as native Negro boys they would not have been able to make business contacts. On the playing field, a few of the Negro players would put on an act and talk a "gibberish" to each other. Because the New York Giants were a popular team of players, the Cubans added the name "Giants." The name "Giants" became attached to nearly every prominent colored team for a quarter of a century. One still remembers the Brooklyn Royal Giants, the Bacharach Giants, the Mohawk Giants, the Chicago American Giants, and others.

Several efforts were made to form leagues of Negro baseball teams. All the early attempts were doomed to failure. In the spring of 1887, a Negro League was formed on paper, but did not reach the field. In 1889, a league of six white and two Negro clubs were organized in the East but folded in a few weeks. About 1906 several of the prominent teams in the East, including the Cuban Giants, the Cuban X-Giants, the Washington Giants, the Royal Giants of Newark, endeavored to form the International League, but before midsummer it collapsed.

SOURCE: Edwin Bancroft Henderson, The Negro In Sports (Washington, D.C.: Associated Publishers, Inc., 1949), Ch. IX, 168–171.

Leaving the East, one finds that on February 13, 1920, in Kansas City, Missouri, the western circuit of the National Negro Baseball League was organized. Seated in that meeting were Tenny Blount of Detroit, L. S. Cobb of the St. Louis Giants, W. A. Kelley of Washington, John Matthews of the Dayton-Monarchs, Joe Greene of the Chicago Giants, C. J. Taylor of the Indianapolis A.B.C.'s, Elwood Knox of Indianapolis, Andrew "Rube" Foster, J. L. Williamson of Kansas City, Missouri, and Charles Marshall, an Indianapolis newspaperman.

The League upon organizing was chartered in the states of Michigan, Illinois, Ohio, Pennsylvania, New York and Maryland. Those signing the constitution of the newly formed league were Rube Foster, Tenny Blount, J. L. Wilkerson, C. I. Taylor, Joe Greene, and Lorenzo Cobb. Each paid $500 to bind them to the league and constitution. Those who helped with the constitution were Dave Wright of Chicago, Ellwood Knox of Indianapolis, Carey B. Lewis of Chicago, and Elisha Scott of Leavenworth. Rube Foster was named president and secretary. The clubs to represent the League during this first year were the American Giants (Chicago), Chicago Giants, Kansas City Monarchs, St. Louis Giants, Detroit Stars, and the Indianapolis A.B.C.'s. The next meeting was on December 4, 1920, in Indianapolis. Foster was re-elected president and secretary for the ensuing year. The association now became the National Association of Colored Professional Baseball and the Negro National League. The following teams were added: the Hilldale Club, Columbus Club, the New York Bacharach Giants, and the Cuban Stars.

In 1921–22, the Eastern League came into being. Ed Bolden of the Hilldale Club organized the Eastern League and was president. It consisted of the Harrisburg Giants, the Hilldales, Lincoln Giants, Brooklyn Royal Giants, Bacharach Giants, Baltimore Black Sox, with the Washington Potomacs as an associate club. There was much shifting of teams due to the lack of organized control. Sometime about 1932, the Negro National League and the Eastern League went down. Subsequent to this dissolution "Cum" Posey brought about the East-West organization. This East-West League consisted of Hilldale, Baltimore Black Sox, Detroit Stars, Columbus, Pittsburgh Crawfords, Homestead Grays, Washington Pilots, and Black Yankees. The first world series between Negro teams was held in 1924 and 1925 between the Negro National and Negro Eastern League champion teams. The first teams in 1924 and 1925 were the Hilldale (Eastern), Kansas City (Western). Contenders in 1926 and 1927 were the Chicago American Giants and the Bacharach Giants.

The 1939 Negro American League located in the West started the following teams with franchises in the cities indicated: Kansas City Monarchs in St. Louis, Atlanta Black Crackers in Louisville, Jacksonville Red Caps in Cleveland, Memphis Giants in Memphis, A.B.C.'s in Indianapolis, and the Chicago American Giants in Chicago.

A Negro National League consisted that year of the following: The Elite Giants in Baltimore, Newark Eagles, Toledo, Homestead Grays, the Philadelphia Stars, the New York Black Yankees, and the New York Cuban Stars team managed by Alexander Pompez. This later day Negro National League contrived to function during subsequent years apparently on firmer ground. The dubs carried from fifteen to twenty salaried players and business associates. In the beginning many of the games were staged for exhibition only. Tom Wilson of the Baltimore Elites was elected president to succeed "Gus" Greenlee, retired.

Another Association existing in the late thirties known as the American Association included the following teams: Baltimore, Hilldale, Greensboro, Winston-Salem, Philadelphia and High Point.

White and Black Education in 1924:
A Comparison

W. E. B. DuBois in 1924 was provided graphic evidence of the disparity in white and black educational appropriations from an unlikely source, the Charleston News and Courier, *when it published figures committed by the state legislature for various institutions.*

The appropriation for public education in South Carolina for 1924 were, according to the <u>Charleston News and Courier</u> as follows:

For White People: [35,000 students]	
The University of South Carolina	$476,025
The Citadel	161,143
Clemson College	91,813
Winthrop College	468,108
[South Carolina] Medical College	120,775
Confederate Home College	5,000
Howe School	48,206
School for Deaf and Blind	125,700
Training School for Feeble Minded	150,310
Industrial School for Boys	129,548
Industrial School for Girls	27,170
	$1,803,798
For Colored People [32,000 students]	
Colored College	$101,150
Reformatory for Negro Boys	52,287
	$153,437

SOURCE: The <u>Crisis</u> (New York) 28, no. 3 (July 1924), 104–105.

Alain Locke Describes the "New Negro" in 1925

Intersecting the recent northward migration of African Americans with the cultural outpouring that would be called the Harlem Renaissance, Howard University professor and literary critic Alain Locke described the ongoing psychological transformation of African America. The following excerpt is from his introduction to the first major anthology that attempted to capture that mood.

In the last decade something beyond the watch and guard of statistics has happened in the life of the American Negro, and the three norms who have traditionally presided over the Negro problem have a changeling in their laps. The Sociologist, the Philanthropist, the Race leader are not unaware of the New Negro, but they are at a loss to account for him. He simply cannot be swathed in their formulae. For the younger generation is vibrant with a new psychology; the new spirit is awake in the masses; and under the very eyes of the professional observers is transforming what has been a perennial problem into the progressive phases of contemporary Negro life.

Could such a metamorphosis have taken place as suddenly as it has appeared to? The answer is no; not only because the New Negro is now here, but because the Old Negro had long become more of a myth than a man. The Old Negro, we must member, was a creature of moral debate and historical controversy. His has been a stock figure perpetuated as an historical fiction partly in innocent sentimentalism, partly in deliberate reactionism. The Negro himself has contributed his share to this through a sort of protective social mimicry forced upon him by the adverse circumstances of dependence. So for generations in the mind of America, the Negro has been more of a formula than a human being – a something to be argued about, condemned or defended, to be "kept down," or "in his place," or "helped up," to be worried with or worried over, harassed or patronized, a social bogey or a social burden...

But while the minds of most of us, black and white, have thus burrowed in the trenches of the Civil War and Reconstruction, the actual march of development has simply flanked these positions, necessitating a sudden reorientation of view.... The mind of the Negro seems suddenly to have slipped from under the tyranny of social intimidation and to be shaking off the psychology of imitation and implied inferiority. By shedding the old chrysalis of the Negro problem we are achieving something like a spiritual emancipation. Until recently, lacking self-understanding, we have been almost as much of a problem to ourselves as we still are to others. But the decade that found us with a problem has left us with only a task...

SOURCE: Alain Locke, ed., <u>The New Negro: An Interpretation</u> (New York: Macmillan, 1925), 3–8.

With this renewed self-respect and self-dependence, the life of the Negro community is bound to enter a new dynamic phase, the buoyancy from within compensating for whatever pressure there may be of conditions from without. The migrant masses, shifting from countryside to city, hurdle several generations of experience at a leap, but more important, the same thing happens spiritually in the attitudes and self-expression of the Young Negro, in his poetry, his art, his education and his new outlook, with the additional advantage, of course, of the poise and greater certainty of knowing what it is all about. From this comes the promise and warrant of a new leadership . . .

. . . The day of "aunties," "uncles" and "mammies" is equally gone. Uncle Tom and Sambo have passed on, and even the "Colonel" and "George" play barnstorm from which they escape with relief when the public spotlight is off. The popular melodrama has about played itself out, and it is time to scrap the fictions, garret the bogeys and settle down to a realistic facing of facts. . . . A main change has been, of course, that shifting of the Negro population which has made the Negro problem no longer exclusively or predominantly Southern. Why should our minds remain sectionalized when the problem no longer is? Then the trend of migration has not only been toward the North and the Central Midwest, but cityward and to the great centers of industry — the problems of adjustment are new, practical, local and not particularly racial. Rather they are an integral part of the large industrial and social problems of our present day democracy . . .

In the very process of being transplanted, the Negro is being transformed. . . . With each successive wave [of migration] the movement of the Negro become more and more a mass movement . . . a deliberate flight not only from countryside to city, but from medieval America to modern.

Take Harlem as an instance of this. Here in Manhattan is not merely the largest Negro community in the world, but the first concentration in history of so many diverse elements of Negro life. It has attracted the African, the West Indian, the Negro American; has brought together the Negro of the North and the Negro of the South; the man from the city and the man from the town and village; the peasant, the student, the business man, the professional man, artist poet, musician, adventurer and worker, preacher and criminal, exploiter and social outcast. Each group has come with its own separate motives and for its own special ends, but their greatest experience has been the finding of one another. Proscription and prejudice have thrown these dissimilar elements into a common area of contact and interaction. Within this area, race sympathy and unity have determined a further fusing of sentiment and experience. So what began in terms of segregation becomes more and more, as its elements mix and react, the laboratory of a great race-welding. Hitherto, it must be admitted that American Negroes have been a race more in name than in fact, or to be exact, more in sentiment than in experience. The chief bond between them has been that of a common condition rather than a common consciousness; a problem in common rather than a life in common. In Harlem, Negro life is seizing upon its first chances for group expression and self-determination. It is — or promises at least to be — a race capital. . . . That is why our comparison is taken with those nascent centers of folk-expression and self-determination which are playing a creative part in the world to-day. Without pretense to their political significance, Harlem has the same role to play for the New Negro as Dublin has had for the New Ireland or Prague for the New Czechoslovakia.

When the race leaders of twenty years ago spoke of developing race-pride and stimulating race-consciousness, and of the desirability of race-solidarity, they could not in any accurate degree have anticipated the abrupt feeling that has surged up and now pervades the awakened centers. Some of the recognized Negro leaders and a powerful section of white opinion identified with "race work" of the older order have indeed attempted to discount this feeling as a "passing phase," an attack of "race nerves" so to speak, an "aftermath of the war," and the like. It has not abated, however, if we are to gauge the present tone and temper of the Negro press, or by the shift in popular support from the officially recognized and orthodox spokesmen to those of the independent, popular, and often radical type who are unmistakable symptoms of a new order. It is a social disservice to blunt the fact that the Negro of the Northern centers has reached a stage where tutelage, even of the most interested and well-intentioned sort, must give place to new relationships, where positive self-direction must be reckoned with in ever increasing measure. The American mind must reckon with a fundamentally changed Negro.

Harlem Renaissance Poetry: "If We Must Die"

In 1919, Senator Henry Cabot Lodge of Massachusetts entered "If We Must Die," the poem of young Claude McKay, into the Congressional Record. *The poem, inspired by the spirited defense blacks mounted in the Chicago race riot of 1919, symbolized the militancy of the "New Negro." However, Georgia Douglas Johnson's poignant poem, which follows McKay's, captures the beauty and passion of renaissance writing as well.*

If we must die, let it not be like hogs
Hunted and penned in an inglorious spot,
While round us bark the mad and hungry dogs,
Making their mock at our accursed lot.

If we must die, O let us nobly die,
So that our precious blood may not be shed
In vain; then even the monsters we defy
Shall be constrained to honor us though dead!

SOURCE: Claude McKay, "If We Must Die," <u>The Liberator</u> 2 (July 1919), 21.

O kinsmen! we must meet the common foe!
Though far outnumbered let us show brave,
And for their thousand blows deal one deathblow!

What though before us lies the open grave?
Like men we'll face the murderous, cowardly pack,
Pressed to the wall, dying but fighting back!

Harlem Renaissance Poetry: "I Want to Die While You Love Me"

The following selection by Renaissance poet Georgia Douglas Johnson suggests that not all of the literature of that era represented racial protest.

I want to die while you love me,
While yet you hold me fair,
While laughter lies upon my lips
And lights are in my hair.

I want to die while you love me.
I could not bear to see,
The glory of this perfect day,
Grow dim—or cease to be.

I want to die while you love me.
Oh! who would care to live
Till love has nothing more to ask,
And nothing more to give.

I want to die while you love me,
And bear to that still bed
Your kisses, turbulent, unspent,
To warm me when I'm dead.

SOURCE: James Weldon Johnson, <u>The Book of American Negro Poetry</u> (New York: Harcourt, Brace & World, Inc., 1922), 183.

The Debate Over "Racial" Art

*Not all black intellectuals supported the Harlem Renaissance. In this account,
we see the exchange of letters in 1926 between Renaissance artist Langston
Hughes and black conservative George S. Schuyler in the magazine* The Nation
over the existence of racially based art.

To THE EDITOR OF THE NATION:

SIR: Langston Hughes, defending racial art in America, forgets that the
Negro masses he describes are no different from the white masses we are all
familiar with. Both 'watch the lazy world go round' and 'have their nip of gin on
Saturday nights' (love of strong liquors is supposed to be a Nordic characteristic).
If there is anything 'racial' about the spirituals and the blues, then there should be
immediate ability to catch the intricate rhythm on the part of Negroes from
Jamaica, Zanzibar, and Sierra Leone. Such is not the case, and we must conclude
that they are the products of a certain American environment: the South. They
are American folk-songs, built around Anglo-Saxon religious concepts.

An artist, if seems, to me, is one who, able to see life about him, and struck
by its quick interchange of comedy, drama, tragedy, attempts to portray it or
interpret it in music, poetry, or prose, on canvas or in stone. He can only use the
equipment furnished him by education and environment. Consequently his
creation will be French, British, German, Russian, Zulu, or Chinese, depending
on where he lives. The work of the artist raised and educated in this country must
necessarily be American.

It is the Afroamericans masses, who consume several millions' worth of hair-
straightener and skin-whitener per anum in an effort to reach the American standard
in pigmentation and hair-texture. This does not look as if they did not care whether
they were like white folks or not. Negro propaganda-art, is hardly more than a
protest against a feeling of inferiority, and such a psychology seldom produces art.

GEORGE S. SCHUYLER

To THE EDITOR OF THE NATION:

Sir: For Mr. Schuyler to say that "the Negro masses . . . are no different from
the white masses" in America seems to me obviously absurd. Fundamentally,
perhaps, all peoples are the same. But as long as the Negro remains a segregated

group in this country he must reflect certain racial and environmental differences which are his own. The very fact that Negroes do straighten their hair and try to forget their racial background makes them different from white people. If they were exactly like the dominant class they would not have to try so hard to imitate them. Again it seems quite as absurd to say that spirituals and blues are not Negro as it is to say that cowboy songs are not cowboy songs or that the folk-ballads of Scotland do not belong to Scotland. The spirituals and blues are American, certainly, but they are also very much American Negro. And if one can say that some of my poems have no racial distinctiveness about them or that 'Cane' is not Negro one can say with equal truth that 'Nize Baby' is purely American."

From an economic and sociological viewpoint it may, be entirely desirable that the Negro become as much like his white American brother as possible. Surely colored people want all the opportunities and advantages that anyone else possesses here in our country. But until America has completely absorbed the Negro and until segregation and racial self-consciousness have entirely disappeared, the true work of art from the Negro artist is bound, if it have any color arid distinctiveness at all, to reflect his racial background and his racial environment.

LANGSTON HUGHES

Zora On "Being Colored"

Zora Neale Hurston's "How It Feels to Be Colored Me," written in 1928, was a declaration of faith and a refreshing reproach of the "racial burden" thesis that informed much of the writing of the Harlem Renaissance. Here is part of her autobiographical essay.

I am colored but I offer nothing in the way of extenuating circumstances except the fact that I am the only Negro in the United States whose grandfather on the mother's side was not an Indian chief. . . . But I am not tragically colored. There is no great sorrow dammed up in my soul, nor lurking behind my eyes. I do not mind at all. I do not belong to the sobbing school of Negroland who hold that nature somehow has given them a lowdown dirty deal and whose feelings are all hurt about it. . . . I have seen that the world is to the strong regardless of a little pigmentation more or less. No, I do not weep at the world – I am too busy sharpening my oyster knife.

Someone is always at my elbow reminding me that I am the granddaughter of slaves. It fails to register depression with me. Slavery is sixty years in the past. The

SOURCE: Zora Neale Hurston, The World Tomorrow XI (May 1928), 215–216.

operation was successful and the patient is doing well, thank you. The terrible struggle that made me an American out of a potential slave said "On the line!" The Reconstruction said "Get set!"; and the generation before said "Go!" I am off to a flying start and I must not halt in the stretch to look behind and weep. Slavery is the price I paid for civilization, and the choice was not with me. It is a bully adventure and worth all that I have paid through my ancestors for it. No one on earth ever had a greater chance for glory. The world to be won and nothing to be lost. It is thrilling to think – to know that for any act of mine, I shall get twice as much praise or twice as much blame. It is quite exciting to hold the center of the national stage, with the spectators not knowing whether to laugh or weep.

I do not always feel colored.... I feel most colored when I am thrown against a sharp white background.... Sometimes it is the other way around. A white person is set down in our midst, but the contrast is just a sharp for me. For instance, when I sit in the drafty basement that is the New World Cabaret with a white person, my color comes. We enter chatting about any little nothing that we have in common and are seated by the jazz waiters. In the abrupt way that jazz orchestras have, this one plunges into a number. It loses no time in circumlocutions, but gets right down to business. It constructs the thorax and splits the heart with its tempo and narcotic harmonies. This orchestra grows rambunctious, rears on its hind legs and attacks the tonal veil with primitive fury, rending it, clawing it until it breaks through to the jungle beyond. I follow those heathen—follow them exultingly. I dance wildly inside myself; I yell within, I whoop; I shake my assegai above my head, I hurl it true to the mark yeeeeooww! I am in the jungle and living in the jungle way. My face is painted red and yellow and my body is painted blue. My pulse is throbbing like a war drum. But the piece ends. The men of the orchestra wipe their lips and rest their fingers. I creep back slowly to the veneer we call civilization with the last tone and find the white friend sitting motionless in his seat, smoking calmly.

"Good music they have here," he remarks, drumming the table with his fingertips. Music. The great blobs of purple and red emotion have not touched him. He has only heard what I felt. He is far away and I see him but dimly across the ocean and the continent that have fallen between us. He is so pale with his whiteness then and I am so colored.

At a certain time I have no race, I am me. When I set my hat at a certain angle and saunter down Seventh Avenue, Harlem City, feeling as snooty as the lions in front of the Forty-second Street Library . . . the cosmic Zora emerges.... Sometimes I feel discriminated against, but it does not make me angry. It merely astonishes me. How can any deny themselves the pleasure of my company? It's beyond me.

Marcus Garvey's Views on Race and Nation

In the following article from the Negro World, *the newspaper of the Universal Negro Improvement Association, Marcus Garvey laid out his beliefs on race and nation.*

The time has come for the Negro to forget and cast behind him his hero worship and adoration of other races, and to start out immediately, to create and emulate heroes of his own.

We must canonize our own saints, create our own martyrs, and elevate to positions of fame and honor black men and women who have made their distinct contributions to our racial history. Sojourner Truth is worthy of the place of sainthood alongside of Joan of Arc; Crispus Attacks and George William Gordon are entitled to the halo of martyrdom with no less glory than that of the martyrs of any other race. Toussaint L'Ouverture's brilliancy as a soldier and statesman outshone that of a Cromwell, Napoleon and Washington; hence, he is entitled to the highest place as a hero among men. Africa has produced countless numbers of men and women, in war and in peace, whose lustre and bravery outshine that of any other people. Then why not see good and perfection in ourselves?

We must inspire a literature and promulgate a doctrine of our own without any apologies to the powers that be. The right is ours and God's. Let contrary sentiment and cross opinions go to the winds. Opposition to race independence is the weapon of the enemy to defeat the hopes of an unfortunate people. We are entitled to our own opinions and not obligated to or bound by the opinions of others.

If others laugh at you, return the laughter to them; if they mimic you, return the compliment with equal force. They have no more right to dishonor, disrespect and disregard your feeling and manhood than you have in dealing with them. Honor them when they honor you; disrespect and disregard them when they vilely treat you. Their arrogance is but skin deep and an assumption that has no foundation in morals or in law. They have sprung from the same family tree of obscurity as we have; their history is as rude in its primitiveness as ours; their ancestors ran wild and naked, lived in caves and in the branches of trees, like monkeys, as ours . . . for centuries even as they accuse us of doing; their cannibalism was more prolonged than ours; when we were embracing the arts and sciences on the banks of the Nile their ancestors were still drinking human blood and eating out of the skulls of their conquered dead; when our civilization had reached the noonday of progress they were still running naked and sleeping in holes and caves with rats, bats . . . and animals. After we had already fathomed the

SOURCE: Marcus Garvey, "African Fundamentalism," <u>Negro World</u> (New York), June 6, 1925.

SOURCE: "At the Crossroads," <u>Negro World</u> (New York), April 14, 1928, 4.

mysteries of the stars and reduced the heavenly constellations to minute and regular calculus they were still backwoodsmen, living in ignorance and blatant darkness.

The world today is indebted to us for the benefits of civilization. . . . Then why should we be ashamed of ourselves? Their MODERN IMPROVEMENTS are but DUPLICATES of a grander civilization that we reflected thousands of years ago, without the advantage of what is buried and still hidden, to be resurrected and reintroduced by the intelligence of our generation and our prosperity. Why should we be discouraged because somebody laughs at us today? Who [is] to tell what tomorrow will bring forth? Did they not laugh at Moses, Christ and Mohammed . . . ? We see and have changes every day, so pray, work, be steadfast and be not dismayed.

As the Jew is held together by his RELIGION, the white races by the assumption and the unwritten law of SUPERIORITY, and the Mongolian by the precious tie of BLOOD, so likewise the Negro must be united in one GRAND RACIAL HIERARCHY. Our UNION MUST KNOW NO CLIME, BOUNDARY, or NATIONALITY. Like the great Church of Rome, Negroes the world over MUST PRACTICE ONE FAITH, that of Confidence in themselves, with One God! One Aim! One Destiny! Let no religious scruples, no political machination divide us, but let us hold together under all climes and in every country, making among ourselves a Racial Empire upon which "the sun shall never set."

There is no humanity before that which starts with yourself. . . . God and Nature first made us what we are, and then out of our own creative genius we make ourselves what we want to be. Follow always that great law. . . . There is no height to which we cannot climb by using the active intelligence of our minds. . . . Being at present the scientifically weaker race, you shall treat others only as they treat you; but in your homes and everywhere possible you must teach the higher development of science to your children; and be sure to develop a race of scientists par excellence, for in science and religion lies our only hope to withstand the evil designs of modern materialism. Never forget your God. Remember, we live, work and pray for the establishing of a great...RACIAL EMPIRE whose only natural, spiritual and political limits shall be God and "Africa, home and abroad."

Marcus Garvey: A Seattle Woman Remembers

In September 1976, Juanita Warfield Proctor was interviewed as part of an oral history project sponsored by the state of Washington. Mrs. Proctor, a Seattle native who at that time was sixty-four years old, discussed her parents as members of the UNIA in that city. Mrs. Proctor was ten years old when Marcus Garvey visited Seattle in 1922. In the following passage, she described that visit and the activities of the Seattle division.

On Sunday morning after Sunday School at First AME Church we Warfield children walked down 14th Avenue to the UNIA Hall where they'd have meetings for the kids.... Sometimes we kids wouldn't want to stay. 'Course, we'd have to stay until my parents came to the meeting. After they came my mother and the other ladies used to fix a big dinner for us kids and then they'd have their meeting. I can remember the large dining room, they had this long table.

My mother was one of the Black Cross Nurses. There were about 50 to 100 women that belonged to the Black Cross Nurses. They practiced first aid and stuff like that. They used to march in the parades, like the Memorial Day Parade, and Fourth of July Parade. And they'd dress in their beautiful white uniforms with the black cross on the forehead, and on the arm a red, black and green sash. And my dad, and the men wore the red, black and green sash across their chest.

INTERVIEWER: Were your mother and father officers in the UNIA?

Well no, they were more of working members, you know, mostly they were very faithful members, because they went every Sunday and they would practice marching. They had march sessions, you know, on Wednesday evenings. I remember sometimes they would take us kids to them and they would practice their march. And then on Fridays they had choir rehearsal. See, they even had choirs too.

SOURCE: Juanita Warfield Proctor Interview, September 22, 1975. Transcript at the Manuscripts and Archives Division, University of Washington Library, Seattle, Washington.

I remember Marcus Garvey coming here. We met [him] at the Union Station, and all the Black Cross Nurses and the men were all there [in uniform] to greet him. And I was the little girl that they gave the flowers to give to him. I though he was going to be a big tall man. He looked big in the pictures, and when I went to give him the flowers he was almost as short as I was.

He spoke at the Washington Hall on 14th and Fir. As for his speech, you know, with kids, when we're kids we don't pay any attention to what they were talking about. They were trying to teach us about Africa, that we should know more about Africa. I remember that, and they were working to . . . free . . . Liberia. And I remember my mother and father talking about Marcus Garvey was getting this ship up to send black people back to Africa, the ones that wanted to go.

A Lunatic or a Traitor

In an editorial in the Crisis *dated May 1924, W. E. B. DuBois made one of his harshest attacks on Marcus Garvey and his program.*

Marcus Garvey is, without doubt, the most dangerous enemy of the Negro race in America and in the world. He is either a lunatic or a traitor. He is sending all over this country tons of letters and pamphlets appealing to Congressmen, business men, philanthropists and educators to join him on a platform whose half concealed planks may be interpreted as follows:

That no person of Negro descent can ever hope to become an American citizen.

That forcible separation of the races and the banishment of Negroes to Africa is the only solution of the Negro problem.

That race war is sure to follow any attempt to realize the program of the N.A.A.C.P.

We would have refused to believe that any man of Negro descent could have fathered such a propaganda if the evidence did not lie before us in black and white signed by this man. . . .

Everybody, including the writer, who has dared to make the slightest criticism of Garvey has been intimidated by threats and threatened with libel suits. Over fifty court cases have been brought by Garvey in ten years. After my first unfavorable article on Garvey, I was not only threatened with death by men declaring themselves his followers, but received letters of such unbelievable filth that they were absolutely unprintable. When I landed in this country from my trip to Africa I learned with disgust that my friends stirred by Garvey's threats had actually compelled to have secret police protection for me on the dock!

SOURCE: W. E. B. DuBois, Crisis (New York), May 1924, 8–9.

Friends have even begged me not to publish this editorial lest I be assassinated. To such depths have we dropped in free black America! I have been exposing white traitors for a quarter century. If the day has come when I cannot tell the truth about black traitors it is nigh time that I died.

The American Negroes have endured this wretch all too long with fine restraint and every effort at cooperation and understanding. But the end has come. Every man who apologizes for or defends Marcus Garvey from this day forth writes himself down as unworthy of the countenance of decent Americans. As for Garvey himself, this open ally of the Ku Klux Klan should be locked up or sent home.

The Messenger: A Black Socialist Newspaper

In the first editorial of The Messenger *titled "Our Reason for Being," co-editors Chandler Owen and A Philip Randolph described their approach to the black situation in the United States.*

First, as workers, black and white, we all have one common interest, viz., the getting of more wages, shorter hours, and better working conditions. Black and white workers should combine for no other reason than that for which individual workers should combine, viz., to increase their bargaining power. The combination of black and white workers will be a powerful lesson to the capitalists of the solidarity of labor. It will show that labor, black and white, is conscious of its interests and power. This will prove that unions are not based upon race lines, but upon class lines. This will serve to convert a class of workers, which has been used by the capitalist class to defeat organized labor, into an ardent, class conscious, intelligent, militant group.

The Industrial Workers of the World commonly termed the I. W. W. draw no race, creed, color or sex line in their organization. They are making a desperate effort to get the colored men into the One Big Union. The Negroes are at least giving them an ear, and the prospects point to their soon giving them a hand. With the Industrial Workers Organization already numbering 800,000, to augment it with a million and a half or two million Negroes, would make it fairly rival the American Federation of Labor. This may still be done anyhow and the reactionaries of this country, together with Samuel Gompers, the reactionary President of the American Federation of Labor, desire to hold back this trend of Negro labor radicalism. . . .

The New York World, the mouth piece of the present administration, and also a plutocratic mouth piece, says in its issue of June 4, 1919, "The radical forces in New York City have recently embarked on a great new field of revolutionary

SOURCE: The Messenger (August 1919), 11–12.

endeavor, the education through agitation of the southern Negro into the mysteries and desirability of revolutionary Bolshevism." There are several different powerful forces in N.Y. City behind this move. The chief established propaganda is being distributed through The Messenger, which styles itself – "The only magazine of scientific radicalism in the world, published by Negroes." With the exception of The Liberator, it is the most radical journal printed in the U.S." ...

There is a new leadership for Negro workers. It is a leadership of uncompromising manhood. It is not asking for a half loaf but for the whole loaf. It is insistent upon the Negro workers exacting justice, both from the white labor unions and from the capitalists or employers.

The Negroes who will benefit from this decision are indebted first to themselves and their organized power, which made them dangerous. Second, to the radical agitation carried on by The Messenger; and third, to the fine spirit of welcome shown by the Industrial Workers of the World, whose rapid growth and increasing power the American Federation of Labor fears. These old line Negro political fossils know nothing of the Labor Movement, do not believe in labor unions at all, and have never taken any active steps to encourage such organizations. We make this statement calmly, coolly and with a reasonable reserve. The very thing which they are fighting is one of the chief factors in securing for Negroes their rights. That is Bolshevism. The capitalists of this country are so afraid that Negroes will become Bolshevists that they are willing to offer them almost anything to hold them away from the radical movement. Nobody buys pebbles which may be picked up on the beach, but diamonds sell high. The old line Negro leaders have no power to bargain, because it is known that they are Republicans politically and job-hunting me-too-boss-hat-in-hand-Negroes, industrially. Booker Washington and all of them have simply advocated that Negroes get more work. The editors of The Messenger are not interested in Negroes getting more work. Negroes have too much work already. What we want Negroes to get is less work and more wages, with more leisure for study and recreation.... In organization there is strength; and whenever Negroes or anybody else make organized demands, their call will be heeded.

Black "Pilgrims" in the Soviet Union

In the following account, historian Allison Blakely describes the migration of a small group of African Americans to the Soviet Union to participate in its "new society."

If some Negroes viewed Russia as a land of promise in the nineteenth century, in the 1920s and 1930s other Negroes, especially from the Americas, saw the Soviet Union, and its idea of the "new society," as "the promised land" itself. ...

SOURCE: Allison Blakely, <u>Russia and the Negro: Blacks in Russian History and Thought</u>, 81–84. Howard University Press, 1986. Copyright © 1986 by Howard University Press. All rights reserved. Reprinted with permission by Howard University Press.

The bright humanitarian ideals of the Soviet Union represented one more alluring option to Negroes seeking a society where they would not be persecuted because of their color. . . . One observer estimated that by the early 1930s several hundred Negroes had visited the Soviet Union. As least a small segment of that number remained for several years or permanently; others followed them in subsequent decades–politicos, technicians, and artists.

There were . . . Negroes who fought in the Red Army during the Russian Civil War. A memoirist recalled that a man named George fought on the Ural front in 1918 as a signal corpsman in an international communist detachment assigned to the division commanded by Vasili Chapaev. . . . Another Negro, this one a cavalry officer who died leading a charge near Voronezh, inspired Boris Kornilov's poem, Moia Afrika [My Africa], published in 1935. In fact, the Soviets claimed to have won over an entire African regiment from the forces the French employed to aid the Whites [White Russian forces] during the Civil War.

In the 1920s several Negroes were among the first foreigners invited to attend special schools established to train Communist Party leaders for various parts of the world. As part of Comintern's training program, in 1921 it founded the Communist University for the Toilers of the East (sometimes called the Far East University). It was intended primarily for students from the Soviet East and from colonial countries. However, it soon admitted four American Negroes and one African then residing in the United States . . .

The communist students represented only a small minority of negroes who have been so fascinated by . . . Soviet society that they paid a visit. Most were neither pro- nor anti-communist; their only definite objective was to find a society where a person's worth was not defined by his skin color. The most interesting and well-documented visit of the type was that of the writer Claude McKay in 1922. . . . He was originally invited to Russia in 1920 by John Reed, after Lenin had raised the issue of the Negro question at the Second Comintern Congress, but at the time McKay felt unqualified for the mission. Having missed that opportunity, in 1922 he raised the fare for what he call his "magic pilgrimage to Russia."

Another American Negro, Otto Huiswood, had come to the Soviet Union as part of the American delegation to the Comintern Congress. However, it soon became obvious that the Soviet leaders preferred McKay as a representative Negro. Huiswood was light-skinned whereas McKay was dark-skinned and therefore better fit the Russian preconception of a Negro. This was highly ironic considering Huiswood's credentials. A native of Dutch Guiana whose father had been born a slave, Huiswood would eventually become one of the most prominent Americans in the Comintern. As a delegate from New York . . . he was the only Negro among the ninety-four founders of the American Communist Party. McKay later claimed that the American delegation tried to have him deported because he had arrived with a British group and not with them. However the prominent Japanese communist Sen Katayama interceded on McKay's behalf and he was allowed to stay. The Soviet leaders apparently had a specific objective in mind; for McKay soon found himself being photographed with Zinoviev, Bukharin, Radek, Katayama, and other Party luminaries. At the opening of the Congress, McKay, and not Huiswood, was seated on the platform as representing the symbolic presence of the black American worker.

Negro Women in Steel

By the late 1930s, African American workers in major Northern cities had finally become part of organized labor, usually joining "industrial" unions such as the United Steelworkers. Mollie V. Lewis's 1938 article in the Crisis titled "Negro Women in Steel," however, wrote of the growing support of the wives of these black unionized steelworkers in Gary, Indiana, suggesting that the incorporation of African American workers and their families into the labor movement also furthered the cause of societal racial integration. Part of her article appears here.

Perhaps you are a Negro woman, driven to the worst part of town but paying the same high rent," writes Jenny Elizabeth Johnstone in her challenging little pamphlet Women in Steel. "You are strong. There is nothing new in suffering to you," she continues. "Your man is driven even harder than the white workers, but your man gets lower pay – hired the last and fired the first," I know these women of the steel towns of which Miss Johnstone writes – these women living dreary lives under the domination of powerful and impersonal corporations. I have been one of them. The conditions under which they live, the excessive rents demanded for cramped and inadequate shelter, the uncertainty of employment for their men folk and the disruptive inconvenience of the mill shifts all combine to make life a hard and uneven road for them. It is because of such conditions, faced by the women of every mill worker's family, that the Steel Workers' Organizing Committee, of the Committee for Industrial Organization has sponsored the formation of women's auxiliaries in the campaign for the unionization of the industry.

Last summer I revisited Gary, that hard and unbeautiful metropolis of steel upon the banks of Lake Michigan. In the mills which line the lake shore, furnaces were going full blast, twenty four hours a day. Steel was pouring from them in molten streams. Thousands of men of both races and many nationalities, sweaty and grimy, were tending the furnaces and conducting the ore through its processes to the finished product.

Something new had come into the lives of these men. Thousands of them had joined the union. For the first time it was possible for them openly to be union men in the mills of the United States Steel Corporation. For the first time this vast corporation for which they worked had recognized their union and entered into an agreement with it.

Only a few miles distant, however, in Indiana Harbor and South Chicago, Little Steel had taken a bitter stand against the union and against the spirit of the New Deal and had engaged in a costly fight which was climaxed by the

SOURCE: Mollie V. Lewis, "Negro Women in Steel," The Crisis (New York) 45 (February 1938), 54. Thomson Publishing wishes to thank that Crisis Publishing Co., Inc., the publisher of the magazine of the National Association for the Advancement of Colored People, for the use of the materials from the Crisis Magazine.

Memorial Day Massacre. The strike was now over and the men were returning to work without the recognition which had been negotiated with Big Steel.

Hand in hand with the campaign to organize the mill workers went the drive to bring the women folk of these men into active participation in the labor movement. The agency for organizing the women was the Women's Auxiliary of the Amalgamated Association of Iron, Steel and Tin Workers of North America. The objectives of the campaign were to organize the women "to lend aid to the union in all possible ways," to help them to maintain the morale of the steel workers, to educate them in the principles of trade unionism, and to weld them into a force for social betterment.

Bringing Races Together

In the matter of race relations, Gary and the adjacent steel towns are by no means utopian. From time to time bitter racial animosities have flared, not only between Negroes and whites, but also between native citizens and the foreign born. In addition many of the foreign born brought with them to this country nationalistic enmities rooted in Old World conflicts. To induce the women of such diverse groups to join the same organization, even for their own benefit, has been no easy task. In Gary I talked with Mrs. Minneola Ingersoll who was in charge of the organization of women's auxiliaries in the Chicago-Calumet district, Mrs. Ingersoll is a young southern white woman and a graduate of the University of Alabama. Together we visited the homes of members of the auxiliary of both races and various nationalities.

"Our policy in the auxiliary, as in the union," Mrs. Ingersoll said, "is to organize all regardless of their race, color, creed or nationality. When it comes to exploitation, the mill owners draw no color line. They exploit the native white workers just as they do the Mexican, Polish and Negro workers."

In Indiana Harbor where Inland Steel had forced its workers into a long and bitter strike rather than grant their demand for recognition, a number of Negro women had been drawn into the auxiliary In Gary, however, Negro women seemed more reluctant to join and the campaign had been less successful among them, Along with the women of other groups, Negro women were represented on the picket lines of the struck plants.

During the strike they cooperated with others behind the lines in the preparation and serving of hot meals to the strikers. They were members of the various committees which sought contributions of money and food to keep the strike going.

Negroes Aided in Strike

... The organizing of white and Negro women in the same units has naturally had its by-product in the field of race relations. While the auxiliaries have by no means eliminated racial barriers in a district where jim crowism flourishes, they have for the first time made it possible for the women of both races to get to know one another on friendly terms.

While the municipal government of Gary continues to keep the children apart in a system of separate schools, their parents are getting together in the union and in the auxiliary. And after school hours, the children meet jointly in a junior lodge under guidance of an instructor. It is noteworthy that the only public eating place in Gary where both races may be freely served is a cooperative restaurant largely patronized by members of the union and auxiliary.

These, it may be true, are of minor importance. But they represent steps toward inter-racial cooperation on a mass basis. When the black and white workers and members of their families are convinced that their basic economic interests are the same, they may be expected to make common cause for the advancement of these interests. Women of both races have, for traditional reasons, been inclined to be more stand-offish than men when it comes to organizing a common body. The efforts of the auxiliary to bring the women together may ultimately prove to be a significant factor in overcoming racial barriers which still retard the advance of the labor movement in this country.

Franklin Roosevelt: Roy Wilkins Remembers

In the following account NAACP officer Roy Wilkins describes the impact of the policies of Franklin Delano Roosevelt's Administration on the nation's African American citizens.

On the subject of the Negro, the Roosevelt record is spotty, as might be expected in an administration where so much power is in the hands of the southern wing of the Democratic Party. And yet Mr. Roosevelt, hobbled as he has been by the Dixie die-hards, has managed to include Negro citizens in practically every phase of the administration program. In this respect, no matter how far behind the ideal he may be, he is far ahead of any other Democratic president, and of recent Republican ones.

The best proof that Mr. Roosevelt has not catered always to the South and has insisted on carrying the Negro along with his program is to be found in the smearing, race-hating propaganda used against him in the 1936 campaign by southern white groups. Both he and Mrs. Roosevelt were targets of filthy mud-slinging simply because they did not see eye-to-eye with the South on the Negro.

This does not mean that the Roosevelt administration has done all that it could have done for the race. Its policies in many instances have done Negroes great injustice and have helped to build more secure walls of segregation. On

SOURCE: Roy Wilkins, "The Roosevelt Record", Crisis 47 (November 1940).
Reprinted with permission by The Crisis Magazine. Thomson Publishing wishes to thank
that Crisis Publishing Co., Inc., the publisher of the magazine of the National Association
for the Advancement of Colored People, for the use of the materials from the Crisis
Magazine.

the anti-lynching bill Mr. Roosevelt has said not a mumbling word. His failure to endorse this legislation, to bring pressure to break the filibuster, is a black mark against him. It does no good to say that the White House could not pass down some word on this bill. The White House spoke on many bills. Mr. Roosevelt might have pressed the anti-lynching bill to a vote, especially during January and February 1938, when there was tremendous public opinion supporting the bill. His failure to act, or even speak, on the anti-lynching bill was the more glaring because, while mobs in America were visiting inhumanities upon Negroes, Mr. Roosevelt periodically was rebuking some foreign government for inhumanity, and enunciating high sentiments of liberty, tolerance, justice, etc. . . .

Full credit must go to the administration for its program of low-cost housing, so sorely needed by low-income families. No one pretends that the American housing program is more than a beginning, but Negroes have shared in it in the most equitable manner. However, there were, outside the slum-clearance program, some damaging practices. The FHA, which insures mortgages for home buyers, has enforced a regulation which puts the power and approval of the government on ghetto life. No Negro family which sought a home outside the so-called "Negro" neighborhood could get a FHA-insured loan . . .

The farm program has not been ideally administered, but colored people have shared in the benefits. More than 50,000 families have been assisted by the Farm Security Administration.

Mr. Roosevelt had the courage to appoint a Negro to a federal judgeship, the first in the history of the country. His nominee was confirmed by a Democratic Senate without a murmur.

Heavily on the debit side is Mr. Roosevelt's approval of the War Department's notorious Jim Crow in the armed services.

[The] most important contribution of the Roosevelt administration to the age-old color line problem in America has been its doctrine that Negroes are a part of the country and must be considered in any program for the country as a whole. . . . For the first time in their lives, government has taken on meaning and substance for the Negro masses.

Segregated Baseball, 1939

In the article reprinted here, Washington Post Sports Writer Shirley Povich described the loss of talented players because of Major League Baseball's color bar. Povich joined a growing chorus of white sports writers who demanded the integration of baseball and other professional sports.

SOURCE: "This Morning with Shirley Povich," <u>Washington Post</u>, April 7, 1939, Section III, 21. Copyright © 1939 by The Washington Post. All rights reserved. Reprinted with permission of The Washington Post Co.

Orlando, Fla., April 6. There's a couple of million dollars worth of baseball talent on the loose, ready for the big leagues yet unsigned, by any major league clubs. There are pitchers who would win 20 games this season for any big league club that offered them contracts, and there are outfielders who could hit .350, infielders who could win quick recognition as stars, and there is at least one catcher who at this writing is probably superior to Bill Dickey.

Only one thing is keeping them out of the big leagues—the pigmentation of their skin. They happen to be colored. That's their crime in the eyes of many club owners and fans.

Their talents are being wasted in the rickety parks in the Negro sections of Pittsburgh, Philadelphia, New York, Chicago and four other cities that comprise the major league of Negro baseball. They haven't got a chance to get into the big leagues of the white folks. It's a tight little boycott that the majors have set up against colored players.

It's a sort of gentleman's agreement among the club owners that is keeping Negroes out of big league baseball. There's nothing in the rules that forbids a club from signing a colored player. It's not down in black and white, so to speak. But it's definitely understood that no club will attempt to sign a colored player. And, in fact, no club could do that, because the elasticity of Judge Landis' authority would forbid it. And the judge can rule out of baseball any character whose presence he may deem 'detrimental' to the game.

Just how a colored player would be detrimental to the game has never been fully explained, but that seems to be the light in which they are regarded by the baseball brass hats. Perhaps it is because there is such an overwhelming majority of Southern boys in big league baseball who would not take kindly to the presence of colored athletes and would flash a menacing spike, or so. Perhaps it's because baseball has done well enough without colored players. It's a smug, conservative business not given to very great enterprise and the introduction of new and novel features.

There have been campaigns aimed at smashing the boycott. One New York newspaper openly advocated the signing of Negro players, and Heywood Broun has often berated the baseball magnates for drawing the color line. But despite the presence of thousands of colored customers in the stands, the club owners have blithely hewed to the color line. They are content, seemingly, to leave well enough alone and make no concerted play for Negro patronage.

A $200,000 Catcher

But in its restricted localities, Negro baseball has flowered. There are Negro teams which now might do very well in big league competition even if they played as a Negro entity. The Homesteads of Pittsburgh are probably the best colored team. They train here in Florida each spring, even as do the American and National League first teams. The other evening at Tinker Field, the Homesteads met the Newark Eagles of the same colored league. Curious Washington players flocked to the game, went away with a deep respect for colored baseball.

Walter Johnson sat in a box at the game, profoundly impressed with growing the talents of the colored players. 'There,' he said, 'is a catcher that any big league club would like to buy for $200,000. I've heard of him before. His name is Gibson. They call him 'Hoot' Gibson, and he can do everything. He hits that ball a mile. And he catches so easy, he might just as well be in a rocking chair. Throws like a rifle. Bill Jim Dickey isn't as good a catcher. Too bad that Gibson is a colored fellow.'

Until last season there was a colored pitcher around named 'Satchel' Page. The colored folks have a penchant for picturesque names for their idols and 'Satchel' Page was so-called because of the size of his feet. He was 6 feet 3, a left-hander and a whale of a pitcher. 'He retired last year at the age of 44,' said Jimmy Wasdell, 'and he was still a great pitcher. I've been on clubs that barnstormed against Negro teams and in a dozen games against this Page we never beat him. He beat Paul and Dizzy Dean one night, 1-0, and we got only one hit off him. I was the only minor leaguer on our club . . . '

4

World War II

The World War II years and the following decade provided the first significant employment advances and civil rights victories since the Reconstruction period. Consequently, the massive edifice of segregation and racial discrimination was beginning to show major fissures.

The first fissure occurred in 1941 when civil rights and labor leader A. Philip Randolph pressured the Franklin Roosevelt Administration to issue Executive Order 8802, which outlawed racial discrimination by private firms receiving defense contracts. His argument is advanced in the vignette **A. Philip Randolph Calls for a March on Washington, 1941**. The second vignette is a cartoon by Theodor Seuss Geisel (Dr. Seuss) titled **"The Old Run Around,"** which satirizes job discrimination by the defense industries. The vignette **Dr. Charles Drew and "Segregated" Blood** profiles the physician who developed blood plasma and thus saved thousands of lives in World War II, while **"Can Negroes Really Fly Airplanes"** relates an episode where First Lady Eleanor Roosevelt is flown by a black pilot to challenge another prevailing stereotype. The growing assertiveness of black women war workers is profiled in **Lyn Childs Confronts a Racist Act**, while **The Liberation of the Death Camps** is a poignant reminder of the black soldier's participation in World War II.

Anticipation of change in the post-war period, including the linking of black domestic struggles with anticolonial campaigns in Asia, Africa, and Latin America, began even while the fighting still raged in Europe and the Pacific as reflected in **African America and International Affairs: A Rising Wind.**

A Conservative's Outlook, 1946 is a critique of the strategies of the leading civil rights organizations of the time, while in **Civil Rights and Organized Labor in the South: Moranda Smith Speaks** profiles the attempt to fuse two increasingly powerful movements for social change. **"Live Anywhere!" High**

Court Rules shows the growing role of the federal government in undermining racial discrimination, while **Army Integration in the Korean War** describes its impact. The table **Black Student Enrollment in Colleges, 1941–1942** palpably illustrates the small number of African Americans who had access to higher education during this period. Finally the international influence of political activist Paul Robeson is displayed in **Paul Robeson Sings on the Border**.

A. Philip Randolph Calls for a March on Washington, 1941

In an article published in the Black Worker *in May 1941, civil rights leader A. Philip Randolph called on African Americans to march to the U.S. capital to demonstrate for the end of employment discrimination in defense employment. Part of that call is reprinted here.*

We call upon you to fight for jobs in National Defense. We call upon you to struggle for the integration of Negroes in the armed forces, such as the Air Corps, Navy, Army, and Marine Corps of the Nation. We call upon you to demonstrate for the abolition of Jim-Crowism in all Government departments and defense employment. This is an hour of crisis. It is a crisis of democracy. It is a crisis of minority groups. It is a crisis of Negro Americans. What is this crisis?

To American Negroes, it is the denial of jobs in Government defense projects. It is racial discrimination in Government departments. It is widespread Jim-Crowism in the armed forces of the Nation. While billions of the taxpayers' money are being spent for war weapons, Negro workers are finally being turned away from the gates of factories, mines and mills–being flatly told, "NOTHING DOING." Some employers refuse to give Negroes jobs when they are without "union cards," and some unions refuse to Negro workers union cards when they are "without jobs . . . "

With faith and confidence of the Negro people in their own power for self-liberation, Negroes can break down the barriers of discrimination against employment in National Defense. Negroes can kill the deadly serpent of race hatred in the Army, Navy, Air and Marine Corps, and smash through and blast the Government, business and labor-union red tape to win the right to equal opportunity in vocational training and re-training in defense employment.

Most important and vital of all, Negroes, by the mobilization and coordination of their mass power, can cause PRESIDENT ROOSEVELT TO ISSUE AN EXECUTIVE ORDER ABOLISHING DISCRIMINATIONS IN ALL GOVERNMENT DEPARTMENTS, ARMY, NAVY, AIR CORPS AND NATIONAL DEFENSE JOBS.

Of course, the task is not easy. In very truth, it is big, tremendous and difficult. It will cost money. It will require sacrifice. It will tax the Negroes' courage, determination and will to struggle. But we can, must and will triumph.

The Negroes' stake in national defense is big. It consists of jobs, thousands of jobs. It may represent millions, yes, hundreds of millions of dollars in wages. It consists of new industrial opportunities and hope. This is worth fighting for. But to win our stakes, it will require an "all-out," bold and total effort and demonstration of colossal proportions. Negroes can build a mammoth machine of mass action with a terrific and tremendous driving and striking power that can shatter and crush the evil fortress of race prejudice and hate, if they will only resolve to do so and never stop, until victory comes . . .

In this period of power politics, nothing counts but pressure, more pressure, and still more pressure, through the tactic and strategy of broad, organized, aggressive mass action behind the vital and important issues of the Negro. To this end, we propose that ten thousand Negroes MARCH ON WASHINGTON FOR JOBS IN NATIONAL DEFENSE AND EQUAL INTEGRATION IN THE FIGHTING FORCES OF THE UNITED STATES. An "all-out" thundering march on Washington, ending in a monster and huge demonstration at Lincoln's Monument will shake up white America. It will shake up official Washington. It will give encouragement to our white friends to fight all the harder by our side, with us, for our righteous cause. It will gain respect for the Negro people. It will create a new sense of self-respect among Negroes.

But what of national unity? We believe in national unity which recognizes equal opportunity of black and white citizens to jobs in national defense and the armed forces, and in all other institutions and endeavors in America. We condemn all dictatorships, Fascist, Nazi and Communist. We are loyal, patriotic Americans all. But if American democracy will not defend its defenders; if American democracy will not protect its protectors; if American democracy will not give jobs to its toilers because of race or color; if American democracy will not insure equality of opportunity, freedom and justice to its citizens, black and white, it is a hollow mockery and belies the principles for which it is supposed to stand.

To the hard, difficult and trying problem of securing equal participation in national defense, we summon all Negro Americans to march on Washington. We summon Negro Americans to form committees in various cities to recruit and register marchers and raise funds through the sale of buttons and other legitimate means for the expenses of marchers to Washington by buses, train, private automobiles, trucks, and on foot.

We [also] summon Negro Americans to stage marches on their City Halls and Councils in their respective cities and urge them to memorialize the President to issue an executive order to abolish discrimination in the Government and national defense. However, we sternly counsel against violence and ill-considered and intemperate action and the abuse of power. Mass power, like physical power, when misdirected is more harmful that helpful. We summon you to mass action that is orderly and lawful, but aggressive and militant, for justice, equality and freedom . . .

Today, we call upon President Roosevelt, a great humanitarian and idealist, to . . . free American Negro citizens of the stigma, humiliation and insult of discrimination and Jim-Crowism in Government departments and national defense. The Federal Government cannot with clear conscience call upon private industry and labor unions to abolish discrimination based on race and color as long as it practices discrimination itself against Negro Americans.

NEGROES' COMMITTEE TO MARCH ON WASHINGTON
FOR EQUAL PARTICIPATION IN NATIONAL DEFENSE.

The Old Run-Around

SOURCE: The Dr. Seuss Collection, Mandeville Special Collections Library, University of California, San Diego.

Dr. Charles Drew and "Segregated" Blood

Many African Americans have long recalled and recounted the story of Dr. Charles R. Drew, the brilliant Howard University surgeon who during World War II developed blood plasma, which saved millions of lives, but who in 1950 died tragically, and by implication unnecessarily because he was refused admittance to a segregated North Carolina hospital after a traffic accident. Historian Spencie Love investigated the story of Drew's death and discovered that he was unsuccessfully treated by white doctors in an otherwise segregated hospital following his accident. She posits that the account of Drew's death was interwoven with the stories of many other less famous African Americans who died or suffered from segregated medical care. Love traces in detail the story of Malthus Reeves Avery, a black North Carolina college student, who did in fact die after being refused admittance to the Duke University Hospital in another traffic accident just months after Drew's death. The Red Cross's segregated blood policy in World War II, and the protests it generated by Drew and others, laid the foundation for the Drew legend. The excerpted portion of her 1992 article, which follows, describes the life of Drew and his brief campaign against the Red Cross's segregation of blood.

SOURCE: Spencie Love, " 'Noted Physician Fatally Injured,' Charles Drew and the Legend That Will Not Die," <u>Washington History: Magazine of the Historical Society of Washington, D.C.</u> 4, no. 2 (Fall/Winter 1992–93): 8–11.

C harles Richard Drew was born on June 3, 1904, at 1806 E Street, N.W., in Washington, D.C. He was the eldest of five children born to Richard Thomas Drew and Nora Rosella Burwell Drew.... The years of Drew's childhood were terrible ... for American blacks as a group. But Drew and many of his peers managed to live in a protected, hopeful environment, thanks to their families, their churches, and excellent black schools. The Washington of this period was describes as having "the most distinguished and brilliant assembly of Negroes in the world."

Drew graduated from Dunbar [High School] in 1922. He attended Amherst College on an athletic scholarship along with several Dunbar friends. Except for intermittent periods of work, Drew spent the next 18 years completing an extremely formal education.... After Amherst came four years of McGill University Medical School in Montreal, Canada and two years of internship. Drew was then chosen for a Rockefeller fellowship at Columbia University Medical School from 1938 to 1940. There he trained under Dr. Allen Whipple, one of the top surgeons in the country. He also undertook the research on blood preservation that earned him a doctor of science degree, the first ever earned by an African American.

In 1939 Drew married Lenore Robbins, a strikingly beautiful, coolly intelligent home economics professor he had met at Spelman College while on a trip south. In characteristic Drew fashion, he fell in love with her within hours of their meeting and a few days later, on his trip back north, woke Lenore in the middle of the night and proposed.

After receiving his degree in 1940, Drew returned briefly to Howard University, resumed his teaching career, and started a family life. He and Lenore already had one daughter. (Two more daughters and finally a son followed later.)

But within a few months, history intervened and took Drew away again. Because of his expertise in blood banking, Drew was called back to New York from Washington to serve as medical director of the Blood for Britain project, a hastily organized effort to send liquid blood plasma to British solders wounded in France. During the fall of 1940, Drew completed this job so successfully that he was chose to serve as medical director of the first American Red Cross blood bank the following winter. This New York City pilot program became the model for Red Cross blood collection programs all over the country once American entered the war in December 1941. . . .

Drew returned to Howard University Medical School in the summer of 1941 as chief of the Department of Surgery and chief surgeon of Freedmen's Hospital. He stayed on that job until his death, spending most of his time training young black doctors to be top-notch surgeons. Drew always felt himself to be a pioneer. He instilled in his students the sense that they too were pioneers, part of a team that would help break down the wall of prejudice and create a tradition of black excellence and humanitarian values. . . .

Some months after Drew left the Red Cross, the organization began a national program of blood collection. Initially, at the instigation of the Armed Forces, the Red Cross collected blood only from white Americans. All African Americans were turned away as donors.

With black soldiers being drafted, this policy caused an uproar. The NAACP, the National Medical Association, and many humanitarian groups protested the policy. After a few months, it was changed: black volunteers could give blood but theirs was stored separately and labeled accordingly.... Charles Drew, as an expert on blood, managed to place himself at the symbolic epicenter of racial fear in American. As a scientist, he knew what nonsense these policies of exclusion and segregation were. From his perspective there was only one kind of blood, human blood, and it made no sense to segregate it.

He spoke out against these discriminatory policies, saying to reporters in 1942: "As you know, there is no scientific basis for the separation of the bloods of different races except on the basis of the individual types or groups." Drew's style was firm and authoritative but also gentle and low-key.

Newspaper stories and magazine articles followed his statement. Wasn't it ironic, they said, that the pioneer of blood plasma would have his blood refused or segregated if he wished to donate it.... Drew was rightly perceived by the black community as having performed sacrificial humanitarian work and yet having been mistreated. He had in a sense *discovered* the blood bank. Yet at first his own blood would not have been accepted at it. The irony was powerful.

"Can Negroes Really Fly Airplanes"

This was the question posed facetiously by Eleanor Roosevelt in April, 1941. The answer to her question appears in this vignette, taken from an account of the black World War II-era Tuskegee Airmen, described by Omar Blair, a Denver resident who became a member of the elite group.

Omar Blair likes to tell the story about Eleanor Roosevelt and the Tuskegee Airmen. He particularly likes the part in which the peripatetic outspoken wife of the president stood on a grass strip in April 1941 near Tuskegee Institute in Alabama and asked an outrageous question: "Can Negroes really fly airplanes?"

Months earlier four black schools – Tuskegee, Hampton Institute, Virginia State, and Howard University – had been named as the schools to offer the Civilian Pilot Training Program to black college students. With the increased threat of U.S. entrance into World War II, the War Department was being pressured to use black officers and pilots in the newly established Army Air Corps. The choice for this training was between Tuskegee and Hampton institutes. Eleanor Roosevelt had been chosen to evaluate their qualifications, to meet with Charles ("Chief") Anderson, the project director of the program, and to ask, as it turned out, the right question. As Anderson told it, he answered: "Certainly we can fly. Would you like to take an airplane ride?" When the Secret Service realized where she was going *this* time, they first forbade it, and

SOURCE: Joan Reese, "Two Enemies to Fight: Blacks Battle for Equality in Two World Wars," Colorado Heritage 1 (1990), 2. Copyright © 1990 by the Colorado Heritage Society. All rights reserved. Reprinted with permission by the Colorado Historical Society.

when that did not work, they called her husband. FDR replied with the wisdom of long experience: "If she wants to, there is nothing we can do to stop her."

Thirty minutes later, Eleanor Roosevelt climbed down from the back seat of Anderson's Piper J-3 Cub, posed for photographers, and with a broad grin reassured everyone that, yes, Negroes could fly. Her return to Washington was followed by the birth of the Tuskegee Airmen, a victory in the history of participation of blacks in the military – except for one glaring failure: this unit, like all others, would be segregated and commanded by white officers. Blair, a former Tuskegee Airman and an imposing figure who led Denver's Board of Education during the 1970s, said with some delight: "But this failure is where the Establishment made its mistake–they put us on our mettle."

Why was this considered a victory? Because for the first time there was a real crack in the armor of white supremacy within the military–only a crack, but destined to widen.

Lyn Childs Confronts a Racist Act

In the following vignette, black San Francisco shipyard worker Lyn Childs describes how she came to the defense of a Filipino employee on the ship she was repairing. Her account also discusses the reaction from her supervisor.

I was working down in the hold of the ship and there were about six Filipino men . . . and this big white guy went over and started to kick this poor Filipino and none of the Black men that was working down there in the hold with him said one word to this guy. And I sat there and was getting madder and madder by the minute. I sprang to my feet, turned on my torch, and I had a flame about six to seven feet out in front of me, and I walked up to him and I said (you want me to say the real language?) I said to him,

"You so-in-so. If you go lift one more foot, I'll cut your guts out." That was my exact words. I was so mad with him.

Then he started to tell me that he had been trained in boot camp that any national group who was dark skinned was beneath all White People. So he started to cry. I felt sorry for him, because he was crying, really crying. He was frightened, and I was frightened. I didn't know what I was doing, so in the end I turned my torch off and I sat down on the steps with him.

About that time the intercom on board the ship started to announce,

"Lyn Childs, report to Colonel Hickman immediately."

So I said, "I guess this is it." So I went up to Colonel Hickman's office, and behind me came all these men, and there lined up behind me, and I said,

SOURCE: Paul R. Spickard, "Work and Hope: African American Women in Southern California during World War II," <u>Journal of the West</u> 32, no. 3 (July 1993): 74–75.

"Where are you guys going?"

They said, "We're going with you."

When we got to the office [Colonel Hickman] said, "I just wanted to see Lyn Childs," and they said, "You'll see all of us, because we were all down there. We all did not have the guts enough to do what she did, [but] we're with her."

Colonel Hickman said, "Come into this office."

He had one of the guards take me into the office real fast and closed the door real fast and kept them out, and he said,

"What kind of communist activity are you carrying on down there?"

I said, "A communist! What is that?"

He said, "You know what I am talking about. You're a communist."

I said, "A communist! Forget you! The kind of treatment that man was putting on the Filipinos, and to come to their rescue. Then I am the biggest communist you ever seen in your life. That is great. I am a communist."

He said, "Don't say that so loud."

I said, "Well, you asked me was I a communist. You're saying I am. I'm saying I'm a . . .

"Shh! Shh! Shh! Hush! Don't say that so loud." Then he said, "I think you ought to get back to work."

"Well, you called me. Why did you call me?"

"Never mind what I called you for," he said, "Go back to work."

The Liberation of the Death Camps

In this passages, death camp survivors Samuel Pisar and Moshe Sanbar describe their initial encounters with black U.S. Army troops in April 1945.

Pisar: I suddenly became aware of a hum, like a swarm of bees, growing in volume, a machine gun opened fire alongside our barn and, when it stopped, there was that hum again, only louder, unearthly metallic.

I peeped through a crack in the wooden slats. Straight ahead, on the other side of the field, a huge tank was coming toward the barn. It stopped, and the humming ceased. From somewhere to one side, machine guns crackled and the sounds of mortar explosions carried across the field. The tank's long cannon lifted its round head, as though peering at me, then turned slowly aside and let loose a tremendous belch. The firing stopped. The tank resumed its advance, lumbering cautiously toward me. I looked for the hateful swastika, but there wasn't one. On the tank's sides, instead, I made out an unfamiliar emblem. It was a five-pointed white star. In an instant, the realization flooded me; I was looking at the insignia of the United States army.

SOURCE: Samuel Pisar, Of Blood and Hope (Boston: Little, Brown & Company, Inc., 1980), 92–93.

My skull seemed to burst. With a wild roar, I broke through the thatched roof, leaped to the ground, and ran toward the tank. The German machine guns opened up again. The tank fired twice. Then all was quiet. I was still running. I was in front of the tank, waving my arms. The hatch opened. A big black man climbed out, swearing unintelligibly at me. Recalling the only English I knew, those words my mother had sighed while dreaming of our deliverance, I fell at the black man's feet, threw my arms around his legs and yelled at the top of my lungs: "God bless America!"

With an unmistakable gesture, the American motioned me to get up and lifted me in through the hatch. In a few minutes, all of us were free.

★   ★   ★

Sanbar: A group of SS soldiers pointed towards the village and said that the tanks parked there were American. I don't think that any of us believed them. It seemed a joke at our expense. Somebody asked if we could get out of the train and in a voice very different from the usual, a soldier replied, "Of course." Some of us got out, without any particular joy, unable to understand the meaning of that fateful moment. Some ran to the grass and began devouring it as if it was the most natural of foods. The Germans stood silent, only looking towards the tanks.

We were free, but we did not know it, did not believe it, could not believe it. We had waited for this such long days and nights that now when the dream had come true it seemed still a dream. We wanted to go to a house to beg something, but just then an American tank approached from which the soldiers motioned us to come nearer. Only then did we understand that it was not a dream. We were free! We were really free! We broke into weeping. We kissed the tank. A Negro soldier gave us a tin of meat, bread and chocolate, and pointed to us the way to the village center. We sat down on the ground and ate up all the food together – bread, chocolate and meat. The Negro watched us, tears in his eyes.

African America and International Affairs: A Rising Wind

In a 1945 book titled A Rising Wind, *Walter White, executive secretary of the NAACP became the latest of a long list of African Americans scholars and activists who established a nexus between domestic civil rights issues and international developments. White was inspired to write the book after a tour of Europe during the final months of World War II. Taking the title from a speech*

SOURCE: Walter White, A Rising Wind (Garden City, NY: Doubleday, Doran and Company, 1945), 144, 147–155.

by Eleanor Roosevelt affirming the rise of global anti-colonialist and anti-imperialist movements, White argued that the struggles of peoples in Asia and Africa to gain independence paralleled the campaign of African Americans for full citizenship in the United States. He added that attempts to restrict black freedom would resonate negatively around the world, and particularly among the emerging nations. Excerpts from the book appear below.

World War II has given to the Negro a sense of kinship with other colored – and also oppressed – peoples of the world. Where he has not thought through or informed himself on the racial angles of colonial policy and master-race theories, he senses that the struggle of the Negro in the United States is part and parcel of the struggle against imperialism and exploitation in India, China, Burma, Africa, the Philippines, Malaya, the West Indies, and South America. The Negro soldier is convinced that as time proceeds that identification of interests will spread even among some brown and yellow peoples who today refuse to see the connection between their exploitation by white nations and discrimination against the Negro in the United States. . . .

Any person of normal intelligence could have foreseen this. With considerable effectiveness, the Japanese by radio and other means have industriously spread in the Pacific stories of lynchings, of segregation and discrimination against the Negro in the American Army, and of race riots in Detroit, Philadelphia, and other American cities. To each of these recitals has been appended the statement that such treatment of a colored minority in the United States is certain to be that given to brown and yellow peoples in the Pacific if the Allies, instead of the Japanese, win the war. No one can accurately estimate at this time the effectiveness of such propaganda. But it is certain that it has had wide circulation and has been believed by many. Particularly damaging has been the circulation of reports of clashes between white and Negro soldiers in the European and other theaters of operation.

Indissolubly tied in with the carrying overseas of prejudice against the Negro is the racial and imperialist question in the Pacific of Great Britain's and our intentions toward India and China. Publication of Ambassador William Phillips' blunt warning to President Roosevelt in May 1944 that India is a problem of the United States as well as of England despite British opposition to American intervention is of the highest significance. It reaffirmed warnings to the Western world by Wendell Willkie, Sumner Welles, Pearl Buck, and Henry Wallace, among others, that grave peril which might bring disaster to the entire world was involved in continued refusal to recognize the just claims for justice and equality by the colored people, particularly in the Orient. These people are not as powerless as some naive Americans believe them to be. In the first place they have the strength of numbers, unified by resentment against the condescension and exploitation by white nations which Pearl Buck calls "the suppression of human rights to a degree which has not been matched in its ruthlessness outside of fascist-owned Europe," which can and possibly will grow into open revolt. The trend of such awakening and revolution is clearly to be seen in the demand which was made by China at the Dumbarton Oaks Conference of August 1944 that the Allied nations unequivocally declare themselves for complete racial equality. It is to be seen in Ambassador Phillips' warning that though there are four million Indians under arms they are wholly a mercenary army whose allegiance to the Allies will last only as long as they are paid; and in his further revelation that all of these as well as African troops must be used to police other Indians instead of fighting Japan.

Permit me to cite a few solemn warnings of the inevitability of worldwide racial conflict unless the white nations of the earth do an about-face on the issue of race. "Moreover, during the years between 1920 and 1940 a period in the history of the Asiatic and Pacific peoples was in any event drawing to its close," says Sumner Welles, former Undersecretary of State, in his epochal book, *The Time* for *Decision*.

> The startling development of Japan as a world power, and the slower but nevertheless steady emergence of China as a full member of the family of nations, together with the growth of popular institutions among many other peoples of Asia, notably India, all combined to erase very swiftly indeed the fetish of white supremacy cultivated by the big colonial powers during the nineteenth century. The thesis of white supremacy could only exist so long as the white race actually proved to be supreme. The nature of the defeats suffered by the Western nations in 1942 dealt the final blow to any concept of white supremacy which still remained.

The distinguished former Undersecretary might well have gone on to point out that had not the Russians and Chinese performed miracles of military offense and defense in World War II, or had not the black Governor-General of French Equatorial Africa, Félix Eboué, retained faith in the democratic process when white Frenchmen lost theirs, the so-called Anglo-Saxon nations and peoples would surely have lost this war. And Mr. Welles could have reminded his readers that brown and yellow peoples in Asia and the Pacific and black peoples in Africa and the West Indies and the United States are not ignorant of the truth that the war was won by men and women – white, yellow, black, and brown. Resumption of white arrogance and domination in the face of such facts may be disastrous to the peace of the world . . .

Will the United States after the war perpetuate its racial-discrimination policies and beliefs at home and abroad as it did during the war? Will it continue to follow blindly the dangerous and vicious philosophy voiced in Kipling's poem, *The White Man's Burden?* Will decent and intelligent America continue to permit itself to be led by the nose by demagogues and professional race-hate mongers-to have its thinking and action determined on this global and explosive issue by the lowest common denominator of public opinion?

Or will the United States, having found that prejudice is an expensive luxury, slough off the mistakes of the past and chart a new course both at home and in its relations with the rest of the world?

What will America's answer be? If already planned race riots and lynchings of returning Negro soldiers "to teach them their place" are consummated, if Negro war workers are first fired, if India remains enslaved, if Eboué's people go back to disease and poverty to provide luxury and ease for Parisian boulevardiers, World War III will be in the making before the last gun is fired in World War II . . .

What to do?

The United States, Great Britain, France, and other Allied nations must choose without delay one of two courses-to revolutionize their racial concepts and practices, to abolish imperialism and grant full equality to all of its people, or else prepare for World War III. Another Versailles Treaty providing for "mandates," "protectorates," and other devices for white domination will make such a war inevitable. One of the chief deterrents will be Russia. Distrustful of Anglo-American control of Europe, many and perhaps all of the Balkan states may through choice or necessity ally themselves with Russia. If Anglo-Saxon practices in China and India are not drastically and immediately revised, it is probable and perhaps certain that the people of India, China, Burma, Malaya, and other parts of the Pacific may also move into the Russian orbit as the lesser of two dangers.

As for the United States, the storm signals are unmistakable. She can choose between a policy of appeasement of bigots-which course she gives every indication now of following-and thus court disaster. Or she can live up to her ideals and thereby both save herself and help to avert an early and more disastrous resumption of war.

A wind is rising – a wind of determination by the have-nots of the world to share the benefits of freedom and prosperity which the haves of the earth have tried to keep exclusively for themselves. That wind blows all over the world. Whether that wind develops into a hurricane is a decision which we must make now and in the days when we form the peace.

A Conservative's Outlook, 1946

Spencer Logan, a former noncommissioned officer in the U.S. Army, wrote A Negro's Faith in America, *which was published in 1946. Logan took issue with civil rights leaders and organizations and argued against political agitation. Instead he counseled African Americans to become better educated while waiting, reminding his readers that white America was, however gradually, nonetheless moving toward societal integration. Logan and newspaper columnist George Schulyer are reminders of the links between black conservatives in the era of Booker T. Washington and the African American neo-conservatives who emerged in the 1970s.*

Have the Negro people developed a man or group of men who can lead them and speak for them in the postwar era which lies just ahead?

The mere development of creative talent, no matter how great, does not, it seems to me, necessarily fit an individual for leadership. Many of the Negroes

SOURCE: Spencer Logan, <u>A Negro's Faith in America</u> (New York: Macmillan Co., 1946), 12, 15–16, 18–19, 60.

who are prominent because of their creative talents or their success as interpretive artists are not in the real sense leaders of the Negro people.

These men and women, including some of the most eminent and distinguished members of the Negro race, are obviously moved by the artist's desire to give of himself to humanity. But I wonder if it is not also from a sense of social frustration–which even with their gifts they cannot shake off–that some of them have attempted a leadership for which they are not emotionally fitted. Between these individuals and the Negro masses which they represent, there is a spiritual gulf. These gifted men and women are not of the people. Their policy of stressing social equality rather than the building of a strong Negro society is indicative of their desire to get away from being Negroes. Any kind of leadership that arises from such frustration is not of the Negro people as I know them. . . .

The ideal of democracy demanded by many Negro leaders is in harmony with the theory of democracy for all; but it ignores reality. The reality of the situation is that many Negro and white people are not ready to assume the responsibility of citizenship in a progressive modern state. One of the first needs of the mass Negro is a better understanding of the present-day crisis in American life and a recognition of his own responsibility in relation to it.

The extent to which Negro leadership has drifted from a program in harmony with the needs of the Negro in this crisis is indicated by certain aspects of the Negro press. Negro editors, aware of the inconsistency between the ideal of democracy as advocated by the Negro leaders and the discrimination and injustice endured by the average Negro, have attempted to emphasize the discrepancy by resorting to a type of headline which stresses the basic defects of Negro-white relationship: "White Policeman Shoots Negro Boy "–" White Man Slays Negro Sweetheart "–" Negro Youth Denied Entrance to White College."

These editors will say that, by political agitation, social and economic equality can be gained. Yet the feeling lingers in the hearts of many responsible Negroes that the problem presented has bread-and-butter roots, and that agitation yields at best only a few jobs. . . .

Dr. George Washington Carver was a leader of quite a different sort. He avoided the many pitfalls of the Negro publicists. He developed his talent to the utmost, then gave freely of his wizardry to all people. He earned the gratitude and respect of white people. Dr. Carver set the highest possible standard for good race relationship, for he, as a Negro, achieved and practiced a concept of democracy which was in harmony with its greatest social and spiritual possibilities. Dr. Carver often said that he gave so freely of his talent because it was given to him by God. He subordinated his racial instincts to the good of democracy, and he believed that by dedicating his energies to the well-being of all mankind he would best serve his race. Dr. Carver more than any other Negro has set an example for Negro leadership of the future.

There are many Negro organizations which are dedicated to the task of obtaining social equality and a fuller share in democracy for the Negro by means of political pressure and court decisions. Such groups operate on the theory that the ideals upon which a government is founded can be enforced through the legal code of that country by test cases which establish definite precedents. They fight segregation by proving that it is legally wrong. They would wipe out lynchings by fining the county involved, or by making prison sentences mandatory for anyone involved in them. They would loosen the economic noose about the neck of the Negro by the passage of more laws designed to make job discrimination illegal.

Negro leaders ruled by this thought pattern are in my opinion guilty, along with their white counterparts, of the gravest injustice to their cause if they attempt to gain by force of law alone the advantages of social equality from people who are not spiritually or morally prepared to grant it. They should realize that those who live by political agitation are by this very fact often handicapped as leaders; for a man who fights for the legal recognition of a principle may in the process lose sight of the human values involved. . . .

If the people of America are to get along with one another, regardless of racial and religious differences, they must become more aware of the need of making their democratic principles a part of their everyday lives. No citizen should be allowed to fail in the realization of his own responsibility for the welfare of the whole, with stress upon mutual respect among all. America has learned the technique of selling the public almost anything. We have been taught lessons of health and cleanliness, have been influenced to spend or save money, and have been united for the purpose of waging war against a common enemy. Why cannot similar educational techniques be used against those attitudes on the part of many of our citizens which may well prove to be as destructive as any foreign foe could have been?

Civil Rights and Organized Labor in the South: Moranda Smith Speaks

After World War II, organized labor began to penetrate into some industrialized areas of the South where it inevitably confronted the issue of race. Unions such as the Food and Tobacco Workers affiliated with The Congress of Industrial Organizations promoted racial integration and helped develop a group of African American labor activists who either led or supported parallel efforts for civil rights. Moranda Smith (1915–1950) of Winston-Salem, North Carolina, was one of these leaders. The following passage, from her address at the CIO's national convention in Boston in 1947, combines the issues of civil rights and labor organizing.

I work for the R. J. Reynolds Tobacco Company in Winston-Salem, North Carolina. I want to say a few words on this resolution for the reason that I come from the South and I live in the South. I live where men are lynched, and the people that lynch them are still free.

SOURCE: <u>Final Proceedings of the 9th Constitutional Convention of the CIO</u>, October 15, 1947. (Pamphlet). Reprinted with permission of the AFL-CIO.

The Taft-Hartley Bill to Local 22 in Winston-Salem is an old, old story. The Taft-Hartley Bill was put before the workers in Winston-Salem about four years ago when the CIO came to Winston-Salem to organize the unorganized workers in the R. J. Reynolds Tobacco plant. We were faced at that time with a lot of court actions. They tried to put fear into the hearts of the workingmen in Winston-Salem.

One of the things in the Constitution of the United States is a guarantee to a human being, regardless of his race, creed or color, of freedom from fear. I say the Taft-Hartley Bill is nothing new to us. When men are lynched, and when men try to strike and walk the picket line, the only weapons that the workers in America, especially in the South, have to protect themselves is action. When they are put in jail, they must protect themselves. If that is the protection of democracy in the United States of America I say it is not enough.

I want to emphasize a few of the things that you have in this resolution. Too long have the Negro people of the South and other workers in America heard a lot of words read to them. It is time for action, and I am now wondering if the CIO is going to stop and do some of the things by action. You talk about political action and you talk about politics. How can there be any action when the Negroes in the South are not allowed to vote? Too long have the workers in the South stopped and looked to Congress for protection. We no longer look to the government in Washington for protection. It has failed. Today we are looking for an organization that says they are organized to fight for the freedom of all men regardless of race, creed or color, and that is the CIO.

I will tell you this and perhaps it will interest you. To the Negro workers in Winston-Salem it means a great deal. They told us, "You cannot vote for this and you cannot vote for that." But last May in the city of Winston-Salem the Negro and white workers, based on a program of unity, were able to put in their city government two labor men. I am proud to say one of those was a Negro. The other was a white labor leader. (Applause.) Yes. We are faced today with this word that they call "democracy." I want to say to this convention let us stop playing around. Each and every one of you here today represents thousands and thousands of the rank and file workers in the plants who today are looking for you to come back to them and give them something to look forward to: not words, but action.

We want to stop lynching in the South. We want people to walk the picket lines free and unafraid and know that they are working for their freedom and their liberty. When you speak about this protection of democracy, it is more than just words. If you have got to go back to your home town and call a meeting of the rank and file workers and say, "This is what we adopted in the convention, now we want to put it into action," if you don't know how to put it into action, ask the rank and file workers. Ask the people who are suffering, and together you will come out with a good program where civil rights will be something to be proud of. When you say "protection of democracy" in your last convention, along with it you can say we have done this or that. The people that lynch Negroes in the South, the people that burn crosses in the South, the people who put men in jail because they wanted 10 or 20 cents an hour wage increase will learn that the workers can walk as free men, because we have done something in action.

One thing more. I have looked over this delegation, and I wonder if you cherish the word "democracy." I say to you it means something to be free. It means a great deal. I do not think you have ever read or have ever heard of a Negro man or a Negro woman that has ever been a traitor to the United States of America. . . .

They can lynch us. They can beat us. They can do anything they want to, but the Negroes of America who have always been true to the American flag, will always march forward. We are just asking your help. We are not asking for charity. We do not want charity. We belong to America.

Our forefathers fought and bled and died for this country and we are proud to be a part of it just as you are. When the civil liberties of Negroes in the South are interfered with [and] you do nothing about it, I say to you, you are untrue to the traditions of America. You have got to get up and do something in action, as I have said before and not by mere words. So we are looking forward to your help and we call on you, because we have called on you before and you have given us aid. We will call on you again, and we ask you not to fail us.

"Live Anywhere!" High Court Rules

In 1945, the Shelleys, an African American family, purchased a home in St. Louis unaware of the racially restrictive covenant on the property since 1911. Neighbors sued to prevent them from occupying the home, triggering a series of court cases that ended with the 1948 U.S. Supreme Court decision in Shelley v. Kraemer, which ruled restrictive covenants unenforceable by state action. The Pittsburgh Courier article here titled, "'Live Anywhere!' High Court Rules," described the decision and its impact.

An American citizen can live anywhere in the U. S . . . if he has the money to buy or build a home. This was the ruling of the United States Supreme Court Monday when it outlawed restrictive covenants in cases arising in Detroit, St. Louis and Washington, D. C. The vote was unanimous in every case!

Reversed were rulings of the Supreme Court of Michigan, upholding the legality of covenants restricting Orsel McGhee and his family from living in a so-called "white" residential area in Detroit, and a similar ruling by the Missouri Supreme Court against J. D. Shelley and his family in St. Louis. All were barred because they were Negroes.

Adding totality to the finality of its decisions the Nation's highest tribunal also reversed the U. S. Circuit Court of Appeals for the District of Columbia in two cases in Washington, D. C., involving James M. Hurd and family and Robert H. Rowe and family.

SOURCE: Lem Graves, Jr.," 'Live Anywhere! High Court Rules," The Pittsburgh Courier, May 8, 1948, 1, 5.

Taken behind closed doors several months ago, the Supreme Court justices had studied the dynamite-laden issue secretly, and when the decision was announced three of the justices did not vote. They were justices Reed, Jackson and Rutledge, who had excused themselves from hearing the case when it was argued, because each was in some manner involved in circumstances which had a bearing on the cases.

Voting unanimously were Chief Justice Vinson, who delivered the Court's opinion; Justices Frankfurter, Burton, Black, Murphy and Douglas.

The far-reaching decision means that a mortal blow has been struck at racial restrictions in homes, artificially created ghettoes, public utilities and public services, restaurants, neighborhood theaters and countless and countless other jim-crow manifestations made possible because of the heretofore enforced segregation in home ownership.

The decision of the Court was that individual property owners could voluntarily enter into covenants, but that Court enforcement of such covenants contravened the Fourteenth Amendment. The Supreme Court further ruled that court action constituted State action, and will not henceforth be permitted in these covenant cases.

Yet to be considered by the Supreme Court is a case from Ohio.

In giving the Court ruling Chief Justice Vinson said:

"Upon full consideration we have concluded that in these cases the State has acted to deny petitioners the equal protection of the laws guaranteed by the Fourteenth Amendment . . . the judgment of the Supreme Court of Missouri and the judgment of the Supreme Court of Michigan must be reversed."

Their decision in the cases in Washington, D. C., was patterned after the Michigan and Missouri reversals.

The ruling of the Supreme Court – which may upset the pattern of residential life in almost every State in the Union – supported a 1917 ruling by the U. S. Supreme Court in which it voided racial restrictive covenant ordinances enacted by the city of Louisville, Ky., and other municipalities.

Army Integration in the Korean War

Although racial integration of the armed services began with President Harry Truman's Executive Order 9981 in 1948, practically speaking the army began to integrate during the Korean War. The accounts that follow provide a glimpse of that integration. The first is by Beverly Scott, a black officer, while the second is by Harry Summers, a white enlisted soldier.

SOURCE: Rudy Tomedi, <u>No Bugle, No Drums: An Oral History of the Korean War</u>.
(New York: John Wiley & Sons, 1993). Copyright © 1993 by John Wiley & Sons, Inc. All
rights reserved. Reprinted with permission of John Wiley and Sons, Inc.

Beverly Scott: The 24th Regiment was the only all-black regiment in the division, and as a black officer in an all-black regiment commanded by whites I was always super sensitive about standing my ground. Being a man. Being honest with my soldiers. . . .

Most of the white officers were good. Taken in the context of the times, they were probably better than the average white guy in civilian life. But there was still that patronizing expectation of failure. White officers came to the 24th Regiment knowing or suspecting or having been told that this was an inferior regiment.

[In September 1951, members of the regiment were integrated into other units.] I was transferred to the 14th [Regiment] and right away I experienced some problems. People in the 14th didn't want anybody from the 24th. I was a technically qualified communications officer, which the 14th said they needed very badly, but when I got there, suddenly they didn't need any commo officers.

Then their executive officer said, "We got a rifle platoon for you. Think you can handle a rifle platoon?"

What the hell do you mean, can I handle a rifle platoon? I was also trained as an infantry officer. He knew that. I was a first lieutenant, been in the army six years. . . . If I had been coming in as a white first lieutenant the question never would have been asked.

Harry Summers: When they first started talking about integration, white soldiers were aghast. They would say, How can you integrate the army? How do you know when you go to the mess hall that you won't get a plate or a knife or a spoon that was used by a Negro? Or when you go to the supply room and draw sheets, you might get a sheet that a Negro had slept on. . . .

I remember a night when our rifle company was scheduled to get some replacements. I was in a three-man foxhole with one other guy, and they dropped this new replacement off at our foxhole. The other guy I was in the foxhole with was under a poncho, making coffee. It was bitterly cold. And pitch dark. He got the coffee made, and he gave me a drink, and he took a drink, and then he offered some to this new replacement, who we literally couldn't see, it was that dark. And the guy said, "No, I don't want any."

"What the hell are you talking about, you don't want any? You got to be freezing to death. Here, take a drink of coffee."

"Well," he said, "you can't tell it now, but I'm black. And tomorrow morning when you find out I was drinking out of the same cup you were using, you ain't gonna be too happy." Me and this other guy kind of looked at each other. "You silly son of a bitch," we told him, "here, take the goddam coffee."

Black Student Enrollment in Colleges, 1941–1942

Twenty Black Institutions with the Largest Black Student Enrollment

School	Enrollment	Degrees to Black Students, 1942
1. Howard University	1,953	155
2. Tennessee A&I State College	1,583	192
3. Tuskegee Institute	1,407	138
4. Prairie View (Tex.) State College	1,151	71
5. Virginia State College	1,097	236
6. Alabama State Teachers College	1,054	48
7. North Carolina A&T College	1,020	93
8. Hampton Institute (Va.)	1,018	127
9. Florida A&M State College	907	79
10. Wiley College (Texas)	906	51
11. South Carolina State College	895	153
12. Lincoln Univ. (Missouri)	734	88
13. Fayetteville (NC) State College	714	83
14. Philander Smith College (Ark.)	686	–
15. Langston University (Okla)	681	68
16. Morgan State College (Md.)	660	84
17. Lane College (Tenn.)	650	52
18. (Ala.) State A&M Institute	644	41
19. Virginia Union University	635	100
20. Winston-Salem (NC) State College	632	74

Twenty White Institutions with the Largest Black Student Enrollment

School	Enrollment	Degrees to Black Students, 1942
1. Wayne University (Mich.)	594	23
2. Ohio State University	431	24
3. City College of New York	250	–
4. Columbia Teachers College (N.Y.)	229	7
5. University of Kansas	159	14
6. University of Illinois	142	11
7. Western Reserve Univ (Ohio)	115	6
8. Indiana University	93	13
9. Boston University	65	5
10. Oberlin College (Ohio)	42	1

11. Kansas State University	41	4
12. Northwestern University (Ill.)	41	3
13. Harvard University	27	1
14. University of Nebraska	26	2
15. University of Denver	21	5
16. Purdue University	21	3
17. Loyola University (Chicago)	21	–
18. University of Arizona	15	3
19. Pacific Union College (Ca.)	14	–
20. Drew University (N.J.)	13	–

SOURCE: "The American Negro in College, 1941–1942," Crisis (New York) 49, no. 8 (August 1942), 252, 266. Thomson Publishing wishes to thank that Crisis Publishing Co., Inc., the publisher of the magazine of the National Association for the Advancement of Colored People, for the use of the materials from the Crisis Magazine.

Paul Robeson Sings on the Border

By the late 1940s, Paul Robeson had emerged as one of the most controversial figures on the American political scene. A Phi Beta Kappa graduate of Rutgers University and the first black All-American football player, an accomplished actor and concert singer, Robeson had an acclaimed career in the theater and motion pictures. Like many of his politically conscious contemporaries, Robeson chose to identify with the Communist Party in the 1930s. By the 1940s, when other public figures renounced such allegiances, Robeson nevertheless reaffirmed his support, making him a major target of the 1950s Red Scare.

In 1950, the U.S. State Department revoked Robeson's passport to prevent him from traveling and speaking abroad. In response, Canadian and U.S. labor activists organized a series of four border concerts between 1952 and 1955 where Robeson sang to thousands of Canadians and Americans at the Peace Arch near Blaine, Washington, which marks the border between the nations. In one concert, Robeson stood on the back of a truck one foot from the border and performed before 40,000 Canadians in attendance on the other side. These remarkable concerts are described here.

It seems so simple that all people should live in full human dignity and in friendship. But somewhere the enemy has always been around who tries to push back the great mass of the people in everyland – we know that.

SOURCE: Ernest A. Jasmin, "Barred at the Border," The Bellingham Herald (Washington), February 24, 1998, C1, C3. All rights reserved. Reprinted by permission of the author.

Before Rosa Parks refused to give up her seat and Martin Luther King Jr., shared his dream with those gathered to march at the nation's capitol, actor-singer-activist Paul Robeson's deep voice rippled over the thousands at the U.S.-Canadian border near Blaine for his second Peace Arch concert, Aug. 16, 1953.

And I want you to know that I'll continue this year fighting for peace, however difficult it may be. And I want everyone in the range of my voice to hear, official or otherwise, that there is no force on Earth that will make me go backward one one-thousandth part of one little inch.

That speech, given in response to government censorship of Robeson, might have faded into historical oblivion if not for the efforts of a handful of people.

One of them, Detroit African-American Museum founder Charles Wright, was determined to keep Robeson's legacy of speaking for the concerns of African-Americans and world laborers alive in the mid-1970s.

"Since I'd seen him in 'Othello' in 1944, I was naturally attuned to look up Robeson everywhere I went," says Wright, 79.

Some time after he learned of the Whatcom County concerts, Wright came to the Pacific Northwest looking for people who had witnessed them. That's how he learned of Harvey Murphy of the United Mine, Mill and Smelters Workers' Union, which would have sponsored a 1952 Robeson concert in Vancouver if the government had allowed the singer to go to Canada. Wright visited Murphy at his Toronto home in 1974.

There Murphy gave Wright a tape of the first two of Robeson's four annual Peace Arch concerts. The tape had been gathering dust in his closet.

This year, which would have been Robeson's hundredth birthday, the recordings have been released commercially for the first time by Illinois-based Folk Era Records. Robeson will also be recognized posthumously Wednesday at the Grammy Awards.

A number of historians, including Wright in his book "Robeson: Labor's Forgotten Champion," have documented the events leading up to the four concerts.

Robeson visited Russia in the 1930s and openly praised his treatment there and the country's policies. The entertainer's political speeches, which continued in following decades, didn't sit well with government officials, which were increasingly agitated by Sen. Joseph McCarthy's communist witch hunts.

Robeson was blacklisted. Eventually, his annual income fell from a reported $100,000 annually to a paltry $6,000. Despite the damage to his career and threats of violence, he continued to speak out.

In 1950 Robeson's passport was revoked to keep him from speaking abroad. In early 1952, the Mine, Mill and Smelters Workers' Union invited him to address its annual meeting, to take place in Vancouver, B.C. Because U.S. citizens weren't required to have passports to enter Canada, Robeson proceeded as planned.

However, he was stopped at the border, on the basis of World War I legislation that allowed the United States to restrict its citizens' travel during times of national emergency.

Many Canadians resented the U.S. restriction of who they could hear speak, recalls Ray Stevenson, who was a union member at the time.

"It was a question of the right of Canadian people to hear Paul Robeson, who was an internationally known world figure," says Stevenson, 79, who lives in Toronto.

After union workers discovered the restriction, they decided to gather at a Vancouver auditorium to protest. Robeson was to call union leaders from Seattle but to everyone's surprise, members of the International Brotherhood of Electrical Workers had rigged the telephone so everyone could hear him speak, Stevenson says.

"All of a sudden Paul's voice is booming over the loudspeakers to this assembled throng," he says.

Robeson spoke for 17 minutes and sang "Joe Hill" before plans for a protest concert were announced.

"The lack of a dissenting vote, Murphy announced – to a roar of laughter – meant that the representatives of the Royal Canadian Mounted Police and the FBI who were present were in support of the resolution," writes Martin Duberman in his biography of Robeson.

"So instead of a couple of hundred people listening to Paul Robeson there were literally thousands and thousands who came to listen to Paul Robeson," says Al King of Vancouver, B.C.

King, also a former union member, attended the first of the Peace Arch Concerts. He recalls a festive atmosphere with about 40,000 on the Canadian side of the border and 10,000 on the U.S. side.

"It turned into a real picnic," says King, 83. "We clogged up the bloody border for hours."

Robeson stood on the back of a truck parked one foot away from the border singing spirituals like "No More Auction Block" and "Old Man River."

At one point, King got to shake the former college football All-American's hand.

"I was absolutely amazed," King recalls. "I'm over 6-feet, but I had to look up to see him. . . . He was an immense man."

Stevenson attended the last two concerts, held in 1954 and 1955.

"It was a very moving experience – one of the great moving experiences of my life," Stevenson says.

Attendance had declined to about 15,000 to 20,000 by Stevenson's recollection, but the audience remained enthusiastic. However, not everyone had come to support Robeson, he says, remembering a handful of attendees suspected of being with the FBI and Royal Canadian Mounted Police.

"We sort of felt, and I think justifiably, that they were something of a hostile force in this sea of pro-Robeson (activity)," Stevenson says.

Robeson was finally allowed to enter Canada in 1956, though Canadian officials were reluctant to allow him to perform at first. Their stance softened, however, with the threat of additional concerts along the border, Stevenson says.

Robeson's passport was restored in 1958.

"If Paul had been allowed to just go naturally amongst the people the impact would not have been nearly as widespread and well-known as when we had to struggle to hear him," Stevenson says.

Years later, Wright says he is happy to see Robeson get more recognition for his efforts.

"This tape will be lost to the public unless something happens to publicize it. . . . So when he gave it to me I promised to try and keep it alive," Wright says. "One of our goals is to make sure that the young people know about Paul Robeson, because he was the greatest role model we've ever had."

Robeson died in 1976 after having a stroke in Philadelphia.

5

We Shall Overcome: 1950–1965

This chapter explores the civil rights campaigns of the 1950s and early 1960s. It begins with **The Montgomery Victory, 1956**, which describes the first successful challenge to segregation in the Deep South. The vignettes **Elizabeth Eckford at Little Rock's Central High School** and **President Eisenhower Sends Troops to Little Rock, 1957** recall this major confrontation between segregationists and the federal government. **With All Deliberate Speed: Integration in Southern Schools, 1960** recalls the slow pace of desegregation.

The next set of vignettes analyzes the turbulent pace of change in the 1960s, particularly in the South. The first one, however, is about the West in the late 1950s. In **The First Sit-In: Wichita, Kansas, 1958,** we see the demonstration that inspired Southern black students to engage in widespread civil disobedience, while **James Meredith at "Ole Miss"** describes the most important university desegregation crisis of the period. In **Letter from a Birmingham Jail** and **Dr. Martin Luther King, Jr., and the FBI,** we see the thoughts of the most famous of the civil rights leaders as well as an example of the federal government's efforts to discredit him. **Letters from Mississippi** reminds us that the campaign for black rights excluded no one willing to participate. **Fannie Lou Hamer Testifies at the Democratic National Convention, 1964** recalls the nation's discovery of one of the leaders of the Mississippi Freedom Democratic Party, while **Murder in Mississippi** describes the brutal killing of three civil rights workers in 1964. The frustrations generated by those murders are revealed in **David Dennis Speaks at the Memorial for James Chaney. President Johnson Proposes the Voting Rights Act** discusses the last major legislative victory by the Civil Rights Movement in the 1960s.

The Montgomery Victory, 1956

In 1956, Montgomery blacks won a year-long boycott of the segregated city-owned bus line, achieving the first victory over discrimination in a Deep South city. In the following document, E. D. Nixon, Dr. Martin Luther King, Jr., and other boycott leaders suggested how blacks should behave on the newly integrated busses.

Within a few days ... each of you will be reboarding integrated buses. This places upon us all a tremendous responsibility of maintaining, in face of what could be some unpleasantness, a calm and loving dignity befitting good citizens and members of our race. If there is violence in word or deed it must not be our people who commit it. For your help and convenience the following suggestions are made. Will you read, study and memorize them so that our non-violent determination may not be endangered. First, some general suggestions:

1. Not all white people are opposed to integrated buses. Accept goodwill on the part of many.

2. The whole bus is now for the use of all people. Take a vacant seat.

3. Pray for guidance and commit yourself to complete non-violence in word and action as you enter the bus.

4. Demonstrate the calm dignity of our Montgomery people in your actions. In all things observe ordinary rules of courtesy and good behavior. Remember that this is not a victory for Negroes alone, but for all Montgomery and the South. Do not boast! Do not brag!

5. Be quiet but friendly; proud, but not arrogant; joyous, but not boisterous.

6. Be loving enough to absorb evil and understanding enough to turn an enemy into a friend.

Now for some specific suggestions:

1. The bus driver is in charge of the bus and has been instructed to obey the law. Assume that he will cooperate in helping you occupy any vacant seat.

2. Do not deliberately sit by a white person, unless there is no other seat. Sitting down by a person, white or colored, say "May I" or "Pardon me" as you sit. This is a common courtesy. If cursed, do not curse back. If pushed, do not push back. Do not get up from your seat! Report all serious incidents to the bus driver.

3. For the first few days try to get on the bus with a friend in whose non-violence you have confidence. You can uphold one another by a glance or a prayer. If another person is being molested, do not arise to go to his defense, but pray for the oppressor and use moral and spiritual force to carry on the struggle for justice.

SOURCE: Leaflet distributed to bus protesters, reprinted in Martin Luther King, <u>Stride Toward Freedom</u> (New York, 1984), 144–45.

4. According to your own ability and personality, do not be afraid to experiment with new and creative techniques for achieving reconciliation and social change.

Elizabeth Eckford at Little Rock's Central High School

In September 1957, Elizabeth Eckford was one of nine African American high school students selected to desegregate Little Rock's Central High School. A photographer's snapshot of Eckford bravely walking through a white mob toward the school house door made her the most recognized of the students, an instant celebrity and enduring symbol of the episode and the era. In this vignette she describes that day.

I was about the first one up. While pressing my black-and-white dress – I had made it to wear on the first day of school – my little brother turned on the TV set. They started telling about a large crowd gathered at the school. The man on TV said he wondered if we were going to show up that morning . . .

Before I left home Mother called us into the living room. She said we should have a word of prayer. Then I caught the bus and got off a block from the school. I saw a large crowd of people standing across the street from the soldiers guarding Central. As I walked on, the crowd suddenly got very quiet. Superintendent [Virgil] Blossom told us to enter by the front door. I looked at all the people and thought, "Maybe I will be safer if I walk down the block to the front entrance behind the guards."

At the corner I tried to pass through the long line of guards around the school so as to enter the grounds behind them. One of the guards pointed across the street. So I pointed in the same direction and asked whether he meant for me to cross the street and walk down. He nodded "yes." So, I walked across the street conscious of the crowd that stood there, but they moved away from me.

For a moment all I could hear was the shuffling of their feet. Then someone shouted, "Here she comes, get ready!" I moved away from the crowd on the sidewalk and into the street. If the mob came at me I could then cross back over so the guards could protect me.

The crowd moved in closer and then began to follow me, calling me names. I still wasn't afraid. Just a little bit nervous. Then my knees started to shake all of a sudden and I wondered if I could make it to the center entrance a block away. It was the longest block I ever walked in my whole life.

SOURCE: From GROWING UP SOUTHERN by Chris Mayfield, copyright © 1976, 1978, 1979, 1980, 1981 by Institute for Southern Studies. Used by permission of Pantheon Books, a division of Random House, Inc.

Even so, I still wasn't too scared because all the time I kept thinking that the guards would protect me.

When I got in front of the school, I went up to a guard again. But this time he just looked straight ahead and didn't move to let me pass him. I didn't know what to do. Then I looked and saw that the path leading to the front entrance was a little further ahead. So I walked until I was right in front of the path to the front door.

I stood looking at the school – it looked so big! Just then the guards let some white students through. The crowd was quiet. I guess they were waiting to see what was going to happen. When I was able to steady my knees, I walked up to the guard who had let the white students in. He too didn't move. When I tried to squeeze past him, he raised his bayonet and then the other guards moved in and they raised their bayonets.

They glared at me with a mean look and I was very frightened and didn't know what to do. I turned around and the crowd came toward me.

They moved closer and closer. Somebody started yelling, "Lynch her! Lynch her!"

I tried to see a friendly face somewhere in the mob–someone who maybe would help. I looked into the face of an old woman and it seemed a kind face, but when I looked at her again she spat on me.

They came closer, shouting, "No nigger bitch is going to get in our school! Get out of here."

I turned back to the guards but their faces told me I wouldn't get any help from them. Then I looked down the block and saw a bench at the bus stop. "If I can only get there I will be safe." I don't know why the bench seemed a safe place to me, but I started walking toward it. I tried to close my mind to what they were shouting, and kept saying to myself, "If I can only make it to the bench I will be safe."

When I finally got there, I don't think I could have gone another step. I sat down and the mob crowded up and began shouting all over again. Someone hollered, "Drag her over to this tree! Let's take care of that nigger." Just then a white man sat down beside me, put his arm around me and patted my shoulder. He raised my chin and said, "Don't let them see you cry."

President Eisenhower Sends Troops to Little Rock, 1957

When angry white parents and Governor of Arkansas Orval Faubus refused to allow eight black students to attend Central High School in Little Rock, Arkansas, after the school was ordered desegregated by a federal court, President Dwight Eisenhower sent in federal troops to

SOURCE: Vital Speeches XXIV (October 15, 1957; address of September 24, 1957), 11–12.

enforce the court decision. Here is Eisenhower's television address to the
nation announcing his decision.

For a few minutes this evening I want to talk to you about the serious situation that has arisen in Little Rock. . . . In that city, under the leadership of demagogic extremists, disorderly mobs have deliberately prevented the carrying out of proper orders from a Federal Court. Local authorities have not eliminated that violent opposition and, under the law, I yesterday issued a Proclamation calling upon the mob to disperse.

This morning the mob again gathered in front of the Central High School of Little Rock, obviously for the purpose of again preventing the carrying out of the Court's order relating to the admission of Negro children to that school.

Whenever normal agencies prove inadequate to the task and it becomes necessary for the Executive Branch of the Federal Government to use its powers and authority to uphold Federal Courts, the President's responsibility is inescapable.

In accordance with that responsibility, I have today issued an Executive Order directing the use of troops under Federal authority to aid in the execution of Federal law at Little Rock, Arkansas. This became necessary when my Proclamation of yesterday was not observed, and the obstruction of justice still continues. . . .

Our personal opinions about the decision have no bearing on the matter of enforcement; the responsibility and authority of the Supreme Court to interpret the Constitution are very clear. Mob rule cannot be allowed to override the decision of our courts.

At a time when we face grave situations abroad because of the hatred that Communism bears toward a system of government based on human rights, it would be difficult to exaggerate the harm that is being done to the prestige and influence and, indeed, to the safety of our nation and the world.

Our enemies are gloating over this incident and using it everywhere to misrepresent our whole nation. We are portrayed as a violator of those standards of conduct which the peoples of the world united to proclaim in the Charter of the United Nations. There they affirmed "faith in fundamental human rights" and "in the dignity and worth of the human person," and they did so "without distinction as to race, sex, language, or religion."

And so, with deep confidence, I call upon citizens of the State of Arkansas to assist in bringing to an immediate end all interference with the law and its processes. If resistance to the Federal Court order ceases at once, the further presence of Federal troops will be unnecessary and the city of Little Rock will return to its normal habits of peace and order-and a blot upon the fair name and high honor of our nation will removed.

With All Deliberate Speed: Integration in Southern Schools, 1960

The phrase "with all deliberate speed" was added to a ruling by the U.S. Supreme Court one year after its famous Brown v. Board of Education decision in 1954. The court's second ruling was intended to amplify the previous ruling and to indicate to segregated districts throughout the country that they should initiate plans immediately to end de jure segregation. However, as the following table indicates, most Southern states reluctantly embraced the decision. Six years after the original ruling and three years after U.S. Army troops were used to enforce a federal court order to integration Little Rock's Central High School, five states—Alabama, Georgia, Louisiana, Mississippi, and South Carolina—had not integrated a single school district.

	Total Black Enrollment	*Number of Blacks in Integrated Schools*
Alabama	267,259	0
Arkansas	104,205	98
Delaware	14,063	6,196
District of Columbia	89,451	73,290
Florida	201,091	512
Georgia	306,158	0
Kentucky	42,778	12,000
Louisiana	261,491	0
Maryland	130,076	28,072
Mississippi	271,761	0
Missouri	82,000	35,000
North Carolina	302,060	34
Oklahoma	39,405	10,246
South Carolina	255,616	0
Tennessee	146,700	169
Texas	279,374	3,300
Virginia	203,229	103
West Virginia	24,010	12,000
Total	3,020,727	181,020

SOURCE: Richard N. Current, T. Harry Williams, and Frank Freidel, <u>American History: A Survey</u> (New York: Knopf, 1961), 848.

The First Sit-In: Wichita, Kansas, 1958

Although the Greensboro, North Carolina, sit-ins in 1960 are generally credited with initiating a spontaneous movement that soon swept across the South, the first sit-ins actually occurred in Wichita, Kansas, in July 1958, followed closely by similar demonstrations in Oklahoma City in September. The following is a personal recollection of the Wichita demonstrations by Professor Ronald Walters, who taught political science at Howard University and who in 1984 became one of the managers of the Jesse Jackson for President Campaign.

Forget the tales of John Brown and the Kansas that bled to keep slavery out of the state—that was the 1850s. In the 1950s, Wichita, Kansas, was a midsize city of more than 150,000 people, of whom only 10,000 were black. Agribusiness and defense industries were its economic base; farmers and defense workers, its social foundation. Isolated in the middle of the country, with an ascetic religious heritage and a tradition of individual farming, its people were genuinely and deeply conservative. Kansas, the family home of war hero and president, Dwight Eisenhower, was the most Republican state in the nation ...

Social and economic progress in those years were exceedingly difficult for Wichita's small, closely knit black community, a product of turn-of-the-century migration. We faced an implacably cold, dominant white culture. Blacks in the '50s attended segregated schools up to high school and were excluded from mixing with whites at movie theaters, restaurants, nightclubs and other places of public accommodation, except for some common sports events. Even though the signs "black" and "white" were not publicly visible as in the South, we lived in separate worlds, just as blacks and whites did in the Southern states.... In the spring of 1958, I started a new job without a car, which anchored me to the downtown area for lunch. I remember going to F. W. Woolworth one day for lunch and standing in a line with other blacks behind a 2-foot board at one end of a long lunch counter. Looking at the whites seated at the counter, some staring up at us, I suddenly felt the humiliation and shame that others must have felt many times in this unspoken dialogue abut their power and our humanity. Excluded from the simple dignity of sitting on those stools, blacks had to take their lunch out in bags and eat elsewhere ...

No flash of insight led me to confront this humiliation. It was, like other defining moments in that era, the growing political consciousness within the black community, born of discrete acts of oppression and resistance. That consciousness told me that my situation was not tolerable, that it was time at last to do something. ... As head of the local NAACP Youth Council and a freshman college student, I knew a range of youths who might become involved in a protest against lunch counter segregation.... We targeted Dockum drugstore,

SOURCE: Ronald Walters, "Standing Up in America's Heartland: Sitting in Before Greensboro," <u>American Visions</u> 8, no. 1 (February 1993), 20–23. All rights reserved.
Reprinted with permission of the Association for African American Museums.

part of the Rexall chain, located on Wichita's main street, Douglas Avenue. Because any action here would swiftly attract attention, we tried to anticipate what we might encounter. In the basement of [St. Peter Claver] Catholic Church we simulated the environment of the lunch counter and went through the drill of sitting and role-playing what might happen. We took turns playing the white folks with laughter, dishing out the embarrassment that might come our way. In response to their taunts, we would be well-dressed and courteous, but determined, and we would give the proprietors no reason to refuse us service, except that we were black.

We were motivated by the actions of other people in struggle, especially by the pictures of people in Little Rock and King's Montgomery bus boycott. . . . Like others who would come after us, we held a firm belief that we would be successful simply because we were right; but our confidence was devoid of both the deep religious basis of the Southern movement and the presence of a charismatic leader . . .

★   ★   ★

Ten of us began the sit-in on Saturday morning at 10 a.m., July 19, 1958. We decided to take the vacant seats one by one, until we occupied them all, and then to just sit until whatever happened, happened. It was the prospect of being taken to jail–or worse–that led some parents to prohibit their sons and daughters from taking part in the protest. . . . The sit-in went as planned. We entered the store and took our seats. After we were settled, the waitress come over and spoke to all of us, saying, "I can't serve you here. You'll have to leave." Prepared for this response, I said that we had come to be served like everyone else and that we intended to say until that happened. After a few hours, the waitress placed a sign on the counter that read, "This Fountain Temporarily Closed," and only opened the fountain to accommodate white customers. This was what we were hoping for–a shut-off of the flow of dollars into this operation.

By the second week of the protest, we felt that we were winning because we were being allowed to sit on the stools for long periods. Surely the store was losing money. As we sat, we seldom spoke to each other, but many things crossed my mind. How would I react if my white classmates came in? How would they react? Would my career in college be affected, and would I be able to get another job? What did my family think about what I was doing? How would it all turn out? I am sure that the others were thinking the same things, but they never wavered. I was proud of our group . . .

Despite the fact that some whites spat at us and used racist taunts, we kept the pressure on as the movement grew. It became a popular movement among youth, especially from Wichita University, and at least two white students came down to participate. What had begun as a two-day-a-week demonstration escalated into several days a week. Just as we were realizing our success in generating a mobilization, I began to worry because school was approaching, and it would be difficult to maintain the pressure with school becoming the main priority. Then suddenly, on a Saturday afternoon, into the fourth week of the protest, a man in his 30s came into the store, stopped, looked back at the manager in the rear, and said, "Serve them. I'm losing too much money." This was the conclusion of the sit-in – at once dramatic and anticlimactic.

What happened in the aftermath of our sit-in was completely typical: blacks and whites were served without incident, giving the lie to the basic reason for our exclusion–that whites would cease to patronize the establishment. . . . Not wanting to rest on our laurels, we targeted another drugstore lunch counter, across from East High School on Douglas Avenue and there segregation was even more quickly ended. Other lunch counters in the city followed suit . . .

The Dockum sit-in was followed in a few days by the beginning of a much longer campaign of sit-ins in Oklahoma City. This protest was also initiated by the NAACP Youth Council, under the leadership of the courageous 16-year-old Barbara Posey. . . . The link between the Midwest actions and the Greensboro sit-in was more than mere sequence. Ezell Blair and Joseph McNeil, two of the four originators of the Greensboro protest, were officers in Greensboro's NAACP Youth Council. It is highly unlikely that they were unfamiliar with the sit-ins elsewhere in the country led by their organizational peers. Indeed, at the 51st Conference of the NAACP held in 1960, the national office recognized its local youth councils for the work they were doing in breaking down lunch counter segregation. In his speech at that conference, Robert C. Weaver, the United States's first black cabinet official, said, "NAACP youth units in Wichita, Kansas, and Oklahoma City started these demonstrations in 1958 and succeeded in desegregating scores of lunch counters in Kansas and Oklahoma." NAACP Executive Director Roy Wilkins paid tribute to the sit-in movements as "giving fresh impetus to an old struggle," and "electrifying the adult Negro community . . ."

By summer 1960, the NAACP Youth Council-inspired protests had occurred in North Carolina, South Carolina, Virginia, Maryland, Arkansas, Florida, Louisiana, West Virginia, Tennessee, Texas, Kentucky and Mississippi. There was one ironic historical twist: On July 21, 1960, the Woolworth Company in Greensboro began to serve everyone without regard to color, nearly two years to the day after the beginning of the "first" sit-in in Wichita.

James Meredith at "Ole Miss"

In October 1962, James Meredith integrated the University of Mississippi only after federal marshals enforced a court decision that allowed his entry. On the weekend that Meredith entered, "Ole Miss" segregationists attacked federal marshals and in the ensuing riot two people were killed and 5,000 federal troops

SOURCE: James Meredith, "I'll Know Victory or Defeat," <u>Saturday Evening Post</u>, November 10, 1962, 14–17. Reprinted from The Saturday Evening Post magazine, © 1962 Saturday Evening Post Society. Used with permission. www.saturdayeveningpost.com.

were called in to restore order and protect Meredith. Here is Meredith's account of his first days at Ole Miss.

. . . Negroes in Mississippi did not have the rights of full citizens, including the right to the best education the state offered. Someone had to seek admission to the University of Mississippi, and I decided to do it. But there were many of us involved. Although the lawsuit was mine, the others were with me, and I sought their advice on every move I made.

People have asked me if I wasn't terribly afraid the night we went to Oxford [location of the University]. No, my apprehensions came a long time before that . . . I was sure that if I were harmed or killed, somebody else would take my place one day. I would hate to think another Negro would have to go through that ordeal, but I would hate worse to think there wouldn't be another who would do it.

When we landed at Oxford [Sunday] it was almost dark. We got in a car and I remember seeing a truckload of marshals in front of us and one behind. I went straight to the university and was taken to my rooms—an apartment, I guess you could call it. Since they knew some Government men would be staying with me, I had two bedrooms and a living room and a bathroom. . . . When the trouble started, I couldn't see or hear very much of it. Most of it was at the other end of the campus. . . . I think I read a newspaper and went to bed around 10 o'clock. I was awakened several times in the night by the noise and shooting outside, but it wasn't near me, and I had no way of knowing what was going on. . . . I woke up about six-thirty in the morning and looked out and saw the troops. There was a slight smell of tear gas in my room, but I still didn't know what had gone on during the night, and I didn't find out until some marshals came and told me how many people were hurt and killed.

Monday morning at eight o'clock I registered, and at nine I went to a class in Colonial American History. I was a few minutes late and took a seat in the back of the room. The professor was lecturing on the background in England . . . and he paid no special attention when I entered. I think there were about a dozen students in the class. One said hello to me, and the others were silent. I remember a girl—the only girl there, I think – and she was crying, but it might have been from the tear gas in the room. I was crying from it myself.

One day a fellow from my home town sat down at my table in the cafeteria. "If you're here to get an education, I'm for you," he said. "If you're here to cause trouble, I'm against you." That seemed fair enough to me.

. . . . In the past the Negro has not been allowed to receive the education he needs. If this is the way it must be accomplished, and I believe it is, then it is not too high a price to pay.

Letter from a Birmingham Jail

By 1963, Dr. Martin Luther King, Jr., had emerged as the most important civil rights leader of the era. However as the campaign to desegregate public accommodations in Birmingham proved far more difficult than King or his followers had anticipated, some white Birmingham clergy openly criticized his efforts as harmful to the harmonious relationship between the races and questioned his commitment to Christianity. In his letter written while he was under arrest for violating Birmingham's segregationist ordinances, King answered the ministers.

I think I should indicate why I am here in Birmingham since you have been influenced by the view which argues against "outsiders coming in." Several months ago the [SCLC] affiliate here in Birmingham asked us to be on call to engage in a non-violent direct-action program if such were deemed necessary. We readily consented, and when the hour came we lived up to our promise.... But more basically, I am in Birmingham because injustice is here.... I cannot sit idly by in Atlanta and not be concerned about what happens in Birmingham. Injustice anywhere is a threat to justice everywhere.... Never again can we afford to live with the narrow, provincial "outside agitator" idea. Anyone who lives inside the United States can never be considered an outsider anywhere within its bounds.

You deplore the demonstrations taking place in Birmingham. But your statement fails to express a similar concern for the conditions that brought about the demonstrations. ... It is unfortunate that demonstrations are taking place in Birmingham, but it is even more unfortunate that the city's white power structure left the Negro community with no alternative.

We know through painful experience that freedom is never voluntarily given by the oppressor; it must be demanded by the oppressed. Frankly, I have yet to engage in a direct-action campaign that was "well-timed" in the view of those who have not suffered from the disease of segregation. For years now I have heard the word "wait!" This "wait" has almost always meant "Never."

We have waited for more than 340 years for our constitutional and God-given rights. The nations of Asia and Africa are moving with jet like speed toward gaining political independence, but we still creep at horse-and-buggy pace toward gaining a cup of coffee at a lunch counter. Perhaps it is easy for those who have never felt segregation to say, "Wait." But when you have seen vicious mobs lynch your mothers and fathers and drown your sisters and brothers at whim; when you have seen hate-filled policemen curse, kick and even kill your black brothers and sisters ... when you have to concoct an answer for a five-year-old son who is asking: "Daddy, why do white people treat colored people so mean?" ... when your first name becomes "boy" (however old you are) and your last name becomes "John," and your wife and mother are never given the respected title "Mrs." – then you will understand why we find it difficult to wait.

Martin Luther King, Jr., and the FBI

In 1964, Dr. Martin Luther King, Jr., shortly after his notification that he was the Nobel Peace Prize recipient, got an anonymous letter suggesting he was a fraud and that he commit suicide. It was later determined that the letter originated with the FBI, which was trying to discredit King and retard the Civil Rights Movement. The letter is reprinted here.

In view of your low grade ... I will not dignify your name with either a Mr. or a Reverend or a Dr. And, your last name calls to mind only the type of King such as King Henry the VIII ...

King, look into your heart. You know you are a complete fraud and a great liability to all of us Negroes. White people in this country have enough frauds of their own but I am sure they don't have one at this time anywhere near your equal. You are no clergyman and you know it. I repeat you are a colossal fraud and an evil, vicious one at that. You could not believe in God.... Clearly you don't believe in any personal moral principles.

King, like all frauds your end is approaching. You could have been our greatest leader. You, even at an early age have turned out to be not a leader but a dissolute, abnormal moral imbecile. We will now have to depend on our older leaders like Wilkins, a man of character and thank God we have others like him. But you are done. Your "honorary" degrees, your Nobel Prize (what a grim farce) and other awards will not save you. King, I repeat you are done.

No person can overcome facts, not even a fraud like yourself. ... I repeat–no person can argue successfully against facts.... Satan could not do more. What incredible evilness.... King you are done. The American public, the church organizations that have been helping–Protestant, Catholic and Jews will know you for what you are–an evil, abnormal beast. So will others who have backed you. You are done.

King, there is only one thing left for you to do. You know what it is. You have just 34 days in which to do (this exact number has been selected for a specific reason, it has definite practical significant [*sic*]). You are done. There is but one way out for you. You better take it before your filthy, abnormal fraudulent self is bared to the nation.

SOURCE: David J. Garrow, The FBI and Martin Luther King, Jr., 125–126. W. W. W. Norton, Inc., 1981. Copyright © 1981 by David J. Garrow. All rights reserved. Reprinted with permission of the author c/o JCA Literary Agency.

Letters from Mississippi

The following letters written between June and August 1964 provide a brief glimpse of the impressions and emotions of the largely white college students who worked in Mississippi during that "Freedom Summer."

June 15

...Us white kids here are in a position we've never been in before. The direction of the whole program is under Negro leadership–almost entirely. And a large part of that leadership is young people from the South–Negroes who've had experience just because they're Negroes and because they've been active in the movement. And here "we" are, for the most part never experiencing any injustice other than "No, I won't let you see your exam paper ..."

Dear Mom and Dad,

A lot of the meetings have been run by a Negro Mennonite minister from Georgia, a member of the National Council of Churches. (The NCC is paying for this orientation, and has some excellent staff people here.) His name is Vincent Harding, plump, bespectacled, and brilliant moderator in discussions because he reacts so honestly and humorously to every question. Yesterday he gave a long talk about people using each other and where to watch out for this within the movement itself (Negro man accuses white girl of being a racist if she won't go to bed with him, or vice versa; or white girl looking for "my summer Negro"; or Negroes in the community using volunteers as the only available victims of their suppressed hostility to whites in general, etc., etc). These are examples of the kind of honesty that characterizes the whole training session. His main point was that people within the movement must not use each other because it is that very exploitation of someone else, which turns him from a human being into an object, that the movement is fighting against.

Love, Susan

June 27

... Before the first bus pulled out last night Bob Moses, his head hanging, his voice barely audible, tried to tell us what he feels about being responsible for the creation of situations in which people get killed.... He talked of the problem of good and evil ... of a book which is one of my greatest favorites, a rather unknown book by the Englishman, J.R.R. Tolkien, *The Lord of the Rings* ... The hero gains a means of ultimate power which he does not want. Yet this power becomes a

SOURCE: Elizabeth Sutherland, ed., <u>Letters From Mississippi</u> (New York, 1965), 3–4, 9, 14, 22–23, 31–32, 68, 93, 119, 157–59, 229–230. All rights reserved. Reprinted with permission of Zephyr Press c/o The Permissions Co.

necessity to him until in the end he is unable to yield it voluntarily, and in a very great sense, he must sacrifice that which is best in himself. . . . For those of use who knew the book, it was a great and beautiful moment and it gave us an understanding which we might otherwise never have had.

Dear Mom and Dad, June 27

This letter is hard to write because I would like so much to communicate how I feel and I don't know if I can. It is very hard to answer to your attitude that if I loved you I wouldn't do this–hard, because the thought is cruel. I can only hope you have the sensitivity to understand that I can both love you very much and desire to go to Mississippi. I have no way of demonstrating my love. It is simply a fact and that is all I can say. . . .

I hope you will accept my decision even if you do not agree with me. There comes a time when you have to do things which your parents do not agree with. . . . Convictions are worthless in themselves. In fact, if they don't become actions, they are worse than worthless–they become a force of evil in themselves. You can't run away from a broadened awareness. . . . This doesn't apply just to civil rights or social consciousness but to all the experiences of life.

Love, Bonnie

Batesville

. . . Fear of The Man, fear of Mr. Charlie. . . . Occasionally it is the irrational fear of something new and untested. But usually it is a highly rational emotion, the economic fear of losing your job, the physical fear of being shot at. Domestic servants know that they will be fired if they register to vote; so will factory workers, so will Negroes who live on plantations. In Mississippi, registration is no private affair.

Mound Bayou

The county superintendent of schools ordered that neither foreign languages nor civics shall be taught in any Negro schools, nor shall American history from 1860 to 1875 be taught.

Moss Point, Monday, July 6

Tonight the sickness struck. At our mass meeting as we were singing "We Shall Overcome" a girl was shot in the side and in the chest. We fell to the floor in deathly fear; but soon we recovered and began moving out of the hall to see what had happened. When I went out I saw a woman lying on the ground clutching her stomach. She was so still and looked like a statute with a tranquil smile on her face. I ran to call an ambulance and police.

Gulfport, August 12

Dear Mother and Father:

I have learned more about politics here from running my own precinct meetings than I could have from any Government professor.... For the first time in my life, I am seeing what it is like to be poor, oppressed, and hated. And what I see here does not apply only to Gulfport or to Mississippi or even to the South.... The people we're killing in Viet Nam are the same people whom we've been killing for years in Mississippi. True, we didn't tie the knot in Mississippi and we didn't pull the trigger in Viet Nam – that is, we personally– but we've been standing behind the knot-tiers and the trigger-pullers too long. This summer is only the briefest beginning of this experience, both for myself and for the Negroes of Mississippi.

Your daughter, Ellen

Fannie Lou Hamer Testifies at the Democratic National Convention, 1964

Fannie Lou Hamer, a Mississippi native, emerged as one of the major leaders of the Mississippi Freedom Democratic Party (MFDP), which represented all the state's voters regardless of race. In 1964, she testified before the Credentials Committee of the National Democratic Convention, urging the party to seat the MFDP delegation rather than the "regular" Democrats who represented the state's white voters. Her testimony, which described the terror campaign against her and other black voters, follows.

Mr. Chairman and the Credentials Committee, my name is Mrs. Fannie Lou Hamer, and I live at 626 East Lafayette Street, Ruleville, Mississippi, Sunflower County, the home of Senator James O. Eastland, and Senator [John] Stennis.

It was the 31st of August in 1962 that eighteen of us traveled twenty-six miles to the county courthouse in Indianola to try to register to try to become first-class citizens. We was met in Indianola by Mississippi men, highway patrolmens, and they only allowed two of us in to take the literacy test at the time. After we had taken this test and started back to Ruleville, we was held up by the City Police and the State Highway Patrolmen and carried back to Indianola, where the bus driver was charged that day with driving a bus the wrong color.

SOURCE: "Testimony of Fannie Lou Hamer Before the Credentials Committee of the Democratic National Convention," August 22, 1964, Joseph Rauh Papers, Library of Congress.

After we paid the fine among us, we continued on to Ruleville, and Reverend Jeff Sunny carried me four miles in the rural area where I had worked as a timekeeper and sharecropper for eighteen years. I was met there by my children, who told me the plantation owner was angry because I had gone down to try to register. After they told me, my husband came, and said the plantation owner was raising cain because I had tried to register, and before he quit talking the plantation owner came, and said, "Fannie Lou, do you know – did Pap tell you what I said?"

I said, "Yes, sir."

He said, "I mean that. If you don't go down and withdraw your registration, you will have to leave." Then he said, "Then if you go down and withdraw, you will—you might have to go because we are not ready for that in Mississippi."

And I addressed him and told him and said, "I didn't try to register for you. I tried to register for myself." I had to leave that same night.

On the 10th of September 1962, sixteen bullets was fired into the home of Mr. and Mrs. Robert Tucker for me. That same night two girls were shot in Ruleville, Mississippi. Also Mr. Joe McDonald's house was shot in.

And in June, the 9th, 1963, I had attended a voter registration workshop and was returning back to Mississippi. Ten of us was traveling by the Continental Trailways bus. When we got to Winona, Mississippi, which is Montgomery County, four of the people got off to use the washroom, and two of the people– to use the restaurant–two of the people wanted to use the washroom. The four people that had gone in to use the restaurant was ordered out. During this time I was on the bus. But when I looked through the window and saw they had rushed out, I got off the bus to see what had happened, and one of the ladies said, "It was a State Highway Patrolman and a chief of police ordered us out."

I got back on the bus and one of the persons had used the washroom got back on the bus, too. As soon as I was seated on the bus, I saw when they began to get the four people in a highway patrolman's car. I stepped off the bus to see what was happening and somebody screamed from the car that the four workers was in and said, "Get that one there," and when I went to get in the car, when the man told me I was under arrest, he kicked me.

I was carried to the county jail, and put in the booking room. They left some of the people in the booking room and began to place us in cells. I was placed in a cell with a young woman. . . . After I was placed in the cell I began to hear sounds of licks and screams. I could hear the sounds of licks and horrible screams, and I could hear somebody say, "Can you say, yes sir, nigger? Can you say yes, sir?"

And they would say other horrible names. She would say, "Yes, I can say yes, sir."

"So say it."

She says, "I don't know you well enough."

They beat her, I don't know how long, and after a while she began to pray, and asked God to have mercy on those people.

And it wasn't too long before three white men came to my cell. One of these men was a State Highway Patrolman and he asked me where I was from, and I told him Ruleville. He said, "We are going to check this." And they left my cell and it wasn't too long before they came back. He said, "You are from Ruleville all right," and he used a curse word, and he said, "We are going to make you wish you was dead."

I was carried out of that cell into another cell where they had two Negro prisoners. The State Highway Patrolman ordered the first Negro to take the blackjack. The first Negro prisoner ordered me, by orders from the State Highway Patrolman for me, to lay down on a bunk bed on my face, and I laid on my face. The first Negro began to beat, and I was beat by the first Negro until he was exhausted, and I was holding my hands behind me at that time on my left side because I suffered from polio when I was six years old. After the first Negro had beat until he was exhausted, the State Highway Patrolman ordered the second Negro to take the blackjack.

The second Negro began to beat and I began to work my feet, and the State Highway Patrolman ordered the first Negro who had beat to set on my feet to keep me from working my feet. I began to scream and one white man got up and began to beat me in my head and tell me to hush. One white man – my dress had worked up high, he walked over and pulled my dress down – and he pulled my dress back, back up . . .

All of this on account we want to register, to become first-class citizens, and if the Freedom Democratic Party is not seated now, I question America. Is this America, the land of the free and the home of the brave, where we have to sleep with our telephone off the hooks because our lives be threatened daily because we want to live as decent human beings, in America?

Murder in Mississippi

During the 1964 Freedom Summer, hundreds of black and white civil rights workers from throughout the United States assisted black Mississippians to register to vote and to challenge the racially discriminatory laws of the state. Three of those workers, Andrew Goodman, Michael Schwerner, and James Chaney, were killed near Philadelphia. This passage, from William Bradford Huie's Three Lives for Mississippi, *describes their deaths.*

The murder was done in the "cut" on Rock Cut Road, less than a mile from Highway 19, about four miles from where the three were taken from the station wagon. It was before midnight, and the moon was still high. Three cars were in the cut. I was told that the three victims said nothing, but that they were jeered by the murderers. Several of the murderers chanted in unison, as though they had practiced it:

"Ashes to ashes, Dust to dust, If you'd stayed where you belonged, You wouldn't be here with us."

Another said: "So you wanted to come to Mississippi? Well, now we're gonna let you stay here. We're not even gonna run you out. We're gonna let you stay here with us."

When Schwerner was pulled from the car and stood up to be shot, I was told that the man with the pistol asked him: "You still think a nigger's as good as I am?" No time was allowed for a reply. He was shot straight through the heart and fell to the ground.

Goodman was next, with nothing said. Apparently he stood as still as Schwerner did, facing his executioner, for the shot that killed him was the same precise shot. I was told that another man fired the shot, using the same pistol, but my opinion remains that one man fired both shots.

Chaney was last, and the only difference was that he struggled while the others had not. He didn't stand still; he tried to pull and duck away from his executioner. So he wasn't shot with the same precision, and he was shot three times instead of once.

The three bodies were tossed into the station wagon and driven along dirt roads to a farm about six miles southwest of Philadelphia. All three bodies were buried in darkness with a bulldozer. They were also uncovered, forty-four days later, with a bulldozer. After the burial the station wagon was driven to a point fifteen miles northeast of Philadelphia, to the edge of the Bogue Chitto swamp. There it was doused with diesel fuel and burned. Afterwards the murderers began drinking though none could be called drunk. They were met by an official of the state of Mississippi.

"Well, boys," he said, "you've done a good job. You've struck a blow for the White Man. Mississippi can be proud of you. . . . Go home now and forget it. But before you go, I'm looking each one of you in the eye and telling you this: the first man who talks is <u>dead</u>! If anybody who knows anything about this ever opens his mouth to any Outsider about it, then the rest of us are going to kill him just as dead as we killed those three sonsofbitches tonight. "Does everybody understand what I'm saying? The man who talks is dead . . . dead . . . dead!"

David Dennis Speaks at the Memorial for James Chaney

On August 7, 1964, David Dennis, the assistant director of the Mississippi Summer Project for COFO, spoke to approximately 120 people who filled a small black church in Meridian, Mississippi, during a memorial service for recently slain James Chaney. His remarks, understandably laced with anger and bitterness over the death a friend,

SOURCE: Elizabeth Sutherland, ed., Letters from Mississippi (New York: McGraw-Hill Book Company, 1965), 191–192. All rights reserved. Reproduced with permission of Zephyr Press c/o The Permission Co.

nonetheless challenged the listeners to turn their grief into a renewed commitment to voter registration.

"I am not here to memorialize James Chaney, I am not here to pay tribute— I am too sick and tired. Do YOU hear me, I am S-I-C-K and T-I-R-E-D. I have attended too many memorials, too many funerals. This has got to stop. Mack Parker, Medgar Evers, Herbert Lee, Lewis Allen, Emmett Till, four little girls in Birmingham, a 3-year old boy in Birmingham, and the list goes on and on. I have attended these funerals and memorials and I am SICK and TIRED.

But the trouble is that YOU are NOT sick and tired and for that reason YOU, yes YOU, are to blame, Everyone of your damn souls. And if you are going to let this continue now then you are to blame, yes YOU. Just as much as the monsters of hate who pulled the trigger or brought down the club; just as much to blame as the sheriff and the chief of police, as the governor in Jackson who said that he 'did not have time' for Mrs. Schwerner when she went to see him, and just as much to blame as the President and Attorney General in Washington who wouldn't provide protection for Chancy, Goodman and Schwerner when we told them that protection was necessary in Neshoba County . . .

Yes, I am angry, I AM. And it's high time that you got angry too, angry enough to go up to the courthouse Monday and register —everyone of you. Angry enough to take five and ten other people with you. Then and only then can these brutal killings be stopped. Remember it is your sons and your daughters who have been killed all these years and you have done nothing about it, and if you don't do nothing NOW, I say God Damn Your Souls.

President Johnson Proposes the Voting Rights Act

On March 7, 1965, Dr. Martin Luther King, Jr. led demonstrations at Selma, Alabama, to secure voting rights for black Americans. One week later, President Lyndon Johnson spoke before a joint session of Congress to urge passage of voting rights legislation that would guarantee that right. Johnson for the first time placed the full support of the presidency behind Dr. King and the Civil Rights Movement. Here is his address to Congress.

SOURCE: Public Papers of the Presidents of the United States: Lyndon B. Johnson (Washington: Federal Register Division, National Archives and Records Service, General Services Administration, 1966), 1:281–287.

Mr. Speaker, Mr. President, Members of the Congress:

I speak tonight for the dignity of man and the destiny of democracy. I urge every member of both parties, Americans of all religions and of all colors, from every section of this country, to join me in that cause.

Wednesday I will send to Congress a law designed to eliminate illegal barriers to the right to vote. This bill will strike down restrictions to voting in all elections ... which have been used to deny Negroes the right to vote. We cannot refuse to protect the right of every American to vote in every election that he may desire to participate in. We have already waited one hundred years and more, and the time for waiting is gone. ...

But even if we pass this bill, the battle will not be over. What happened in Selma is part of a far larger movement which reaches into every section and State of America. It is the effort of American Negroes to secure for themselves the full blessings of American life.

Their cause must be our cause too. Because it is not just Negroes, but really it is all of us, who must overcome the crippling legacy of bigotry and injustice.

And we shall overcome.

As a man whose roots go deeply into Southern soil I know how agonizing racial feelings are. I know how difficult it is to reshape the attitudes and the structure of our society.

But a century has passed, more than a hundred years, since the Negro was freed. And he is not fully free tonight.

The time of justice has now come. I tell you that I believe sincerely that no force can hold it back. It is right in the eyes of man and God that it should come. And when it does, I think that day will brighten the lives of every American.

For Negroes are not the only victims. How many white children have gone uneducated, how many white families have lived in stark poverty, how many white lives have been scarred by fear, because we have wasted our energy and our substance to maintain the barriers of hatred and terror?

So I say to all of you here, and to all in the Nation tonight, that those who appeal to you to hold on to the past do so at the cost of denying you your future.

This great, rich, restless country can offer opportunity and education and hope to all: black and white, North and South, sharecropper and city dweller. These are the enemies: poverty, ignorance, disease. They are the enemies and not our fellow man, not our neighbor. And these enemies too, poverty, disease and ignorance, we shall overcome.

6

Black Power, 1965–1975

This chapter assesses the changing civil rights struggle throughout the nation as symbolized by the phrase "Black Power." The term would mean different things to various groups, which is reflected in the vignettes. The first vignette suggests one definition even before the term itself came into widespread use. In **Malcolm X "On White Oppression,"** we see the contrast between the then dominant strategies and goals of organizations such as the NAACP and leaders like Martin Luther King, Jr. **The Assassination of Malcolm X** reminds us of the shadow of violence that followed all who called for change in that era. In **Watts: A City Explodes, A Singer Dies** we get a snapshot of a single incident in what would become the first of a series of urban conflagrations through the 1960s. The vignettes **Stokely Carmichael on Black Liberation** and **The Black Panther Party** describe the emergence of post-Watts leaders with new agendas. The nexus of the black liberation struggle and the antiwar effort is seen in the vignette **SNCC Statement on Vietnam.**

The vignette **Black Power Comes to Cleveland: The Election of Carl Stokes** illustrates the ways in which black electoral politics changed during the period. The college and university campuses were profoundly influenced by Black Power, as seen in the vignettes **"Death Was a Distinct Possibility Last Night"** and **The University of Washington Black Student Union.** Black Power's influence on gender questions is seen in myriad ways in the final two vignettes, **Black Feminists Organize** and **Elaine Brown: Black Panther.**

Malcolm X "On White Oppression"

Malcolm X had emerged by the early 1960s as the leading proponent of black nationalist politics. In a speech in Harlem on February 14, 1965, just seven days before his assassination, he explained his position. The full text of this speech can be found at TheBlackPast.org, http://www.blackpast.org.

Attorney Milton Henry, distinguished guests, brothers and sisters, ladies and gentlemen, friends and enemies: I want to point out first that I am very happy to be here this evening, and I am thankful to the Afro-American Broadcasting Company for the invitation to come here this evening. As Attorney Milton Henry has stated – I should say Brother Milton Henry because that's what he is, our brother – I was in a house last night that was bombed, my own. It didn't destroy all my clothes, but you know what fire and smoke do to things. The only thing I could get my hands on before leaving was what I have on now . . .

So I ask you to excuse my appearance. I don't normally come out in front of people without a shirt and tie. I guess that's somewhat a holdover from the Black Muslim movement which I was in. That's one of the good aspects of the movement. It teaches you to be very careful and conscious of how you look, which is a positive contribution on my part. But that positive contribution on their part is greatly offset by too many liabilities . . .

Look right now what's going on in and around Saigon and Hanoi and in the Congo and elsewhere. They [white Americans] are violent when their interests are at stake. . . . They're violent in Korea, they're violent in Germany, they're violent in the South Pacific, they're violent in Cuba, they're violent wherever they go. But when it comes time for you and me to protect ourselves against lynchings, they tell us to be nonviolent.

That's a shame. Because we get tricked into being nonviolent, and when somebody stands up and talks like I just did, they say, "Why, he's advocating violence . . ." I have never advocated violence. I have only said that black people who are the victims of organized violence perpetrated upon us by the Klan, the Citizens Councils, and many other forms should defend ourselves. . . . I wouldn't call on anybody to be violent without cause. But I think the black man in this country, above and beyond people all over the world, will be more justified when he stands up and starts to protect himself, no matter how many . . . heads he has to crack. . . .

Now, for saying something like that, the press calls us racist and people who are "violent in reverse." They make you think that if you try to stop the Klan from lynching you, you're practicing violence in reverse. . . . Well, if a criminal comes around your house with his gun, brother, just because he's got a gun and he's robbing your house ... it doesn't make you a robber because you grab your gun and run him out.... With skillful manipulating of the press they're able to make the victim look like the criminal and the criminal look like the victim....

Now, what effect does [the struggle over Africa] have on us? Why should the black man in America concern himself since he's been away from the African continent for three or four hundred years...? Number one, you have to realize that up until 1959 Africa was dominated by the colonial powers. Having complete control over Africa, the colonial powers of Europe projected the image of Africa negatively.... We didn't want anybody telling us anything about Africa, much less calling us Africans. In hating Africa and in hating the Africans, we ended up hating ourselves, without even realizing it.... You can't hate your origin and not end up hating yourself . . .

After 1959 the spirit of African nationalism was fanned to a high flame, and we then began to witness the complete collapse of colonialism. France began to get out of French West Africa, Belgium began to make moves to get out of the Congo, Britain began to make moves to get out of Kenya, Tanganyika, Uganda, Nigeria, and some of these other places . . .

One of the things that made the Black Muslim movement grow was its emphasis upon things African. This was the secret to the growth of the Black Muslim movement. African blood, African origin, African culture, African ties. And you'd be surprised – we discovered that deep within the subconscious of the black man in this country, he is still more African than he is American. . . . He's telling him, "You're an American, you're an American. . ." Just because you're in this country doesn't make you an American. No, you've got to go farther than that before you can become an American. You've got to enjoy the fruits of Americanism. You haven't enjoyed those fruits. You've enjoyed the thorns . . .

Brothers and sisters, let me tell you, I spend my time out there in the streets with people, all kinds of people, listening to what they have to say. And they're dissatisfied, they're disillusioned, they're fed up, they're getting to the point of frustration where they begin to feel, "What do we have to lose?" When you get to that point, you're the type of person who can create a very dangerously explosive atmosphere. This is what's happening in our neighborhoods, to our people . . .

And it is for this reason that it is so important for you and me to start organizing among ourselves, intelligently.... I say again that I'm not a racist, I don't believe in any form of segregation or anything like that. I'm for brotherhood for everybody, but I don't believe in forcing brotherhood upon people who don't want it. Let us practice brotherhood among ourselves, and then if others want to practice brotherhood with us, we're for practicing it with them also. But I don't think that we should run around trying to love somebody who doesn't love us.

The Assassination of Malcolm X

In February 1965, Malcolm X was assassinated as he was about to deliver an address to the Organization of Afro-American Unity, the group he had recently formed following his separation from the Nation of Islam. This excerpt is an eyewitness account by Larry Neal, a Harlem poet, writer, and black nationalist.

An obvious commotion had started down in the front rows. Malcolm was standing at a podium. He stepped from behind the podium to quiet the commotion. He said something like, "Peace, be cool, brothers." Then it came. The strongest possible message, direct. The shots came rapid fire. Malcolm fell back, his arms flung outward like wings from the impact of the bullets hitting him square in the chest. Then there was the rumbling of scuffling feet, and the chairs were overturned.

After it happened there seemed to be a pause, then the fear was everywhere. People scrambled for cover on the floor under the tables in the back, shouting. Screams came from the women and children. It seemed like the shots were coming from all over the ballroom (a smoke bomb in the rear, found later, didn't go off). Security guards were trying to reach Malcolm, trying to stop the assassins who now were safely escaping in the confusion. Ahada's [Ahada and her daughter Amina accompanied Neal to the presentation] daughter bolted out of the seat beside us. Ahada managed to catch the child before she could be trampled by the mob.

A gunman ran by us, shooting and hurdling over chairs in his way. He twisted and turned, and fired at a knot of black men chasing him. The man was still firing as he ran out of the door toward the 165th Street entrance. He was being chased by several of Malcolm's men. They caught him at the top of the steps, and he was wounded in the thigh. Another assassin left by the side door, waving his gun, daring anyone to follow him. The whole room was a wailing woman. Men cried openly.

SOURCE: Larry Neal, <u>Visions of a Liberated Future: Black Arts Movement and Writings</u>, 127–128. Thunder's Press, 1989. Copyright © 1989 by Thunder's Press. All rights reserved. Reprinted with permission of Avalon Publishing Group, Inc.

Watts: A City Explodes, A Singer Dies

The four days of rioting that swept the Watts section of Los Angeles in August 1965 proved a turning point in the civil rights struggle. The nation's attention, which had previously been focused on the rural South, now shifted to the ghettos of the North and West as African Americans demonstrated their anger with the prevailing political and economic status quo. The following passage describes the death of Charles Patrick Fizer, one of the thirty-four people killed during the riot.

Charles Patrick Fizer, born in Shreveport Louisiana, sang because he loved to – and for money. People paid to hear Charles Fizer sing. For a brief time, he made it big. Most of the Fizer family migrated to California during World War II to take jobs in the buzzing Los Angeles area aircraft plants and shipyards. In 1944, when he was only three, Charles Fizer was taken there by his grandparents. He lived with them for a time. Then, when he was seven, he moved to Watts with his mother.

The Fizer family was a religious one. Charles attended the Sweet Home Baptist Church and became an enthusiastic choir member. He had a good voice. By the time he was fifteen, he was singing in night clubs. . . . He became part of a successful group of entertainers. He broke in singing second lead with the Olympics, as the group was known. . . . Came the Olympics' recording of "Hully Gully," and Charles Fizer was something to be reckoned with as an entertainer. The record sold nearly a million copies. The Olympics won television guest shots. Charles came up with a snaky dance to fit the "Hully Gully" music. Other hit songs followed, and it seemed nothing could stop Charles Fizer from reaching the top. [But] Charles became restless. With his fellow performers, he became impatient. His testy attitude and souring views cost him his job with the singing group. He and another entertainer formed a night-club duo, but it flopped. The summer of the Los Angeles riot, he hit bottom. He served six months at hard labor on a county prison farm after being arrested with illegal barbiturates.

He was released Thursday, August 12. The riot already was in progress. Even as the violence spread in Los Angeles, Charles Fizer wakened early Friday, went job-hunting and found work as a busboy. . . . But there would be no work Saturday, the restaurant manager decided to close until peace was restored in the city. . . . But that night Charles Fizer drove through Watts after the curfew hour. In the center of the fire-blackened community, he stopped short of a National Guard roadblock at 102nd and Beach Streets. Inexplicably, he backed the Buick away from the barricade. Suddenly, he turned on the car's headlights and shifted into forward gear. What compelled him to jam the accelerator to the floor only he could say, and soon he was past explaining. Too many white faces challenging him?

SOURCE: From BURN, BABBY, BURN! by Jerry Cohen and William S. Murphy, copyright © 1966 by Jerry Cohen & William S. Murphy. Used by permission of Dutton, a division of Penguin Group (USA) Inc.

Perhaps. A white man giving him an order? Perhaps. In any event, he pointed the car straight for the roadblock. Guardsmen cried to him to halt and fired warning shots into the air. Then came the roar of M-1 carbines. The Buick spun crazily and rammed a curb. Charles Fizer never realized his resolve to make a new life. Inside the car he lay dead, a bullet in his left temple. The time was 9:15 P.M.

Stokely Carmichael on Black Liberation

In the spring of 1966, Stokely Carmichael became chairman of the Student Non-Violent Coordinating Committee and soon afterward advanced the concept of Black Power. In an article published later that year, he discussed its ramifications for America.

The history of every institution of this society indicates that a major concern . . . has been the maintaining of the Negro community in its condition of dependence and oppression. This has not been on the level of individual acts of discrimination between individual whites against individual Negroes, but as total acts by the White community against the Negro community.

Let me give you an example of the difference between individual racism and institutionalized racism. . . . When unidentified white terrorists bomb a Negro Church and kill five children, that act is widely deplored by most segments of the society. But when in that same city, Birmingham, Alabama, not five but 500 Negro babies die each year because of lack of proper food, shelter and medical facilities . . . that is a function of institutionalized racism.

We must organize black community power to end these abuses, and to give the Negro community a chance to have its needs expressed. A leadership which is truly "responsible" – not to the white press and power structure, but to the community – must be developed. Such leadership will recognize that its power lies in the unified and collective strength of that community.

The single aspect of the black power program that has encountered most criticism is this concept of independent organization. This is presented as third-partyism which has never worked, or a withdrawal into black nationalism and isolationism. . . . When the Negro community is able to control local office, and negotiate with other groups from a position of organized strength, the possibility of meaningful political alliances on specific issues will be increased. That is a rule of politics and there is no reason why it should not operate here. The only difference is that we will have the power to define the terms of these alliances.

SOURCE: Thomas R. Frazier, <u>Afro-American History: Primary Sources</u> (New York: Harcourt, 1970), 414, 419–420.

The next question usually is, "So – can it work, can the ghettoes in fact be organized?" The answer is that this organization must be successful, because there are no viable alternatives – not the War on Poverty, which was at its inception limited to dealing with effects rather than causes, and has become simply another source of machine patronage. And "Integration" is meaningful only to a small chosen class within the community.

[The] "inner city" in most major urban areas is [*sic*] already predominately Negro, and with the white rush to suburbia, Negroes will in the next three decades control the heart of our great cities. These areas can become either concentration camps with a bitter and volatile population whose only power is the power to destroy, or organized and powerful communities able to make constructive contributions to the total society. Without the power to control their lives and their communities, without effective political institutions through which to relate to the total society, these communities will exist in a constant state of insurrection. This is a choice that the country will have to make.

SNCC Statement on Vietnam, January 6, 1966

SNCC became the first black civil rights organization to criticize the war in Vietnam. Its statement on the war is reprinted here.

The Student Nonviolent Coordinating Committee assumes its right to dissent with the United States foreign policy on any issue, and states its opposition to United States involvement in the war in Vietnam on these grounds:

We believe the United States government has been deceptive in claims of concern for the freedom of the Vietnamese people, just as the government has been deceptive in claiming concern for the freedom of the colored people in such other countries as the Dominican Republic, the Congo, South Africa, Rhodesia and in the United States itself.

We of the Student Nonviolent Coordinating Committee have been involved in the black people's struggle for liberation and self-determination in this country for the past five years. Our work, particularly in the South, taught us that the United States government has never guaranteed the freedom of oppressed citizens and is not yet truly determined to end the rule of terror and oppression within its own borders.

We ourselves have often been victims of violence and confinement executed by U.S. government officials. We recall the numerous persons who have

SOURCE: Statement on Vietnam, SNCC position paper, January 6, 1966.

been murdered in the South because of their efforts to secure their civil and human rights, and whose murderers have been allowed to escape penalty for their crimes. The murder of Samuel Younge in Tuskegee, Alabama is no different from the murder of people in Vietnam, for both Younge and the Vietnamese sought and are seeking to secure the rights guaranteed them by law. In each case, the U.S. government bears a great part of the responsibility for these deaths.

Samuel Younge was murdered because U.S. law is not being enforced. Vietnamese are being murdered because the United States is pursuing an aggressive policy in violation of international law. The U.S. is no respecter of persons or law when such persons or laws run counter to its needs and desires. We recall the indifference, suspicion and outright hostility with which our reports of violence have been met in the past by government officials.

We are in sympathy with and support the men in this country who are unwilling to respond to the military draft which would compel them to contribute their lives to U.S. aggression in the name of the "freedom" we find so false in this country.

We ask: Where is the draft for the Freedom fight in the United States?

We therefore encourage those Americans who prefer to use their energy in building democratic forms within the country. We believe that work in the civil rights movement and other human relations organizations is a valid alternative to the draft. We urge all Americans to seek this alternative knowing full well that it may cost them their lives, as painfully as in Vietnam.

The Kerner Commission on Race in America, 1967

By September 1967, the United States had witnessed three continuous summers of racial rioting in its largest cities. In response to these uprisings, President Lyndon B. Johnson established the eleven-member National Advisory Commission on Civil Disorders to investigate racial unrest and recommend remedial action. The Kerner Commission, so named after its chairman, Illinois Governor Otto Kerner, said the United States was "moving toward two societies, one black, one white, separate and unequal." Here is the introduction to the Commission's Report.

SOURCE: Report of the National Advisory Commission on Civil Disorders (Washington, D.C.: Government Printing Office, 1968), 1–2.

The summer of 1967 again brought racial disorders to American cities, and with them shock, fear and bewilderment to the nation. The worst came during a two-week period in July, first in Newark and then in Detroit. Each set off a chain reaction in neighboring communities.

On July 28, 1967, the President of the United States established this Commission and directed us to answer three basic questions: What happened? Why did it happen? What can be done to prevent it from happening again?

To respond to these questions, we have undertaken a broad range of studies and investigations. We have visited the riot cities; we have heard many witnesses; we have sought the counsel of experts across the country. This is our basic conclusion: Our nation is moving toward two societies, one black, one white – separate and unequal. Reaction to last summer's disorders has quickened the movement and deepened the division. Discrimination and segregation have long permeated much of American life; they now threaten the future of every American.

This deepening racial division is not inevitable. The movement apart can be reversed. Choice is still possible. Our principal task is to define that choice and to press for a national resolution. To pursue our present course will involve the continuing polarization of the American community and, ultimately, the destruction of basic democratic values. The alternative is not blind repression or capitulation to lawlessness. It is the realization of common opportunities for all within a single society.

This alternative will require a commitment to national action – compassionate, massive and sustained, backed by the resources of the most powerful and the richest nation on this earth. From every American it will require new attitudes, new understanding, and, above all, new will.

The vital needs of the nation must be met; hard choices must be made, and, if necessary, new taxes enacted.

Violence cannot build a better society. Disruption and disorder nourish repression, not justice. They strike at the freedom of every citizen. The community cannot – it will not – tolerate coercion and mob rule. Violence and destruction must be ended – in the streets of the ghetto and in the lives of people.

Segregation and poverty have created in the racial ghetto a destructive environment totally unknown to most white Americans. What white Americans have never fully understood but what the Negro can never forget – is that white society is deeply implicated in the ghetto. White institutions created it, white institutions maintain it, and white society condones it.

It is time now to turn with all the purpose at our command to the major unfinished business of this nation. It is time to adopt strategies for action that will produce quick and visible progress. It is time to make good the promises of American democracy to all citizens-urban and rural, white and black, Spanish-surname, American Indian, and every minority group.

The Black Panther Party

By 1967, the black nationalist movement dominated earlier by Malcolm X and the Nation of Islam had divided into two major factions. One group, the cultural nationalists, led by Imamu Amiri Baraka and Maulana Karenga, argued that blacks must "liberate their minds" before embarking on the inevitable armed revolutionary struggle. The Black Panther Party, founded by Huey Newton and Bobby Seale, however, called for revolutionary nationalism, claiming that the armed struggle and mental liberation must occur simultaneously and immediately. Huey Newton explained the Panther Party philosophy, and particularly the party's relationship with revolutionary whites, in an interview in 1968, part of which is reprinted here.

The imperialistic or capitalistic system occupies areas. It occupies Vietnam now. It occupies areas by sending soldiers there, by sending policemen there. The policemen or soldiers are only a gun in the establishment's hand, making the racist secure in his racism, the establishment secure in its exploitation. The first problem, it seems, is to remove the gun from the establishment's hand. Until lately, the white radical has seen no reason to come into conflict with the policeman in his own community. I said "until recently," because there is friction now in the mother country between the young revolutionaries and the police; because now the white revolutionaries are attempting to put some of their ideas into action, and there's the rub. We say that it should be a permanent thing.

Black people are being oppressed in the colony by white policemen, by white racists. We are saying they must withdraw.

As far as I'm concerned, the only reasonable conclusion would be to first realize the enemy, realize the plan, and then when something happens in the black colony – when we're attacked and ambushed in the black colony – then the white revolutionary students and intellectuals and all the other whites who support the colony should respond by defending us, by attacking the enemy in their community.

The Black Panther Party is an all black party, because we feel, as Malcolm X felt, that there can be no black-white unity until there first is black unity. We have a problem in the black colony that is particular to the colony, but we're willing to accept aid from the mother country as long as the mother country radicals realize that we have, as Eldridge Cleaver says in <u>Soul on Ice</u>, a mind of our own. We've regained our mind that was taken away from us and we will decide the political, as well as the practical, stand that we'll take. We'll make the theory and we'll carry out the practice. It's the duty of the white revolutionary to aid us in this.

SOURCE: Thomas R. Frazier, <u>Afro-American History: Primary Sources</u> (Chicago, 1988), 400–401.

Black Power Comes to Cleveland:
The Election of Carl Stokes

In November 1967, Carl Stokes became the first African American mayor of a major American city. The following vignette from the Cleveland Plain Dealer *describes his victory over Seth C. Taft, the grandson of a former president. That same day, Richard Hatcher was elected mayor of the smaller Midwest city of Gary, Indiana.*

In a spectacular windup to the city's most spectacular mayoral contest in decades, Carl B. Stokes last night won the honor of being the nation's first big-city chief executive. His wafer-thin win over Republican Seth C. Taft was in doubt for more than five hours after the polls closed in a historic election. Almost certain to be headed for a recount, the final tally showed Stokes the winner by the skinny margin of 2,500 votes.

All night long, Taft led in both the figures coming unofficially from the Board of Elections and the projections being guessed at all over the city. But, as the number of unreported precincts dwindled, so did Taft's margin. Then, almost miraculously for Stokes, it flipped and declared Stokes the winner. Unofficial figures from the Board of Elections showed: MAYOR (All of 903 polling places) Stokes – 129,825, Taft – 127,328.

Wearing a yard-wide smile, Stokes, his wife Shirley at his side hugging him, told cheering partisans at 3 a.m.: "It's a wonderful feeling." As if on cue, a massive response went up: "Amen!" He promised to fulfill the heritage of serving all Clevelanders, regardless of their backgrounds. Minutes later, Taft, his wife Frances at his side too, conceded defeat and pledged to "do what I can" to help Stokes govern the nation's eighth largest city.

From 7:30 p.m. on, the pundits were predicting a Taft victory, in hushed voices. Even the candidates, popping up on T.V. screens with regularity, had only one thing to say to the breathless audience: Wait a while longer. The waiting nearly unbearable, produced at first hysteria, then gloom in each head-quarters as reports of 25 new precincts figures dribbled in at the election board. It seemed as though the result reflected the Stokes tactic of combining a massive Negro voter base of support with a doubled share of white votes, compared with what he got in the Democrats' primary. Taft, who had sought to lead the GOP into City Hall for the first time in a quarter-century, had counted on winning over most of the traditionally Democratic – but white – voters.

The general election, conducted on a cold, snow-whipped day, did not appear to be headed toward the 275,000 total vote figure forecast by many experts. But it seemed likely to involve a significantly larger total vote than in 1965, when 237,000 Clevelanders elected Locher. The increased turnout was understandable in the general election. It was, by all odds, one of the city's most fiery mayoral contests.

Stokes, winner of the Democratic primary by an almost unbelievable 18,000-vote margin over Mayor Ralph S. Locher, was figured to be the favorite shortly after the Oct. 3 vote. But in the month-long campaign against Taft his image, among the front-line politicians, slipped somewhat.... The issue, of course, beneath it all was race. It was a question whether the electorate would choose a Democrat who happened to be a Negro or a Republican who happened to have the normally unpopular – in Cleveland – name of Taft. The clash between a grandson of President William Howard Taft and the great-grandson of a slave was history in the making. It attracted the attention of the world, and newsmen from all over the United States and as far as Sweden came to find out about it. Last night, as the drama unfolded at the Board of Elections, the out-of-town newsmen watched with Cleveland as history's newest page was written.

"Death was a Distinct Possibility Last Night"

After Watts, the nation's attention shifted to Northern ghettos. Yet student protests continued in the South and grew increasingly confrontational in the latter part of the 1960s. One such protest occurred in the South Carolina college town of Orange-burg in 1968. When students at South Carolina State College took to the streets to protest a segregated local bowling alley, as they pelted cars with rocks and bottles as their anger exploded on the night of February 7. The next day, police backed by the South Carolina National Guard occupied the campus. When one policeman was struck by a canister thrown by a student protestor, his fellow officers began firing on other students, shooting thirty-three demonstrators and killing three of them in what would be termed the Orangeburg Massacre. Ironically, the Chicago Defender published a story of the February 7 demonstration in which it quoted South Carolina State College President M. Maceo Nance, who said, "Death was a distinct possibility last night." Nance did not know that the possibility would become real the next night. The Defender article appears here.

*O*rangeburg, S.C: The National Guard was alerted Wednesday to head off further violence resulting from an attempt by college students to integrate a bowling alley.

Guard units within a 40 mile radius were told to report to their armories and standby in the event new trouble flares.

More than 10 persons were injured, including a policeman, and 16 arrests were made Tuesday night when seven hundred students from predominantly Negro South Carolina State College clashed with police outside the All-Star Bowling Alley, owned by Harry Floyd. Floyd said he didn't know what the students were protesting, but one said the "rebellion" was against a "hardcore, Reconstruction-day segregationist."

Prior to the melee, students had been picketing the bowling alley, located in a shipping center in a white section near downtown Orangeburg. They contended that Floyd would not permit Negroes to use the facility.

The president of South Carolina State, urged students to boycott the town, a farm center of 13,000 residents, rather than return to the street and risk more violence. Most of the students voiced support of the boycott at a mass meeting, but others wanted to march on City Hall.

Police said the clash with students occurred when demonstrators tried to force their way into the bowling alley, breaking a glass door in the attempt. Students maintained the violence was started by police.

College President M. Maceo Nance, Jr., who suspended classes so students could meet with city officials Wednesday, told the students he wanted the city to know that window-smashing in the area began only after "the ladies (women students) were beaten by policemen."

"Death was a distinct possibility last night," Nance said.

"I am very, very disturbed about some of the brutality that took place."

Nance told students the smartest thing would be to "seal ourselves off from the local community until some action is taken on the grievances."

Mayor E. P. Pendarvis addressed the students and told them that he had been working during his two years in office to improve race relations. He said "city government is interested and it will work with you." There were some catcalls.

Pendarvis said as far as the privately-owned bowling alley was concerned, he had "done all I could."

The clash was the first racial outburst in South Carolina this year.

Although the students' main complaint was the bowling alley, they presented Pendarvis a list of other grievances, asking for establishment of a fair employment commission in the city, and investigation into alleged police brutality, establishment of a human relations committee, and the closing of the bowling lane unless it serves "the total community."

Pendarvis said he does not condone police brutality and would investigate the charges. He said he thought a human relations commission already had been established.

There had been discontent at the college, located on a tree-shaded plot near downtown Orangeburg, since the beginning of the school term.

Cleveland Sellers of the Student Non-Violent Coordinating Committee had been in the area for months, and had been instrumental in forming a "black awareness" group on the campus of the college in 1966.

The University of Washington Black Student Union

By 1968, black student unions had emerged on virtually every major university campus in the United States, including the University of Washington. In the spring of that year, the UW BSU staged a brief takeover of the university's administration building, barricading the president and other university officials into his office. At the end of the student takeover, the University agreed to recruit and admit larger numbers of students of color, hire additional African American faculty, and create a Black Studies Program. The BSU sent a letter to U.W. President Charles Odegaard outlining their call for change on the campus fourteen days before the takeover. The letter appears here.

University of Washington
Black Student Union
Room 92 - Husky Union Bldg.
May 6, 1968

President Charles Odegaard
University of Washington
Seattle, Washington

Dear President Odegaard:

The University of Washington has been, and is a racist institution. Its function has been, and is to preserve and extend a racist status quo. Through its administration, faculty, curriculum, and admission policies, the University has sent white and black students into society with the racist notion that white, middle-class, Western ideals and practices are superior. The average white student leaves the University with the absurd notion that he is superior. The average black student leaves the University with an equally absurd notion that he is inferior.

The phenomenon in the last paragraph can be understood by taking a look at key aspects of the University. First, the administration. Psychologists talk about the need for youth to have adult models. At this point a non-white student has no model at a high administrative level to imitate and relate to. This is important because non-whites need models they can identify with. They need a non-white administrator who has had similar problems and conflicts.

A second point about the present administration must be made. When a non-white youth comes into contact with administration officials, he is subtly told that he is inferior. He sees white people giving orders and running the school. From this realization, comes the mistaken idea that there are no non-white people who can run institutions, who can successfully carry out large assignments. The overall effect of this idea is the stifling of initiative, the decrease and bringing to a halt of positive dreams and desires. The same effect comes from the non-white student's contact with the faculty. A non-white sitting under a 99% white faculty is subtly being told that only white people can teach him the things he needs to know.

A third point must also be made. The faculty are products of a racist-society. Faculty trained in the twenties and thirties came up through an educational system based on the assumption of non-white inferiority. Consciously and/or unconsciously the faculty transmits their racism to black and white students. One way in which they transmit racism is their ignorance. A professor in Classics, enthused over the wonders of Rome, in many cases is unaware of the great achievements of African Universities such as the University of Timbuktu. This university was a magnet for scholars and philosophers while Europeans were running around in caves. A professor in Contemporary Literature praising the works of Hemingway or Faulkner, would do well to consider the beauty and power of a Richard Wright or a Claude McKay. Omissions, distortions, and outright lies produce students that feel all the great ideas came from whites, and came from the West. As we indicated earlier, the white student believes in the lie of his superiority, and the black student in the lie of his inferiority.

A fourth aspect the Black Student Union feels strongly about is the University admission policies. We've been told that the University does not "discriminate" and that they take all students who are Qualified. We realize that standards are necessary if the University is to produce well-trained people, but we also realize that the present elementary and secondary educational system stifles the desire and creativity necessary for achievement.

The majority of non-white students who pass through the present educational system do not: (1) gain a knowledge of their past (2) get encouragement from the faculty and administration. For example, a non-white student is taught only the achievements of whites, he learns about Lincoln (a racist), George Washington (a slaveowner), etc. When we see these things clearly, we realize that the educational system from kindergarten to graduate school must be changed.

The Black Student Union feels that a good starting place for change is at the university level. Although the administration, faculty, and admission policies have been racist in effect, the Black Student Union feels the University should be given a chance to change, to prove its "good intentions." As long as we feel the University is making an honest effort to change, the Black Student Union will cooperate and work closely with the University. However, when the University begins to make phony excuses and racist needed changes, we will be forced to look at the University as an enemy to black people, and act accordingly. In short there will be political consequences for political mistakes.

With this last point in mind, the Black Student Union submits the following demands:

(1) All decisions, plans, and programs affecting the lives of black students, must be made in consultation with the Black Student Union. This demand reflects our feeling that whites for too long have controlled the lives of non-whites. We reject this control, instead we will define what our best interests are, and act accordingly.

(2) The Black Student Union should be given the financial resources and aids necessary to recruit and tutor non-white students. Specifically, the Black Student Union wants to recruit: (1) 300 Afro-American, (2) 200 American Indian, and (3) 100 Mexican students by September. Quality education is possible through an interaction of diverse groups, classes, and races. Out of a student population of 30,000, there are about 200 Afro-Americans, about 20 American Indians, and about 10 Mexican-Americans. The present admission policies are slanted toward white, middle-class, Western ideals, and the Black Student Union feels that the University should take these other ideals into consideration their admission procedures.

(3) We demand that a Black Studies Planning committee be set up under the direction and control of the Black Student Union. The function of this Committee would be to develop a Black Studies Curriculum that objectively studies the culture and life of non-white Americans. We make this demand because we feel that a white, middle-class education cannot and has not met the needs of non-white students. At this point, as American Indian interested in studying the lives of great Indians like Sitting Bull and Crazy-Horse has to go outside the school structure to get an objective view. Afro-American members of the Black Student Union have had to go outside the school structure to learn about black heroes like Frederick Douglas, W. E. B. DuBois, and Malcolm X. One effect of going outside the normal educational channels at the University has been to place an extra strain on black students interested in learning more about their culture. We feel that it is up to the University to re-examine its curriculum and provide courses that meet the needs of non-white students.

(4) We want to work closely with the administration and faculty to recruit black teachers and administrators. One positive effect from recruiting black teachers and administrators is that we will have models to imitate, and learn from.

(5) We want black representatives on the music faculty. Specifically, we would like to see Joe Brazil and Byron Polls hired. The black man has made significant contributions to music (i.e. jazz and spirituals), yet there are no black teachers on the music faculty.

The five demands above are legitimate and worthwhile, and we hope you will consider them carefully. In view of the seriousness of these demands, and the need for the University to change, we have set a five day deadline for a reply from you. We have set this time limit because the University in the past has moved too slowly, has avoided facing key issues squarely.

Sincerely,
Black Student Union

Black Feminists Organize

In 1973, Eleanor Holmes Norton, a Washington, D.C., attorney, brought together African American women from across the nation to create the National Black Feminist Organization to challenge what they called the racism of white feminists and the sexism of black male political activists. The organization's statement of purpose appears here.

The distorted male-dominated media image of the Women's Liberation Movement has clouded the vital and revolutionary importance of this movement to Third World women, especially black women. The Movement has been characterized as the exclusive property of so-called white middle-class women and any black women seen involved in this movement have been seen as "selling out," "dividing the race," and an assortment of nonsensical epithets. Black feminists resent these charges and have therefore established The National Black Feminist Organization, in order to address ourselves to the particular and specific needs of the larger, but almost cast-aside half of the black race in Amerikkka, the black woman.

Black women have suffered cruelly in this society from living the phenomenon of being black and female, in a country that is *both* racist and sexist. There has been very little real examination of the damage it has caused on the lives and on the minds of black women. Because we live in a patriarchy, we have allowed a premium to be put on black male suffering. No one of us would minimize the pain or hardship or the cruel and inhumane treatment experienced by the black man. But history, past or present, rarely deals with the malicious abuse put upon the black woman. We were seen as breeders by the master; despised and historically polarized from/by the master's wife; and looked upon as castrators by our lovers and husbands. The black woman has had to be strong, yet we are persecuted for having survived. We have been called "matriarchs" by white racists and black nationalists; we have virtually no positive self-images to validate our existence. Black women want to be proud, dignified, and free from all those false definitions of beauty and woman hood that are unrealistic and unnatural.

We, not white men or black men, must define our own self-image as black women and not fall into the mistake of being placed upon the pedestal which is even being rejected by white women. It has been hard for black women to emerge from the myriad of distorted images that have portrayed us as grinning Beulahs, castrating Sapphires, and pancake-box Jemimas. As black feminists we realized the need to establish ourselves as an independent black feminist organization. Our above ground presence will lend enormous credibility to the current Women's Liberation Movement, which unfortunately is not seen as the serious political and economic revolutionary force that it is. We will strengthen the

SOURCE: The National Black Feminist Organization, "Statement of Purpose"
(New York: The National Black Feminist Organization, 1973).

current efforts of the Black Liberation struggle in this country by encouraging *all* of the talents and creativities of black women to emerge, strong and beautiful, not to feel guilty or divisive, and assume positions of leadership and honor in the black community. We will encourage the black community to stop falling into the trap of the white male Left, utilizing women only in terms of domestic or servile needs. We will continue to remind the Black Liberation Movement that there can't be liberation for half the race. We must, together, as a people, work to eliminate racism, from without the black community, which is trying to destroy us as an entire people; but we must remember that sexism is destroying and crippling us from within.

Elaine Brown: Black Panther

The following vignette recounts Elaine Brown's assumption of the leadership of the Black Panther Party in Oakland, California, in August 1974.

"I have all the guns and all the money. I can withstand challenge from without and from within. Am I right, Comrade?" Larry snapped back his answer to my rhetorical question: "Right on!" His muscular body tilted slights as he adjusted the .45 automatic piston under his jacket.

I was standing on the stage, with him at my side. Several of the key Brothers from the security squads were standing just in the back of us. To my left I found Big Bob, Huey Newton's personal bodyguard, all six feet eight inches and four hundred pounds of him. In front of me, extending all the way to the back of the auditorium, were several hundred other members of the Black Panther Party, a sea of predominately male faces. They were black men and women from the party's Central Committee and from various local leadership cadres, from the West Side of Chicago, from North Philadelphia, Harlem, New Orleans, Los Angeles, Washington, D.C., and elsewhere. They had come to Oakland this August of 1974 at my command.

I watched them carefully, noting that no one moved in response to my opening remarks. Here I was, a woman, proclaiming supreme power over the most militant organization in America. It felt natural to me. I had spent the last seven years as a dedicated member of the Black Panther Party, the last four at Huey's right hand.

"I haven't called you together to make threats, Comrades," I continued. "I've called this meeting simply to let you know the realities of our situation. The fact is, Comrade Huey is in exile. The other fact is, I'm taking his place until we make it possible for him to return."

SOURCE: From A TASTE OF POWER by Elaine Brown, copyright © 1992 by Elaine Brown. Used by permission of Pantheon Books, a division of Random House, Inc.

I allowed them a moment to grasp the full meaning of my words. "I'm telling you this because it's possible some of you may balk at a woman as the leader of the Black Panther Party. . . . If this is your attitude, you'd better get out of the Black Panther Party. Now. I am saying this also because there may be some individuals in our ranks who have private ambitions and, in Comrade Huey's absence, may imagine themselves capable of some kind of coup." I paused again. No one spoke.

Cocking my head to the side, I continued in the manner I knew was required. "If you are such an individual, you'd better run – and fast. I am, as your chairman, the leader of this party as of this moment. My leadership cannot be challenged. I will lead our party above ground and underground. I will lead the party not only in furthering our goals but also in defending the party by any and all means . . ."

I watched a few of the Brothers slap their palms together in common recognition. A subdued laughter of agreement rippled through the auditorium. I began to walk up and down the stage, purposely emphasizing my words with the sound of the heels of my black leather boots. I punctuated each sentence with a nod to one or another of the soldiers standing on stage with me, backing me up.

"I repeat, I have control over all the guns and all the money of this party. There will be no external or internal opposition I will not resist and put down. I will deal resolutely with anyone or anything that stands in the way. So if you don't like what we're going to do, here is your chance to leave. You'd better leave because you won't be tolerated."

They began to applaud loudly, then louder, and then suddenly they were standing. The Sisters *and* the Brothers were on their feet. "Return to your chapters and branches throughout this country with renewed dedication. . . . Let us get busy and prepare a place for the return of Comrade Huey. Let us get busy and prepare a place for the introduction of revolution!" I raised my fist in the air and shouted: "All power to the people! Panther power to the vanguard!"

They leaped to their fee, fists raised in salute: "POWER TO THE PEOPLE! POWER TO THE PEOPLE! POWER TO THE PEOPLE!"

7

African America in a Conservative Era

This chapter addresses the paradox of change in black America in the 1980s and 1990s, when there was simultaneously greater opportunity than ever before and continuing challenges facing significant segments of the community. The first vignette, **Affirmative Action: A Brief History,** attempts a definition and discussion of one of the major issues generating racial acrimony between 1970 and 2000. The vignette **Race and the Suburbanization of America** illustrates one way in which black home ownership equity has been compromised, while **Black Wealth and Poverty, 1993** reflects the mixed economic news for African Americans during the Reagan Years. Yet the vignette **The Reginald Lewis Story** highlights the remarkable financial achievement of one African American in the face of adversity.

Black politics in the 1980s is the topic of two vignettes: **Jesse Jackson and the Rainbow Coalition, 1984** and **The Governor of Virginia.** In **South Africa and African Americans,** we see a growing sophistication in international affairs as blacks joined other groups to impose economic sanctions successfully on South Africa. African American rivalry with other people of color is explored in **Asian Americans and African Americans: Differences and Similarities** and **The Shrinking Minority.** The rise of a new generation of black conservatives is analyzed in **The New Black Conservatives** and **Clarence Thomas Speaks Out.**

The next vignettes address the continuing poverty faced by approximately 20 percent of African Americans commonly called "the underclass" by social scientists. **The Language of Segregation** illustrates the relationship of income, residence, speech, and behavior to the black underclass. The vignettes **Crippin':**

The Rise of Black Gangs in Post-Watts Los Angeles and **"Crack is Just Jim Crow in a Pipe"** describe the nexus between drugs and crime in impoverished African American neighborhoods. Finally, **The Million Man March Pledge** represents the attempt by organizations such as the Nation of Islam to address the deterioration of the social fabric of African American communities in the 1980s and early 1990s.

Affirmative Action: A Brief History

Affirmative action has come to symbolize for blacks and whites the continuing dilemma of race in America. Blacks generally perceive it as a just and reasonable attempt to eliminate the consequences of America's racial past, but many whites feel it provides undue advantage to blacks and thus is "reverse racism." Here is a brief history of the concept.

Affirmative action had first been developed at a time of a growing economy in response to the paucity of blacks in many jobs. Back in the early 1960s it was relatively easy to get into law school. Just about anyone with a college degree and a high *C* average could get into law school somewhere. Bolt Hall, the law school of the University of California at Berkeley, and one of the top-ranked schools in the nation accepted anyone with a *B* average – three quarters of those who applied. Yet in 1965, in all the country's accredited white law schools, there were only 434 black students. Blacks made up 11 percent of the country's population, but only 2 percent of its lawyers and 1.3 percent of its law school enrollees. In the late 1960s, driven by the gains of the civil rights movement and protests on campus, colleges and universities adopted a range of "affirmative" measures to attract more black students (the phrase "affirmative action" stemmed from an executive order signed by President Johnson in 1965, ordering federal contractors to take aggressive measures to hire black employees. Colleges set up special training programs for blacks, increased financial aid, and recruited blacks aggressively.

But at the same time colleges and universities were increasing their efforts to recruit and accept black students, the competition for jobs and places in law and medical school was stiffening. Between 1964 and 1975, the number of students taking the LSAT, the exam to get into law school, increased by more than threefold. Law schools expanded their classes to meet the demand, but they could not meet it all. By 1970, 70,000 students nationwide were applying for 35,000 law school spots. At prestigious law schools like Bolt Hall it was not unusual for five people to apply for every spot.

The upshot was that standards rose. A *B* average was no longer good enough. Only the best and the brightest could get in.

That placed in a quandary liberals committed to expanding opportunities for blacks. The metaphor invoked in the 1960s envisioned preparing blacks before the race so they could make it to the starting line. But by the late 1970s, the starting line kept being pushed up. Programs that might have given disadvantaged blacks the skills to get into law school in 1965 were insufficient to get them into the far more competitive law schools of 1970. Moreover, many blacks believe that racism was deeply entrenched in universities. The only way to guarantee that blacks entered universities and colleges, they argued, was to establish goals, timetables, and quotas. In the late 1960s and early 1970s, many universities adopted preferential policies that brought in minority students under quota, or near-quota programs. They set aside places for "disadvantaged" students and explicitly directed their admissions committees to seek out blacks and other minorities to fill a certain number of seats.

Race and the Suburbanization of America

Few federal initiatives have had a more paradoxical impact than the efforts of the U.S. government beginning in the 1930s to encourage home ownership through the Home Owners Loan Corporation and its successor agency, the Federal Housing Authority. Both agencies dramatically increased the ability of the "average" American to purchase and own homes and thus helped fashion a middle-class majority in the nation. Yet those same agencies reinforced racial discrimination by "redlining" areas where African Americans and other people of color lived, making it exceedingly difficult for them to access this money for home purchases or improvements. Moreover, the availability of mortgage money encouraged whites to move to rapidly expanding suburbs, particularly in the post-World Wars period that were usually off limits to African Americans through restrictive covenants and other legal and extralegal strategies. These agencies did not "invent" housing discrimination. They did, however, cement it in place and expand it to heighten the physical separation of whites and blacks in the major urban centers throughout the nation. That story is told in brief here.

The suburbanization of America was principally financed and encouraged by actions of the federal government, which supported suburban growth from the 1930s through the 1960s, by way of taxation, transportation, and housing policy.... While these governmental policies collectively enabled over thirty-five million families between 1933 and 1978 to participate in homeowner equity accumulation, they also had the adverse effect of constraining black Americans' residential opportunities to central-city ghettos of major U.S. metropolitan communities and denying them access to one of the most successful generators of wealth in American history, the suburban tract home.

This story begins with the government's initial entry into home financing. Faced with mounting foreclosures, President Roosevelt urged passage of a bill that authorized the Home Owners Loan Corporation (HOLC). According to Kenneth Jackson's *Crabgrass Frontier,* the HOLC "refinanced tens of thousands of mortgages in danger of default or foreclosure." Of more importance to this story, however, it also introduced standardized appraisals of the fitness of particular properties and communities for both individual and group loans. In creating "a formal and uniform system of appraisal, reduced to writing, structured in defined procedures, and implemented by Individuals only after intensive training, government appraisals institutionalized in a rational and bureaucratic framework a racially discriminatory practice that all but eliminated black access to the suburbs and to government mortgage money." Charged with the task of determining the "useful or productive life of housing" they considered to finance, government agents methodically included in their procedures the evaluation of the racial composition or potential racial composition of the community. Communities that were changing racially or were already black were deemed undesirable and placed in the lowest category. The categories, assigned various colors on a map ranging from green for the most desirable, which included new, all-white housing that was always in demand, to red, which included already racially mixed or all-black, old, and undesirable areas, subsequently were used by Federal Housing Authority (FHA) loan officers who made loans on the basis of these designations.

Established in 1934, the FHA aimed to bolster the economy and increase employment by aiding the ailing construction industry. The FHA ushered in the modern mortgage system that enabled people to buy homes on small down payments and at reasonable interest rates, with lengthy repayment periods and full loan amortization. The FHA's success was remarkable: housing starts jumped from 332,000 in 1936 to 619,000 in 1941. The incentive for home ownership increased to the point where it became, in some cases, cheaper to buy a home than to rent one. As one former resident of New York City who moved to suburban New Jersey pointed out, "We had been paying $50 per month rent, and here we come up and live for $29.00 a month." This included taxes, principal, insurance, and interest.

This growth in access to housing was confined, however, for the most part to suburban areas. The administrative dictates outlined in the original act, while containing no anti-urban bias, functioned in practice to the neglect of central cities. Three reasons can be cited: first, a bias toward the financing of single-family detached homes over multifamily projects favored open areas outside of the central city that had yet to be developed over congested central-city areas; second, a bias toward new purchases over repair of existing homes prompted people to move out of the city rather than upgrade or improve their existing residences; and third, the continued use of the "unbiased professional estimate" that made older homes and communities in which blacks or undesirables were located less likely to receive approval for loans encouraged purchases in communities where race was not an issue.

While the FHA used as its model the HOLC's appraisal system, it provided more precise guidance to its appraisers in its *Underwriting Manual*. The most basic sentiment underlying the FHA's concern was its fear that property values would decline if a rigid black and white segregation was not maintained. The *Underwriting Manual* openly stated that "if a neighborhood is to retain stability, it is necessary that properties shall continue to be occupied by the same social and racial classes" and further recommended that "subdivision regulations and suitable restrictive covenants" are the best way to ensure such neighborhood stability. The FHA's recommended use of restrictive covenants continued until 1949, when, responding to the Supreme Court's outlawing of such covenants in 1948 *(Shelly v. Kraemer)*, it announced that "as of February 15, 1950, it would not insure mortgages on real estate subject to covenants."

Even after this date, however, the FHA's discriminatory practices continued to have an impact on the continuing suburbanization of the white population and the deepening ghettoization of the black population. While exact figures regarding the FHA's discriminations against blacks are not available, data by county show a clear pattern of "redlining" in central-city counties and abundant loan activity in suburban counties.

The FHA's actions have had a lasting impact on the wealth portfolios of black Americans. Locked out of the greatest mass-based opportunity for wealth accumulation in American history, African Americans who desired and were able to afford home ownership found themselves consigned to central-city communities where their investments were affected by the "self-fulfilling prophecies" of the FHA appraisers: cut off from sources of new investment their homes and communities deteriorated and lost value in comparison to those homes and communities that FHA appraisers deemed desirable. One infamous housing development of the period – Levittown [on Long Island, New York] provides a classic illustration of the way blacks missed out on this asset-accumulating opportunity. Levittown was built on a mass scale, and housing there was eminently affordable, thanks to the FHA's . . . accessible financing, yet as late as 1960 not a single one of . . . Levittown's 82,000 residents was black.

Black Wealth and Poverty, 1993

The following article by Essence *writer Audrey Edwards summarized the various reasons for continuing black poverty, even in the face of growing incomes and apparent prosperity.*

B lack folks seem to have as many jokes that underscore the fragility of our economic condition as we do race jokes that reveal our obsession with skin color: "When America's in a recession, Black America's in a depression." "I'm just a paycheck away from poverty." "What money can't buy, I don't want." This last one is perhaps prophetic, for what money clearly has not been able to buy in American society is Black economic parity with whites. Despite the Black middle class's being larger than ever before in terms of sheer numbers; despite the gain in Black upper-middle-class income between 1970 and 1989 that outpaced

SOURCE: Audrey Edwards, "The Black-White Money Gap," <u>Essence</u>, April 1993, 85–86.

the growth in white upper-middle-class income by almost two to one; and despite what can now be considered a true African American wealth class, the bottom line remains largely red when it comes to overall Black economic reality: White net worth outdistanced Black net worth by a staggering 1,200 percent. Net worth (the value of assets – home, car, savings accounts, pension fund, insurance policies or any other instrument that generates income – minus the debts owed) is the crucial barometer by which to gauge economic progress, for it measures financial wealth – the monetary worth of the assets, resources and benefits that have been accumulated to enhance economic well-being. Historically, the gap between the economic well-being of whites and that of Blacks has remained a chasm.

Racism and its lethal partner discrimination are still guilty as charged when it comes to ambushing Black economic development. But the gap between Black and white wealth is the result of more than just racism, discrimination or an uneven playing field. It is the result of 246 years – or two and a half centuries and 12 generations – in which a race of people labored for virtually no income. Twelve generations of Blacks produced wealth for a land in which it was illegal for them either to accumulate or to share in that wealth. Twelve generations of African-Americans built the schools that denied them access to an education and tilled the soil that denied them the opportunity to own property, to vote, to travel freely, to earn a living. In the American "democracy" that fought a revolution over the issue of "no taxation without representation," African-Americans were taxed at the maximum rate of 100 percent with no representation, no pay, no acknowledgement of their humanity. And 400 years later we have yet to recover from the economic devastation that was the scourge of slavery, or the vicious Jim Crow discrimination that haunted emancipation. This is the ground on which we find ourselves still trying to play catch-up.

If the gap between Black and white wealth remains deep and wide, the good news is that more African-Americans than ever before have successfully leaped across the chasm to land in the solid middle class. The disturbing news is that just as many are falling into the great void of what has been called the "underclass," an economic pit from which some economists say there is no escape. Indeed, given the fact that African-Americans have been free only half as long as we were enslaved, it may be another hundred years before we can significantly narrow the wealth gap between Blacks and whites, if that gap can even be significantly narrowed. Radical economists believe that nothing short of a Black tax revolt and a demand for reparations can ever remedy the disastrous effects of the 200 plus years that whites had an economic head start over Blacks in America. The arguments are compelling: Because 12 generations of Blacks were taxed to the maximum that was humanly possible and did labor that resulted in no income, shouldn't the income taxes that are levied on succeeding generations of Blacks be adjusted to compensate for the two centuries their ancestors "paid in full"? And aren't reparations owed for America's 246-year theft of human capital?

Given this legacy, the economic progress of Blacks in the last 30 years has nevertheless been considerable and remarkable. The decade of the seventies was something of an economic boom time for African-Americans, with the percentage of Black families earning middle-class incomes of $25,000 to $50,000 climbing as high as 30.5 percent in 1976. Some of the gain was wiped out during the recessionary eighties, however, and by 1988 the percentage of Black families that were in the middle-class $25,000-to-$50,000 income range had slipped to 26.7 percent.

It was the upper middle class, though, fueled by expanded opportunities in education and employment due to the Civil Rights Movement that became the pinnacle reached by an ever-increasing number of Blacks. During the 20 years between 1970 and 1989 the percentage of Blacks who had upper-middle-class annual household incomes of $50,000 or more grew by 182 percent. Numbers can be misleading, however, for a growth in income is not the same as a growth in net worth, nor does Black income growth mean African-Americans are catching up with whites in any significant way. For example, in 1989 the median household income for whites was $30,406, compared with $18,083 for Blacks. Put another way, a Black household made 63 cents for every one dollar a white household made. In 1979, it was 62 cents for every dollar. And in 1988 the median net worth of Black households was only $4,169, compared with $43,279 for white households; and 29 percent of Black families actually had a zero or negative net worth.

So why, despite the recent but real growth in the total numbers of Blacks who now earn middle-class to upper-middle-class incomes, do African-Americans remain relatively poor when it comes to net-worth? Why do even the presumably wealthy among us pass from this life, as Sammy Davis, Jr., and Alex Haley did, insolvent, leaving their heirs only an inheritance of debt? The truth is, we continue to be shaped by not only the legacy of slavery and the reality of racism, but by attitudes and buying habits that hold us back economically. We are less likely than whites, for instance, to invest in such money-making vehicles as stocks and bonds, mutual funds, individual retirement accounts . . . the kinds of instruments that generate income without generating sweat. A large part of the problem is that we are less likely to have the extra or discretionary income to make such investments and often lack access to the critical information needed to do so. We are also much less likely to inherit the kind of resources that allow families to accumulate or perpetuate wealth, since our ancestors died literally owning nothing to pass on. We also tend as a people to invest in the trappings of success – clothes, expensive cars, electronic equipment, household gadgets, fine liquor – rather than the substance of success. This is due largely to a history of deprivation that has resulted in our needing to make a visible statement about economic success once we achieve it. And even when we haven't achieved it, looking as if we're an unqualified success has always made us feel better.

It will probably take as long to change our economic habits as it does our economic fortunes. But changing both are [sic] critical if we want to ensure that the labor of our ancestors does not continue to go for nothing, and that our children do not continue to inherit the wind.

The Reginald Lewis Story

The following vignette is an introduction to Reginald Lewis, one of the most successful corporate leveraged buyout specialists of the 1980s.

Strolling briskly along one of Manhattan's better known boulevards, 44-year-old Reginald Francis Lewis reared back and unleashed a quick right uppercut. A crisply executed left jab followed, but both punches struck only air, leaving eddies of August humidity in their wake. Continuing down the Avenue of the Americas in his $2,000 dark blue Italian-made suit, his ruggedly handsome features tinged orange from the mercury street lights, Lewis threw punch after exuberant punch until he grew arm weary. All the while he flashed a gap-toothed grin and emitted a booming belly laugh as a phalanx of well-dressed business partners accompanying him chuckled too, or looked on with bemused expressions.

Trailing about 50 feet behind with its parking lights on, Lewis's black Mercedes limousine shadowed the group. Inside the car, where the air conditioner was set at precisely 70 degrees and classical music played on the radio – per Lewis's instructions – the driver watched attentively for a casual wave of the hand indicating Lewis was tired of walking and ready to ride.

But on the night of August 6, 1987, Reginald Lewis was in the throes of such an invigorating adrenaline rush he could have walked all night and into the day. A successful corporate lawyer who remade himself into a financier and buyer of corporations, Lewis had bought the McCall Pattern Company for $22.5 million, guided it to record earnings and recently sold it for $65 million, fetching a 90-1 return on his investment.

But even that improbable achievement was small potatoes compared with what Lewis had pulled off a few hours earlier. This audacious African American born to a working-class family in Baltimore had just won the right to buy Beatrice International Foods, a global giant with 64 companies in 31 countries, for just under $1 billion.

Now – foregoing his plush limousine – Lewis preferred to walk the six blocks … to the Harvard Club, located at 44th Street. A richly appointed bastion of Manhattan's old boy network, the Harvard Club invariably reminded Lewis of just how far he had come from his blue-collar youth in segregated Baltimore and just how far he intended to go.

Lewis outbid several multinational companies, including Citicorp, that were aided by squads of accountants, lawyers and financial advisors. Lewis had won by relying on moxie, financial and legal savvy, and the efforts of a two-man team consisting of himself and a recently hired business partner. In fact, when Lewis tendered his bid, a representative of one of the investment banking firms handling

SOURCE: Reginald F. Lewis and Blair S. Walker, "Why Should White Guys Have All the Fun?" How Reginald Lewis Created a Billion-Dollar Business Empire (New York: John Wiley & Sons, 1995), xiii–xv. All rights reserved. Reprinted with permission of Loida Nicolas Lewis.

the auction called Lewis's office and said, "We have received from your group an offer to buy Beatrice International for $950 million. We have a small problem – nobody knows who the hell you are!"

The world knew who Lewis was by the time he succumbed to brain cancer in January 1993, at the relatively young age of 50. His net worth was estimated by Forbes at $400 million when he died, putting him on the magazine's 400 list of wealthiest Americans.

Jesse Jackson and the Rainbow Coalition, 1984

In 1984, Reverend Jesse Jackson campaigned for the Democratic nomination for the presidency. Although he entered the Democratic convention at San Francisco with little hope of winning, his appeals on behalf of the dispossessed of America, whom he characterized as the "Rainbow Coalition," ensured that his influence in Democratic Party politics would continue. Part of his speech to the convention appears here.

This is not a perfect party. We are not a perfect people. Yet, we are called to a perfect mission: our mission, to feed the hungry, to clothe the naked, to house the homeless, to teach the illiterate, to provide jobs for the jobless, and to choose the human race over the nuclear race.

My constituency is the damned, disinherited, disrespected and the despised. They are restless and seek relief. They've voted in record numbers. They have invested the faith, hope, and trust that they have in us. The Democratic Party must send them a signal that we care. I pledge my best not to let them down. . . .

Throughout this campaign, I have tried to offer leadership to the Democratic Party and the nation. If in my high moments, I have done some good, offered some service, shed some light, healed some wounds . . . then this campaign has not been in vain. . . . If in my low moments, in word, deed or attitude, through some error of temper, taste or tone, I have caused anyone discomfort, created pain, or revived someone's fears, that was not my truest self. . . .

Our flag is red, white and blue, but our nation is rainbow – red, yellow, brown, blacks and white – we're all precious in God's sight. America is not like a blanket – one piece of unbroken cloth, the same color, the same texture, the same size. America is more like a quilt – many patches, many pieces, many colors, many sizes, all woven and held together by a common thread.

SOURCE: Jessie Jackson, "The Rainbow Coalition," Vital Speeches of the Day, 51, no. 3 (November 15, 1984), 77–81.

We should not act as if nuclear weaponry is negotiable and debatable. We must choose developed minds over guided missiles, and think it out and not fight it out. It's time for a change.

When we look at Africa, we cannot just focus on apartheid in southern Africa. We must fight for trade with Africa, and not just aid to Africa. We cannot stand idly by and say we will not relate to Nicaragua unless they have elections there and then embrace military regimes in Africa, overthrowing Democratic governments in Nigeria, and Liberia and Ghana. We must fight for democracy all around the world, and play the game by one set of rules.

I have a message for our youth. I challenge them to put hope in their brains, and not dope in their veins. I, too, was born in a slum, but just because you're born in a slum, does not mean the slum is born in you, and you can rise above it if your mind is made up.... Exercise your right to dream. You must face reality – that which is. But then dream of the reality that ought to be, that must be. Live beyond the pain of reality with the dream of a bright tomorrow. Use hope and imagination as weapons of survival and progress. Use love to motivate you and obligate you to serve the human family.

The Governor of Virginia

On November 8, 1989, Douglas Wilder was elected governor of Virginia, becoming the first African American in the twentieth century to hold that post and the first in the nation's history to be chosen by a majority of the state's voters. Here is a description of the historic event taken from two articles in the Washington Post.

Virginia Democratic Lt. Gov. L. Douglas Wilder, a grandson of slaves, won a razor-thin victory over Republican J. Marshall Coleman yesterday to become the first elected black governor in U.S. history.

"I am here to claim to be the next governor of Virginia," an exultant Wilder told supporters at a Richmond hotel last night. "The people of Virginia have spoken."

... With all of the state's 1,967 precincts counted, Wilder defeated Coleman by 7,732 votes out of a record 1.77 million cast, or 50.2 percent to 49.8 percent.

★　★　★

"If he wins, I will cry," teacher Carolyn Simons said after voting for L. Douglas Wilder in Portsmouth's predominately black Precinct 2A. "I just feel

SOURCE: <u>Washington Post</u>, November 8, 1989, A1; A25. Copyright © 1989 by The Washington Post. All rights reserved. Reprinted with permission of The Washington Post Co.

like I'm making history this morning whether he wins or not." In Newport News, Darlene Waddle said, "I voted for J. Marshall Coleman because of abortion. I'm against abortion. If I can help save someone's life, I think God would want me to do it."

Simons, 43 and Waddle, 37 were among scores of Virginians across the state who spoke from the heart as much as the intellect yesterday in explaining their votes for governor. For some, it was easy to vote the straight party ticket out of habit, for others, the choices were more difficult. In random interviews as they emerged from the polls, some indicated that they were deeply stirred by the prospect of voting for Wilder to be the first black elected governor. Others were troubled by the abortion issue.

Tony Whitehead, 51, a Portsmouth truck driver, said after voting for Wilder, "I just feel great about this. . . . A lot of us civil rights activists died in order to see this day." Eleanor Ross, 55, of Reston said she voted for Wilder, but said she was glad Wilder is more conservative than prominent black politicians such as D. C. Mayor Marion Barry and Jesse L. Jackson. "Jesse Jackson, I'm glad he stayed out of the race because he definitely would've turned me against Wilder," she said.

Fred Kellerman, 62, of Alexandria, a drywall contractor, said, "I don't want a black governor. I'm afraid he's going to bring his helpers from all over the country and put them in office. . . . Colored people lie too much. They always have their hands out." An Oakton woman, who declined to give her name, said, "I don't want a black man there. He may be a very capable man, but we'll have another Washington, D.C. We'll have another welfare state. . . . He's got all those kinfolk to look out for."

But James Lamb, 49, a chemical worker in Portsmouth said, "This says to me that people are beginning to accept black people into the mainstream of government – as we should be. It's time for black people to be accepted as just people."

South Africa and African Americans

One indication of the growing political sophistication of African Americans in the 1980s, and their identification with African liberation struggles, was their ability to organize a broad coalition to support economic sanctions against the South African regime. The radically differing views Americans held about South African apartheid and the role the United States should play in ending the system are reflected in the following two passages. The first is an excerpt from a speech by

SOURCE: Ronald Reagan speech July 22, 1986, and Representative William H. Gray's (Pennsylvania) response to Reagan's speech.

President Ronald Reagan on July 22, 1986, opposing sanctions. The second passage is the response of Pennsylvania Congressman William Gray, then chair of the Congressional Black Caucus and chief sponsor of the Comprehensive Anti-Apartheid Act, which proposed sanctions. The act was passed despite President Reagan's strenuous opposition.

President Reagan: The root cause of South Africa's disorder is apartheid, that rigid system of racial segregation wherein black people have been treated as third-class citizens in a nation they helped to build. America's view of apartheid has been, and remains, clear: apartheid is morally wrong and politically unacceptable. The United States cannot maintain cordial relations with a government whose power rests upon the denial of rights to a majority of its people, based on race. . . . The Prime Minister of Great Britain has denounced punitive sanctions as immoral and utterly repugnant. Well, let me tell you why we believe Mrs. Thatcher is right.

The primary victims of an economic boycott of South Africa would be the very people we seek to help. Most of the workers who would lose jobs because of sanctions would be black workers. We do not believe the way to help the people of South Africa is to cripple the economy upon which they and their families depend for survival.

. . . In recent years there's been a dramatic change. Black workers have been permitted to unionize, to bargain collectively and build the strongest free trade union movement in all of Africa. The infamous pass laws have been ended, as have many of the laws denying blacks the right to live, work and own property in South Africa's cities. Citizenship wrongly stripped away has been restored to nearly 6 million blacks. Segregation in universities and public facilities is being set aside. Social apartheid laws prohibiting interracial sex and marriage have been struck down.

. . . But by Western standards, South Africa still falls short – terribly short – on the scales of economic and social justice. . . . But the South African Government is under no obligation to negotiate the future of the country with any organization that proclaims a goal of creating a Communist state, and uses terrorist tactics and violence to achieve it. . . .

. . . But let me outline what we believe are necessary components of progress toward political peace. *First,* a timetable for elimination of apartheid laws should be set. *Second,* all political prisoners should be released. *Third,* Nelson Mandela should be released to participate in the country's political process. *Fourth,* black political movements should be unbanned. *Fifth,* both the Government and its opponents should begin a dialogue about constructing a political system that rests on the consent of the governed, where the rights of majorities and minorities and individuals are protected by law. And the dialogue should be initiated by those with power and authority, the South African Government itself. *Sixth,* if post-apartheid South Africa is to remain the economic locomotive of southern Africa, its strong and developed economy must not be crippled. And therefore, I urge the Congress and the countries of Western Europe to resist this emotional clamor for punitive sanctions. If Congress imposes sanctions it would destroy America's flexibility . . . and deepen the crisis. To make a difference, Americans who are a force for decency and progress . . . must remain involved.

★   ★   ★

Representative Gray: Today President Reagan declared the United States and Great Britain co-guarantors of apartheid. By joining Mrs. Thatcher in opposing economic sanctions, the President protects Pretoria from the one weapon it fears most. . . . In 1985 the Congress bipartisanly passed the Anti-Apartheid Act, changing our policy and opposing sanctions . . . [and] just one month ago the House of Representatives passed the toughest possible economic sanctions: total divestment and a trade embargo, the measures we already have imposed on Cuba, North Korea, Cambodia and Libya. However, the President tells us that sanctions will only hurt the blacks, the people we are trying to help.

But blacks have suffered for years, not because of sanctions, but because of apartheid. They suffer because by law they cannot vote. They suffer because they are 72 percent of the population squeezed onto 13 percent of South Africa's most barren land. They suffer because they can be arrested without charge or trial. More than 6,000 blacks have been detained in the past month alone. They are allowed no contact with lawyers or families. . . . Under a sweeping state of emergency, they simply have disappeared. Killings, detentions, people disappearing – a modern-day Holocaust is unfolding before our very eyes. How can sanctions hurt black South Africans when apartheid is killing them?

. . . Out of 28 million black South Africans, only 47,000 – one tenth of 1 percent – hold jobs with American companies. These numbers alone tell us that the issue in South Africa is not jobs, but the loss of life and the denial of justice. Archbishop Tutu, Reverend Boesak, Doctor Naude, Winnie Mandela, countless other South African leaders have pleaded with us to impose sanctions and raise the cost of apartheid . . .

. . . President Reagan tells us that sanctions don't work. Why then have we imposed sanctions against Libya, Nicaragua, Poland and Cuba, and some 20 nations throughout the world? Those sanctions express our profound distaste of the policies and the actions of those nations. We imposed them not because we thought they would bring down those Governments, but to disassociate us from all that those Governments stand for while raising the cost of behavior we abhor. Why not South Africa? Why the double standard? That's the question the oppressed majority keeps asking the land of freedom and liberty.

The President has preached that the Reagan doctrine is to fight for freedom wherever it is denied. Why is the doctrine being denied in Pretoria? What is needed is not simply a condemnation of apartheid, while we provide economic support for South Africa's oppression through our loans and investments. What is needed is a new policy that clearly dissociates us from apartheid and calls for the complete dismantlement of that system, not cosmetic reforms.

Blacks and Jews: The Politics of Resentment

The title of this vignette comes directly from an article that appeared in
Reform Judaism *in the fall of 1991. The article is a collage of statements
by various Jewish and black authors and activists on the divisions between the
two groups that formed a major political alliance during the Civil Rights
Movement. Included here are the statements of Julius Lester, Professor of
Judaic Studies at the University of Massachusetts, who is both black and
Jewish, and of New York-based writer Anne Roiphe as examples of the
dialogue on this issue.*

Lester: To speak of "the escalating rife between Jews and African-Americans"
is to be unnecessarily polite about the painful truth. We are witnessing the open
expression of outright hatred toward Jews by too many African-Americans.
Where one could understand that perhaps Jesse Jackson's past anti-Semitic
utterances came from ignorance, short-sightedness, or insensitivity, the recent
screams of Minister Farrakhan, Khalid Abdul Muhammad, Tony Martin, and
others are deliberate and intentional. The issue is not so much why Farrakhan,
et al. speak, but why large black audiences applaud them.

When I ask black college students to explain to me Farrakhan's appeal, they
say: "Farrakhan makes the white man listen. When Farrakhan comes to town,
the white man pays attention." It does not seem to have occurred to these
students that the attention is, by and large, condemnatory and negative. To
them, opprobrium is better than invisibility. Although black college students
say they ignore Farrakhan's anti-Semitism, when asked why they do not
repudiate it and Farrakhan, their response is instructive: "We can't reject
Farrakhan because it'll look like others are telling us who we can and can't
have as leaders." In other words, having the power to say who one's leaders is more
important that what those leaders say. There is something almost childishly obstinate
about such an attitude, but to dismiss it as such would be to ignore the depths of
powerlessness and hopelessness that beset major segments of black youth . . .

The overriding question is does America care about black life? Does America
care how blacks live? Does America care if blacks live? When the nation is able to
respond with a resounding YES, Farrakhan and his ilk will find themselves speaking
to near empty auditoriums. The task we as Jews face is to resist the temptation to
take the anti-Semitic bait and recognize that black hopelessness and despair represent a far greater threat to our well-being and safety than hateful tirades. Our efforts
must be directed toward alleviating that hopelessness and despair.

Roiphe: So now we were slave traders as well as plantation owners! Will it never end? It breaks the heart. Listening to Farrakhan threaten to grind us to bits or to Steven Cokely say that Jewish doctors have been injecting black babies with AIDS is to relive our long history of blood libels and pogroms. The success of Jewish students in the American school system mocks the black student. Jewish success in all areas of American life rubs hard against the all too common black experience of failure. Racism exists, of course, but even the most simplistic of black demagogues worries that there is more to the collapse of black culture than the violence of slavery and the prejudice of centuries. If Jews are so smart, then what are blacks? The contrast rankles. Black pride demands that Jews be evil and their gains ill-gotten. This is an old matter. The burdened peasants of Poland and the Ukraine also begrudged and mythologized us.

It may be safer to rant at us. It may be more popular to demonize us. It may make the black preacher feel closer to his God or Christian white America to point his rhetorical finger at us, but it will get him nowhere. It won't win the drug war or assuage his hurt pride, keep him out of jail or nurture his fatherless children. We can't be trusting liberals in a world where empathy with the underdog seems to make the underdog think you're dog food.

Protesting alliances with Farrakhan or publicizing the lies of crazed black professors are necessary actions but they probably won't help us much. . . . We have to protect vulnerable Jews in areas like Crown Heights. We can reach out to those willing to listen. We can continue to be ourselves, remembering that all blacks are not anti-Semites and that all Jews are not free from racism. The massacre at Hebron by Baruch Goldstein reminds us that some of us too can go with rage and turn the other into a faceless stranger. Our reaction to black belief in the Judas Jew may shift the way we play the political game in America, but it should not change the way we feel about other human beings. It frightens me that I will begin to hate back, to look at the black woman on the bus and think she is my enemy, to believe that I should stop her from making a good living, from getting better schools for her children, from a life of dignity and hope.

I don't want Farrakhan to change me. I will therefore assume that this wave of anti-Semitism, pathetic and ugly, unforgivable as it is, will pass like a storm, will cause heavy rain, some damage, but leave standing my human convictions that we are responsible for one another's fate; that injustice, inequality, and racism are the real enemies; and that my Jewish obligation remains to repair the world, to reach my hand out, fixing what is morally broken.

Asian Americans and African Americans: Differences and Similarities

In the following account, Ronald Takaki, a historian of Asian America analyzes the current trend among historians and social observers to compare Asians favorably to blacks. Takaki challenges the convention wisdom that argues since Asians were once an oppressed racial minority who have now achieved significant economic and educational success through hard work and perseverance, blacks and other groups should cease complaints about discrimination and simply follow their example.

Recently Asian Americans have been congratulated for their successful entry into the mainstream of society. In 1982, for example, *Newsweek* proclaimed Asian Americans a "Model Minority" as it reported that they enjoyed the nation's highest median family income: $22,075 a year compared with $20,840 for whites. Two years later, in a speech to a group of Asian and Pacific Island Americans, President Ronald Reagan declared that they represented the immigrants' search for the American dream, a vision of hope and new opportunity symbolized by the Statue of Liberty. "Asian and Pacific Americans," he said, "have helped preserve that dream by living up to the bedrock values that make us a good and worthy people," values such as "fiscal responsibility" and "hard work." Praising them for their economic achievement, Reagan added: "It's no wonder that the median income of Asian and Pacific American families is much higher than the total American average."

This celebration of Asian American "success" had led William Raspberry of the *Washington Post* to ask: If Asian Americans can make it, why can't blacks? Blacks can, Raspberry has contended. What they must do is stop blaming "racism" for their plight, and start imitating law-abiding, hard working, and self-reliant Asian Americans. Noting that "in fact" West Coast Asian American have "outstripped" whites in income, Raspberry has exhorted his fellow blacks to view the successful Asian American minority as a "model." But what are the facts in this case? Data from the 1980 Census ... can help us determine what the facts may be in this case. If we take median household incomes for California, we find that Asian Americans earned $20,790 in 1979, compared to $19,552 for whites and $12,534 for blacks. But does this mean that Asian Americans have "outstripped" whites? These income figures mean very little unless they are analyzed in relation to the number of workers per household. Here we find that Asian Americans had 1.70 workers per household, compared with only 1.28 for whites and 1.20 for blacks. Thus, Asian Americans actually earned only $12,229 per worker, while whites received $15,275. In other words, Asian American income per household worker was only 80% of white income.

But should Asian Americans be used as a model for blacks? Not only does this advice pit the two groups against each other; it also overlooks important socio-logical differences between them. Forty-six percent of black families have a female head of household compared to only 11% of Asian American families (15% for whites). Sixty-four percent of all female-headed black families are below the poverty line, and currently over half of all black children are born to single women. The differences in family sociology between blacks and Asian Americans, due mainly to each group's particular location in the economy and its social or class composition rather than simply its cultural values or degree of dependency on welfare, affects a group's ability to use education as a strategy for social mobility. Furthermore, Asian Americans have increasingly become an immigrant population, and large numbers of recent Chinese, Filipino, and Korean immigrants have carried both skills and capital with them to the United States. For example, in 1973, 65% of the Korean immigrants had been professionals and managers in their home country. Thus, many recent Asian immigrants have resources – education, employable skills, and finances – which underclass blacks do not have.

These differences in social and economic composition between Asian Americans and blacks – only two of several differences – warn us that strategies for one group may not be applicable for another group. They also show that education and individual effort alone may not be sufficient for racial minorities to achieve income equality.

The Shrinking Minority

In the following account, Stephen Buckley discusses the political and racial impact of the rapidly growing Asian-American and Latino populations on African America.

At the University of North Carolina-Chapel Hill a few weeks ago, black students protested a proposal being weighed by school officials to place a cultural center at the edge of an already crowded campus, as opposed to a more visible and convenient location. The demand for physical centrality is, in a way, a metaphor for blacks' conception of their dominant and privileged position in the world of minority politics – a conception that is increasingly out of touch with reality.

On college campuses and elsewhere, blacks are loath to acknowledge what has become abundantly clear. America is becoming a society in which groups once considered "minor" are becoming the major majorities. Blacks make up 12% of the U.S. population today, but 3% of the nation is Asian and 9% is Hispanic. While the black population remains relatively static, the other groups are gaining fast. Already, Asians and Hispanics combined outnumber their black classmates on college campuses. In 1982 blacks made up 8.9% of the college

SOURCE: <u>Eugene Register-Guard</u>, July 25, 1993, 1B.

student population, while Hispanics totaled 4.2% and Asians 2.8%. In 1991, according to the U.S. Department of Education, blacks made up 9.3% of the university enrollment, Hispanics 6% and Asians 4.4%.

Prior to the rush of Asians and Hispanics, blacks sought – and received – black studies programs and cultural centers. We formed black alumni associations and student alliances. And when blacks were the dominant – often the only minorities on white college campuses, such groups made sense, because blacks at white colleges often spent a lot of time confronting racism and fighting off isolation and loneliness. Now, Asians and Hispanics, following the example of their African-American peers, are battling for similar treatment. At the University of California at Los Angeles a month ago, 93 students were arrested during a protest over the administration's refusal to approve a Chicano Studies program. That scenario will become increasingly familiar as the numbers of Asians and Hispanics explode on college campuses over the next few years.

Given the reality of the numbers, blacks can no longer pretend to be the preeminent ethnic group. Our history as an enslaved people in this country has compelled politicians and other leaders to pay especially close attention when we've raised our voices. But that can't, and won't, remain true much longer. Whites, particularly middle- and working-class whites, no longer swallow the argument that blacks are more oppressed than other minorities. White Americans think they see blacks everywhere: in corporate offices as middle- and top-level executives, on television as news anchors, in schools as principals and superintendents, in city halls as mayors, on college campuses as students. And these whites ask, "What oppression?" African-Americans can legitimately argue that blacks in the United States still face a myriad of woes that are the residue of legal oppression but blacks also can't deny progress – not without being intellectually dishonest.

Meanwhile, Asians and Hispanics are gaining influence both economically and politically. Hispanics have achieved enough of a critical mass – 19 members – to create their own congressional caucus. And Asians have harnessed enormous economic clout over the past two decades as their median income has surpassed that of all other groups, including whites. In many of our nation's inner cities, economic muscle belongs to Korean and Vietnamese and Chinese shopkeepers and businessmen, not blacks. This has enraged many African American, who note that Asians are building successful businesses with the dollars spent by blacks in those neighborhoods.

Today, blacks are faced with a somber choice. We can go it alone, fighting against the swelling tide of Asian and Hispanic power, or we can forge coalitions with those groups – and with whites who are sympathetic to minority concerns. We can admit, at least tacitly, that blacks can't maintain or expand our power without their help. What if the NAACP expanded its efforts to embrace issues that affected Hispanics and Asians? What if the black and Hispanic congressional caucuses merged? What if historically black universities, some of which are student-short, launched serious efforts to recruit Hispanics and Asians? Blacks have worked for decades to build and support such institutions, and for many, to become more inclusive is tantamount to dismissing centuries of our ancestors' toil and tears. Besides, many minority leaders would argue that each of these groups faces unique problems, and that forming integrated coalitions . . . would hurt many and help few.

That's partly true. Yet there exists many more issues, social, political and economic, in which the concerns of Asians, Hispanics and blacks intersect. If the Los Angeles riots are anything to go by, it's indeed in the best interest of Asians, for instance, to support more black-owned businesses in African American neighborhoods. A more cogent coalition between black and Asian businesses in South Central LA surely would have reduced riot damage.

Since we remain the most politically potent and sophisticated of the three major ethnic groups, we must then take the lead in forming interracial coalitions. If we don't, the day will come when the powers-that-be, on college campuses and in corporate offices, will greet our demands and concerns with shrugs. They will watch without sympathy as we doom ourselves to social, political and economic stagnancy. And we will have primarily ourselves to blame.

The New Black Conservatives

The confirmation hearings for Supreme Court Justice Clarence Thomas have focused national attention on the rise of black "neo-conservatives." In the following discussion, political scientist Charles P. Henry describes their emergence and impact on black America.

Early in this century, Howard University Dean Kelly Miller reported that "when a distinguished Russian was informed that some American Negroes are radical and some conservative, he could not restrain his laughter. "What on earth" he exclaimed in astonishment, "have they to conserve?" An objective of black institutions like Howard and much of the modern black studies movement has been to answer the Russian's question.... Black accommodationists like Booker T. Washington developed a number of black institutions and had programs for advancement – no matter how flawed. Today's black neo-conservatives lack a base in black institutions and only serve to legitimate the status quo. In this they differ even from liberal black Republicans – Andrew Brimmer, Art Fletcher, James Farmer, William T. Coleman, and in the Senate, Edward Brooke – who served under Presidents Nixon and Ford. These black Republicans generally sought to support affirmative action programs, civil rights legislation, and federal assistance to black colleges and black-owned businesses. They were, in short, able to combine a sense of individualism with a sense of group identity and government responsibility.

Today's black neoconservatives properly belong to the right wing of the Republican party and have severed ties with almost all black institutions. They can generally be placed in three categories: academics, government or party bureaucrats, and business executives. The best known among the academics are economists Thomas Sowell and Walter Williams, political scientist Martin Kilson ... Robert Woodson of the American Heritage Institute.... Among the government and party leaders are Thelma Duggin, Melvin Bradley, Thaddeus Garrett, Clarence Pendleton, Jr. Henry Lucas, Jr. and Samuel Pierce. Black neoconservatives in the business community are Wendell Willkie Gunn, Gloria E. A. Toote, William Packard, Constance Newman.

. . . Black conservatives appear unwilling to credit the liberal programs of the past for having any positive effect. In fact, the expansion of welfare programs is seen as a cause for the deterioration of black culture, especially the black family. Other specific issues black neoconservatives are concerned with include education, affirmative action, and minimum wage. On all of these issues, the position of black neoconservatives runs counter to black public opinion.... By focusing on [these] issues of racial policy... black conservatives have isolated themselves from the traditional views of the black community. In failing to find anything worth conserving in black culture they have ignored the very social issues on which a true black conservatism might rest. For example ... on the issue of school prayer blacks are more conservative than whites.

Blacks also oppose the legalization of marijuana, [support] tougher penalties for law violators...and reject legal abortions. While blacks want the courts to be tougher on criminals, less than a majority favor the death penalty because of its disproportionate use against blacks and the poor. Thus blacks' views on social issues are mediated by their belief in the fairness and equality of policy implementation.

Clarence Thomas Speaks Out

In this 1986 interview, Clarence Thomas, destined to be a Justice on the U.S. Supreme Court but then chairman of the Equal Employment Opportunity Commission, gave his views on affirmative action and other issues affecting African Americans.

I was raised by my grandparents, who played the single most important role in my life. My grandfather... had a third grade education and was barely literate. He believed in this country and its values. He believed that this is the land of opportunity – and fought hard for equal opportunity. He knew that discrimination existed and that its existence undermined the values in which he believed.... His efforts were all but neutralized by racial discrimination and prejudice. So he turned to fight discrimination. As he fought, I fight today. And like my grandfather, I am firmly committed to preserving and advancing the fundamental values of this country – values rooted in the rights of the individual, but values so often paid only lip service.

SOURCE: Jeffrey M. Elliot, ed., <u>Black Voices in American Politics</u> (New York, 1986), 148–156.

I adhere to the principle that individuals should be judged on the basis of individual merit and individual contact. No one should be rewarded or punished because of group characteristics. Unfortunately, this principle has not been made a reality. So today we are faced with the challenge of making this country color-blind after it has seen color for so long. And the critical question facing us is how to approach this challenge. Should we push for immediate *parity* or the fairness that has never really existed? Parity tends to show quicker change at least on paper. But is unfairness under the guise of parity any better than just plain unfairness? Should you concede your promotion in the name of parity for those who traditionally have been discriminated against?

I opt for fairness – that is, treating individuals as individuals. . . . But I choose this option knowing full well that fairness, though an underpinning of this country, has never been a reality. I choose this option with the painful awareness of the social and economic ravages which have befallen my race and all who suffer discrimination. . . .

Long ago, I decided not to become defensive about my own press coverage. I have been zapped. I sometimes wonder why this bigot is using my name when he talks to the press and why people are surprised to learn upon meeting me that I am not *the* Clarence Thomas they read about. More important, however, the press must realize that there is not total agreement, even within the black community, on the merits of all civil rights strategies or social programs. We are not a monolith and we certainly are not clones. . . . It is critical to balance these varying opinions in our national debate. . . . My image as a black Republican, working in the Reagan Administration, is not the important fact. . . . I do not believe that black Americans will accept or reject my ideas on the basis of my party affiliation. They are far too intelligent for that. They know that the great problems facing our country cannot be solved through narrow-minded partisan proposals from either party. I am a black Republican and proud of it. . . . While I am aware that we are presented to the American people as uncaring, unfair, and even *unjust*, I refuse to live with such an untrue image – either personally or politically. However I gladly accept this iconoclasm and abuse to do what I believe is right and necessary. It is a small price to pay.

The Language of Segregation

In the following vignette, sociologists Douglas S. Massey and Nancy A. Denton describe "Black English" as one consequence of the continuing segregation of impoverished African Americans from the rest of the nation.

SOURCE: Douglas S. Massey and Nancy A. Denton, American Apartheid: Segregation and the Making of the Underclass, 162–165. Harvard University Press, 1993. Copyright © 1993 by Harvard University Press. All rights reserved. Reprinted with permission of Harvard University Press.

The depth of isolation in the ghetto is . . . evident in black speech patterns, which have evolved steadily away from Standard American English. Because of their intense social isolation, many ghetto residents have come to speak a language that is increasingly remote from that spoken by American whites. . . . Whereas white speech has become more regionally specialized over time, with linguistic patterns varying increasingly between metropolitan areas . . . Black English has become progressively more uniform across urban areas. Over the past two decades, the Black English Vernaculars of Boston, Chicago, Detroit, New York, and Philadelphia have become increasingly similar in their grammatical structure and lexicon, reflecting urban blacks' common social and economic isolation within urban America. Although black speech has become more uniform internally, however, as a dialect it has drifted farther and farther away from the form and structure of Standard American English. . . . Blacks and whites in the United States increasingly speak different tongues, with different grammatical rules, divergent pronunciations, and separate vocabularies. . . . The less contact blacks have with whites, the greater their reliance on Black English Vernacular and the less their ability to speak Standard American English. Blacks who live within the ghetto, in particular, display speech patterns that are quite remote from the dialect spoken by most white Americans. Because of segregation, the languages spoken by blacks and whites are moving toward mutual unintelligibility.

The educational barriers facing ghetto children are exacerbated by teachers and school administrators who view Black English as "wrong," "bad," or "inferior," thereby stigmatizing black children and further undermining their motivation to learn. In many school settings, Black English is pejoratively stereotyped and taken to indicate a lack of intelligence, an absence of motivation or the presence of a learning disability . . .

The difficulties caused by a reliance on Black English do not stop at the classroom door. Facility with Standard English is required for many jobs in the larger economy, especially those that carry good prospects for socioeconomic advancement and income growth. . . . Employers . . . assume that people who speak Black English carry a street culture that devalues behaviors and attitudes consistent with being a "good worker," such as regularity, punctuality, dependability, and respect for authority.

The inability to communicate in Standard American English, therefore presents serious obstacles to socioeconomic advancement. Black Americans who aspire to socioeconomic success generally must acquire a facility in Standard English as a precondition of advancement, even if they retain a fluency in black speech. Successful blacks who have grown up in the ghetto literally become bilingual, learning to switch back and forth between black and white dialects depending on the social context. This "code switching" involves not only a change of words but a shift between contrasting cultures and identities. Although some people acquire the ability to make this shift without difficulty, it causes real social and psychological problems for others. For someone raised in the segregated environment of the ghetto, adopting white linguistic conventions can seem like a betrayal of black culture, a phony attempt to deny the reality of one's "blackness." As a result, black people who regularly speak Standard American

English often encounter strong disapproval from other blacks. Many well-educated blacks recall with some bitterness the ridicule and ostracism they suffered as children for the sin of "talking white."

Crippin': The Rise of Black Gangs in Post-Watts Los Angeles

In the following account, historian Mike Davis describes the rise of the Los Angeles-based 50,000 member Crips, the nation's largest street gang with "affiliations" in 32 states and 113 cities. His discussion includes an analysis of the historical circumstances, including the "managerial revolution" that gave rise to this "mega-gang."

It is time to meet L.A.'s "Viet Cong." Although the study of barrio gangs is a vast cottage industry, dating back to Emory Bogardus's 1926 monograph... *The City Boy and His Problems,* almost nothing has been written about the history of South central L.A.'s sociologically distinct gang culture. The earliest reported references to a "gang problem" in the Black community press, moreover, deal with gangs of *white* youth who terrorized Black residents along the frontiers of the southward-expanding Central Avenue ghetto.... Indeed, from these newspaper accounts and the recollections of old timers, it seems probable that the first generation of Black street gangs emerged as a defensive response to white violence in the schools and streets during the late 1940s. The [California] *Eagle,* for example, records "racial gang wars" at Manual Arts High in 1946, Canoga Park High (in the Valley) in 1947, and John Adams High in 1949, while Blacks at Fremont High were continually assaulted throughout 1946 and 1947. Possibly as a result of their origin in these school integration/transition battles, Black gangs, until the 1970s, tended to be predominantly defined by school-based turfs rather than by the neighborhood territorialities of Chicago gangs.

Aside from defending Black teenagers from racist attacks (which continued through the 1950s under the aegis of such white gangs as the "Spook hunters"), the early South central gangs – the Businessmen, Slausons, Gladiators, Farmers, Parks, Outlaws, Watts, Boot Hill, Rebel Rousers, Roman Twenties, and so forth–were also the architects of social space in new and usually hostile settings. As tens of thousands of 1940s and 1950s Black immigrants crammed into the overcrowded, absentee-landlord-dominated neighborhoods of the ghetto's Eastside, low-rider gangs offered "cool worlds" of urban socialization for poor young newcomers from rural Texas, Louisiana and Mississippi. Meanwhile, on the other side of Main Street, more affluent Black youngsters from the Westside bungalow belt created an [imitation] white "car club" subculture of Los Angeles in the 1950s . . . While "rumblin" (usually non-lethally) along this East-West socio-economic divide . . . the Black gangs of the 1950s also had to confront the implacable (often lethal) racism of Chief [William A] Parker's LAPD. In the days when the young Daryl Gates was driver to the great Chief, the policing of the ghetto was becoming simultaneously less corrupt but more militarized and brutal. . . . More-over, as Black nationalist groups, like the Muslims, began to appear in the ghetto in the late 1950s, Parker, like [J. Edgar] Hoover, began to see the gang problem and the "militant threat" as forming a single, overarching structure of Black menace . . .

South central gang youth, coming under the influence of the Muslims and the long-distance charisma of Malcolm X, began to reflect the generational awakening of Black Power. The "New Breed" of gang members in the 1960s, "were changing: those who formerly had seen things in terms of East and West were now beginning to see many of the same things in Black and White . . ."

The turning-point, of course, was the festival of the oppressed in August 1965 that the Black community called [the Watts] rebellion and the white media a riot. . . . Up to 75,000 people took part in the [Watts] uprising, mostly from the solid Black working class. For gang members it was "The Last Great Rumble," as formerly hostile groups forgot old grudges and cheered each other on against the hated LAPD and the National Guard. Old enemies, like the Slausons and the Gladiators (from the 54th Street area), flash[ed] smiles and high signs as they broke through Parker's invincible "blue line."

This ecumenical movement . . . lasted three or four years. Community work-ers, and even the LAPD themselves, were astonished by the virtual cessation of gang hostilities as the gang leadership joined the Revolution. Two leading Slausons, Alprentice "Bunchy" Carter (a famous warlord) and Jon Huggins became the local organizers of the Black Panther Party, while a third, Brother Crook (aka Ron Wilkins) created the Community Alert Patrol to monitor police abuse. Meanwhile an old Watts gang hangout near Jordan Downs, the "parking lot," became a recruiting center for the Sons of Watts who organized and guarded the annual Watts Festival.

It is not really surprising, therefore, that in the late 1960s the doo-ragged, hardcore street brothers and sisters, who for an extraordinary week in 1965 had actually driven the police out of the ghetto, were visualized by Black Power theorists as the strategic reserve of Black Liberation, if not its vanguard. . . . There was a potent moment in this period, around 1968–9, when the Panthers – their following soaring in the streets and high schools – looked as if they might become the ultimate revolutionary gang. Teenagers, who today flock to hear Eazy-E rap, "It ain't about color, it's about the color of money. I love the green" – then filled the Sports Arena to listen to Stokely Carmichael, H. Rap Brown, Bobby Seale and James Forman adumbrate the unity program of SNCC and the Panthers. The Black Congress and the People's Tribunal (convened to try the LAPD for the murder of Gregory Clark) were other expressions of the same aspiration for unity and militancy.

But the combined efforts of the FBI's notorious COINTELPRO program and the LAPD's Public Disorder Intelligence Division (a super-Red Squad that until 1982 maintained surveillance on every suspicious group from the Panthers to the National Council of Churches) were concentrated upon destroying Los Angeles's Black power vanguards. The February 1969 murders of Panther leaders Carter and Huggins on the UCLA campus by members of a rival nationalist group (which Panther veterans still insist was actually police-instigated) was followed a year later by the debut of LAPD's SWAT team in a day-long siege of the Panthers' South central headquarters. Although a general massacre of the Panthers cadre was narrowly averted by an angry community outpouring into the streets, the Party was effectively destroyed.

As even the [Los Angeles] *Times* recognized, the decimation of the Panthers led directly to a recrudescence of gangs in the early 1970s. "Crippin," the most extraordinary new gang phenomenon, was a bastard offspring of the Panthers' former charisma.... There are various legends about the original Crips, but they agree on certain particulars. As Donald Bakeer, a teacher at Manual Arts High, explains in his self-published novel about the Crips, the first "set" was incubated in the social wasteland created by the clearances for the Century Freeway – a traumatic removal of housing and destruction of neighborhood ties that was the equivalent of a natural disaster. His protagonist, a second-genera-tion Crip, boasts to his "homeboys": "My daddy was a member of the original 107 Hoover Crip Gang, the original Crips in Los Angeles, O.G. (original gangster) to the max." Secondly, as journalist Bob Baker has determined, the real "O.G." number one of the 107 (who split away from an older gang called the Avenues) was a young man powerfully influenced by the Panthers in their late sixties heyday.:

> He was Raymond Washington, a Fremont High School student who had been too young to be a Black Panther but had soaked up some of the Panther rhetoric about community control of neighborhoods. After Washington was kicked out of Fremont, he wound up at Washington High, and something began to jell in the neighborhood where he lived, around 107th and Hoover Streets.

Although it is usually surmised that the name Crip is derived from the 107 Hoovers' "crippled" style of walking, Bakeer was told by one O.G. that it originally stood for "Continuous Revolution in Progress." However apocryphal this translation may be, it best describes the phenomenal spread of Crip sets across the ghetto between 1970 and 1972. A 1972 gang map, released by the LAPD's 77th Street Division, shows a quiltwork of blue-ragged Crips, both Eastside and Westside, as well as miscellany of other gangs, some descended from the pre-Watts generation. Under incessant Crip pressure, these independent gangs – the Brims, Bounty Hunters, Denver Lanes, Athens Park Gang, the Bishops, and, especially, the powerful Pirus – federated as the red-handkerchiefed Bloods. Particularly strong in Black communities peripheral to the South central core, like Compton, Pacoima, Pasadena and Pomona, the Bloods have been primarily a defensive reaction-formation to the aggressive emergence of the Crips.

It needs to be emphasized that this was not merely a gang revival, but a radical permutation of Black gang culture. The Crips, however perversely, inherited the Panther aura of fearlessness and transmitted the ideology of armed vanguardism (shorn of its program). In some instances, Crip insignia continued to denote Black Power, as during the Monrovia riots in 1972 or the L.A. Schools bussing crisis of 1977–9. But too often Crippin' came to represent an escalation of intra-ghetto violence to *Clockwork Orange* levels (murder as a status symbol, and so on) that was unknown in the days of the Slausons and anathema to everything that the Panthers had stood for.

Moreover the Crips blended a penchant for ultra-violence with an overweening ambition to dominate the entire ghetto. Although . . . Eastside versus Westside tensions persist, the Crips, as the Panthers before them, attempted to hegemonize as an entire generation. In this regard, they achieved, like the contemporary Black P-Stone Nation in Chicago, a managerial revolution in gang organization. If they began as a teenage substitute for the fallen Panthers, they evolved through the 1970s into a hybrid of teen cult and proto-Mafia. At a time when economic opportunity was draining away from south central Los Angeles, the Crips were becoming the power resource of last resort for thousands of abandoned youth.

"Crack Is Just Jim Crow in a Pipe"

These two articles address the crack cocaine epidemic that swept across the African American community of Los Angeles in the 1990s. The first article is an interview by Los Angeles Times *staff writer Darrell Dawsey with a crack addict called "Ron." The second passage is part of a speech by California State Senator Diane Watson, who represented Ron's district, to the Southern Christian Leadership Conference. She titled her speech, "Crack Is Just Jim Crow in a Pipe."*

On a chilly February night, a tall young man named Ron sits in MacArthur Park, his hands stuffed into the pockets of his thin red jacket. In an interview with Times staff writer Darrell Dawsey, he tells a story that's familiar in the netherworld of drug abuse.

I'm from a small town in Louisiana, but the fast life got me. I wanted to hang with the fast people. I had a job at the Southern California Gas Co. I had a job paying $30,000 a year. I had two years of college at Southern University (in Baton Rouge).

I lost all of it because I got hooked on dope, crack.

SOURCE: Los Angeles Times, March 12, 19, 1990. Both articles appear on 7.

That's — is a double-edged sword. It makes you feel so good, but it'll tear your life apart. I've met every challenge in my life, man, and won. But I was not able to beat this drug thing. I started off selling it. I was making a little money, but then I started getting high too much. Pretty soon, I was smoking more than I was selling.

My company paid $20,000 for me to spend 30 days at a rehabilitation clinic, $29,000 for the next 30. But they got tired of me going to rehab. I wasn't making any improvement. I was still smoking and messing up my life. So they fired me. That's why I'm living like I do. I can't get a job.

I heard that they were trying to legalize drugs. That would be the worst thing. Think about it. If they got better cocaine, everybody would try it. You won't have anybody in this country who isn't on their way to getting strung out. That's a lie, when people tell you, you won't have crime (with decriminalization).

I had a heart operation, had a valve replaced. And I'm still smoking. Coke is a cruel mistress, man. She don't care who she takes from. And she doesn't give anything back.

These kids who sell it, they'll tell you. They don't sell it because they are bad people. They sell it to stay alive. How else are people going to make money? Nobody wants to hire too many black people. So they think we are supposed to starve because they won't give us jobs? Naw. People are going to try to stay alive, any way they can. That doesn't make you a villain.

(The drug epidemic) is a tough problem. I really can't say what the solution is. I think you need more education. Enforcement doesn't work. People need jobs. I think that's one of the main things: jobs. I blew mine, but that doesn't mean I don't know how important a job is. After the jobs, though, I don't know. It's tough.

★ ★ ★

"Crack Is Just Jim Crow in a Pipe"

Since the mid-1960s, American blacks have been fighting not a legal war against segregation, nor an insurmountable economic war against discrimination, but a profound psychological war for our own sense of self-worth.

We are fighting to free ourselves of the psychological bondage to which Africans were subjected in this country. It is the damage that results when you distort a people's belief in the cause-and-effect principle of the universe. It is the faith in this principle that motivates achievement and enables self-respect. It is the belief that effort produces results. It is the notion that "I can get what I want if I work hard enough, smart enough, long enough." It is what teaches a human being to believe in productive labor. It is self-discipline.

When racism teaches a man that he must labor not for self-improvement, but because it is the unique doom of his race, that man will hate labor and loathe his race. When a woman comes to perceive that no matter how hard she works she can only marginally improve her lot in life, that woman will come to believe that effort is an evil. When children learn that their status in society will always be determined more by the color of their skin than by their achievements, such children will grow up convinced that achievement is futile. When a culture is ingrained with the concept that there is no cause-and-effect relationship between effort and reward, that culture will fit its people for survival at the lowest, meanest level of existence and fail to teach the value of self-discipline.

I submit that as you ponder how we shall win the war against crack, you will be deciding strategy to win what I dare hope is the final battle in the African American war against racism.

Crack is just Jim Crow in a pipe. It is late in the day. Use well your time.

The Million Man March Pledge

On October 16, 1995, Minister Louis Farrakhan of the Nation of Islam led the following pledge to the thousands of African American men gathered at Washington, D.C., for the Million Man March.

I pledge that from this day forward, I will strive to love my brother as I love myself.

I, from this day forward, will strive to improve myself spiritually, morally, mentally, socially, politically, and economically for the benefit of myself, my family, and my people.

I pledge that I will strive to build businesses, build houses, build hospitals, build factories, and enter into international trade for the good of myself, my family, and my people.

I pledge that from this day forward, I will never raise my hand with a knife or a gun to beat, cut, or shoot any member of my family or any human being except in self-defense.

I pledge from this day forward, I will never abuse my wife by striking her, disrespecting her, for she is the mother of my children and the producer of my future.

I pledge that from this day forward, I will never engage in the abuse of children, little boys, or little girls for sexual gratification. I will let them grow in peace to be strong men and women for the future of our people.

I will never again use the B-word to describe any female-but particularly, my own Black sister.

I pledge from this day forward that I will not poison my body with drugs or that which is destructive to my health and my well-being.

SOURCE: Louis Farrakhan, "The Million Man March Pledge," in <u>Million Man March/Day of Absence: A Commemorative Anthology</u> (Chicago: Third World Press, 1996), 29.

I pledge from this day forward, I will support Black newspapers, Black radio, Black television. I will support Black artists who clean up their act to show respect for their people and respect for the heirs of the human family.

I will do all of this, so help me God.

8

Into the Twenty-First Century, Complicating Identities

This final chapter introduces the evolving history of African America as it enters the twenty-first century by exploring new directions, new issues, and new identities. The first vignette points this out by describing the changing pattern of black internal migration. For most of the twentieth century, African Americans moved from farm to city and from the South to the North and eventually to the West. Sometime in the 1970s, that tide reversed. Black people from northern and western cities are returning to, and in some instances moving to, the urban South. This change is profiled in **Black Migration: The Return to the South.** Although feminism is hardly a new direction for black women, this perspective was dramatically sharpened by the Anita Hill-Clarence Thomas episode. Two vignettes, **Anita Hill Testifies Before Congress** and **African American Women in Defense of Ourselves** reflect that trend. Two additional vignettes suggest themes that grow out of the changing gender dynamic in the black community. **The Gender Gap in the Twenty-First Century** explores the relative success of black women in higher education and the workplace in comparison to black men, while **The Sexist in Me** addresses the largely silent but nonetheless widespread issue of violence between the genders.

In the three decades since *Loving v. Virginia*, there has been an exponential increase in interracial marriage and a growing population of biracial children. That development is addressed in **The 2000 Census: Two or More Races Population** and **Which Side Are You On?** Identity issues around sexual preference are addressed in two vignettes, **Huey P. Newton on the Gay and Women's Liberation Movements** and **Does Your Mama Know About Me?**

The rapid growth of the African-born population in the United States, and its impact is explored in three vignettes, **Out of Africa: African Immigration to the United States, Goodwin Ajala at the World Trade Center** and **Barack Obama's Keynote Address at the Democratic National Convention, 2004**. The two final vignettes address the environment in differing ways. **African Americans and Environmental History: A Manifesto** argues that both traditional environmentalist organizations and African Americans need to find common ground. **In the Eye of the Storm: Race and Hurricane Katrina** shows the disproportionate impact of a hurricane on the fortunes of thousands of African Americans.

Black Migration: The Return to the South

The following vignette acknowledges a movement of African Americans to the South that has been accelerating for the past three decades.

D ecades of vacating Dixie are reversing, reports The Brookings Institution, a nonpartisan research organization. According to "The New Great Migration: Black Americans' Return to the South, 1965–2000," during the latter part of the 1990s, the South was the only region in the U.S. that saw an increase in black residents.

In fact, the study shows that over the last three decades, the South has become a "magnet" for black Americans, particularly college-educated professionals. In the 20th century, there was an exodus of blacks from the South, while the Northeast, Midwest, and West saw an increase in African Americans during the Great Migration.

The tide started turning during the 1970s, mostly due to economic factors. The Northeast and Midwest regions of the country began losing manufacturing jobs to the Sunbelt, which led to black migrants preferring Southern destinations in the late '90s: 8.5% of blacks residing in the Northeast headed south. For the first time in several decades, the Western and Midwestern parts of the country saw decreases in black residents. From 1995 to 2000, urban areas around Los Angeles, Chicago, and San Francisco lost 3% to 6% of their residents. Conversely, newcomers made up 5.5%, 7.6%, and 9.6% of the growing black populations in Dallas, Charlotte, and Atlanta, respectively.

This reverse migration, primarily attributed to an improved racial climate, employment opportunities, and historical ties, differs greatly from the large numbers of blacks who initially headed north, says Roderick Harrison, director of Databank at the Joint Center for Political and Economic Studies in Washington, D.C. Migration north was mainly rural to urban, but movement south has been primarily from major cities to growing metropolitan areas.

SOURCE: Cliff Hocker "Black Migration in Reverse", Black Enterprise (May, 2005), 40.

Anita Hill Testifies Before Congress

What follows are excerpts from the testimony of University of Oklahoma Law Professor Anita Hill before the Senate Judiciary Hearings on the confirmation of Judge Clarence Thomas for the U.S. Supreme Court in 1991.

Ms. HILL. Mr. Chairman, Senator Thurmond, members of the committee, my name is Anita F. Hill, and I am a professor of law at the University of Oklahoma. I was born on a farm in Okmulgee County, Oklahoma, in 1956. I am the youngest of 13 children. I had my early education in Okmulgee County. My father, Albert Hill, is a farmer in that area. My mother's name is Erma Hill. She is also a farmer and a housewife.

My childhood was one of a lot of hard work and not much money, but it was one of solid family affection as represented by my parents. I was reared in a religious atmosphere in the Baptist faith, and I have been a member of the Antioch Baptist Church, in Tulsa, Oklahoma, since 1983. It is a very warm part of my life at the present time.

For my undergraduate work, I went to Oklahoma State University, and graduated from there in 1977.... I graduated from the university with academic honors and proceeded to the Yale Law School, where I received my J.D. degree in 1980.

Upon graduation from law school, I became a practicing lawyer with the Washington, DC, firm of Wald, Harkrader & Ross. In 1981, I was introduced to now Judge Thomas by a mutual friend. Judge Thomas told me that he was anticipating a political appointment and asked if I would be interested in working with him. He was, in fact, appointed as Assistant Secretary of Education for Civil Rights. After he had taken that post, he asked if I would become his assistant and I accepted that position....

After approximately 3 months of working there, he asked me to go out socially with him.... I declined the invitation to go out socially with him, and explained to him that I thought it would jeopardize...a very good working relationship.... I was very uncomfortable with the idea and told him so. I thought that by saying "no" and explaining my reasons, my employer would abandon his social suggestions. However, to my regret, in the following few weeks he continued to ask me out on several occasions. He pressed me to justify my reasons for saying "no" to him.... My working relationship became even more strained when Judge Thomas began to use work situations to discuss sex. On these occasions, he would call me into his office...or he might suggest that...we go to lunch to a government cafeteria. After a brief discussion of work, he would turn the conversation to a discussion of sexual matters.

SOURCE: "Testimony of Anita F. Hill," Hearings before the Committee on the Judiciary, United States Senate on the nomination of Clarence Thomas to be Associate Justice of the Supreme Court of the United States (October 11, 1991).

His conversations were very vivid. He spoke about acts that he had seen in pornographic films involving such matters as women having sex with animals, and films showing group sex or rape scenes. He talked about pornographic materials depicting individuals with large penises, or large breasts and individuals in various sex acts. On several occasions Thomas told me graphically of his own sexual prowess. Because I was extremely uncomfortable talking about sex with him at all, and particularly in such a graphic way, I told him that I did not want to talk about these subjects. I would also try to change the subject to education matters or to nonsexual personal matters. . . . My efforts to change subject were rarely successful. . . .

When Judge Thomas was made chair of the EEOC, I needed to face the question of whether to go with him. I was asked to do so and I did. The work, itself, was interesting, and at that time, it appeared that the sexual overtures, which had so troubled me had ended. . . . For my first months at the EEOC, where I continued to be an assistant to Judge Thomas, there were no sexual overtures. However, during the fall and winter of 1982, these began again. . . . He commented on what I was wearing in terms of whether it made me more or less sexually attractive. The incidents occurred in his inner office at the EEOC.

One of the oddest episodes I remember was an occasion in which Thomas was drinking a Coke in his office, he got up from the table at which we were wording, went over to his desk to get the Coke, looked at the can and asked, "Who has put pubic hair on my Coke?" On other occasions he referred to the size of his own penis as being larger than normal and he also spoke on some occasions of the pleasures he had given to women with oral sex. At this point, late 1982, I began to feel severe stress on the job. . . . I began to be concerned that Clarence Thomas might take out his anger with me by degrading me or not giving me important assignments. I also thought that he might find an excuse for dismissing me.

In January 1983, I began looking for another job. . . . In February 1983, I was hospitalized for 5 days on an emergency basis for acute stomach pain which I attributed to stress on the job. Once out of the hospital. I became . . . committed to find other employment and sought further to minimize my contact with Thomas. In the spring of 1983, an opportunity to teach at Oral Roberts University opened up. . . . I agreed to take the job, in large part, because of my desire to escape the pressures I felt at EEOC due to Judge Thomas. On . . . the last day of my employment at the EEOC in the summer of 1983, I did have dinner with Clarence Thomas. We went directly from work to a restaurant near the office. . . . He said, that if I ever told anyone of his behavior that it would ruin his career. This was not an apology, nor was it an explanation. That was his last remark about the possibility of our going out, or reference to his behavior . . .

It is only after a great deal of agonizing consideration that I am able to talk of these unpleasant matter to anyone, except my closest friends. . . . I may have used poor judgment early on in my relationship with this issue. I was aware, however, that telling at any point in my career could adversely affect my future career. . . . It would have been more comfortable to remain silent. It took no initiative to inform anyone. I took no initiative to inform anyone. But when I was asked by a representative of this committee to report my experience I felt that I had to tell the truth. I could not keep silent.

African American Women in Defense of Ourselves

The legacy of challenge to both sexism and racism by African American women continues into the contemporary era as reflected in this statement placed in the November 17, 1991, issue of the New York Times *in the aftermath of the Anita Hill-Clarence Thomas controversy. This statement was signed by over 1,600 black women.*

We are particularly outraged by the racist and sexist treatment of Professor Anita Hill, an African American woman who was maligned and castigated for daring to speak publicly of her own experience of sexual abuse. The malicious defamation of Professor Hill insulted all women of African descent and sent a dangerous message to any woman who might contemplate a sexual harassment complaint.

We speak here because we recognize that the media are now portraying the Black community as prepared to tolerate both the dismantling of affirmative action and the evil of sexual harassment in order to have any Black man on the Supreme Court. We want to make clear that the media have ignored or distorted many African American voices. We will not be silenced.

Many have erroneously portrayed the allegations against Clarence Thomas as an issue of either gender or race. As women of African descent, we understand sexual harassment as both. We further understand that Clarence Thomas outrageously manipulated the legacy of lynching in order to shelter himself from Anita Hill's allegations. To deflect attention away from the reality of sexual abuse in African American women's lives, he trivialized and misrepresented this painful part of African American people's history. This country, which has a long legacy of racism and sexism, has never taken the sexual abuse of black women seriously. Throughout U.S. history black women have been sexually stereotyped as immoral, insatiable, perverse, the initiators in all sexual contacts – abusive or otherwise. The common assumption in legal proceedings as well as in the larger society has been that black women cannot be raped or otherwise sexually abused.

SOURCE: New York Times, November 17, 1991. Reprinted in Essence 22, no. 11 (March 1992), 56.

As Anita Hill's experience demonstrates, Black women who speak of these matters are not likely to be believed.

In 1991, we cannot tolerate this type of dismissal of any one Black woman's experience or this attack upon our collective character without protest, outrage and resistance.

We pledge ourselves to continue to speak out in defense of one another, in defense of the African American community and against those who are hostile to social justice, no matter what color they are. No one will speak for us but ourselves.

The Gender Gap in the Twenty-First Century

In a Newsweek *article from 2003, Ellis Cose described the growing economic divide between African American women and men and its implications for gender relations between the two groups. An excerpt of his article appears here.*

"I know what every colored woman in this country is doing.... Dying. Just like me. But the difference is they dying like a stump. Me, I'm going down like one of those redwoods." America was in a very different place in 1973, when novelist Toni Morrison put those words in the mouth of the doomed yet defiant Sula, whose triumph lay solely in the fact that she could meet death on her own terms. Who then could have imagined that an African-American female would one day stand atop the nation's foreign-policy pyramid? Who could have predicted that black women would, educationally, so outstrip black men? Who could have dreamed the day would come when black women would lay claim to "white men's" jobs-the phrase used by banking executive Malia Fort's former boss as he reminded her of the time when "the only thing a black woman could have done in a bank is clean up"? Today a black woman can be anything from an astronaut to a talk-show host, run anything from a corporation to an Ivy League university. Once consigned to mostly menial work, black women (24 percent of them, compared with 17 percent of black men) have ascended to the professional-managerial class.

This is not to say that black women have climbed the storied crystal stair.... Nearly 14 percent of working black women remain below the poverty level. And women don't yet out-earn black men. But the growing educational-achievement gap portends a monumental shifting of the sands. College educated

SOURCE: Ellis Cose, "The Black Gender Gap," <u>Newsweek</u> 141, no. 9 (March 3, 2003), 46–51. Copyright © 2003 by Newsweek, Inc. All rights reserved. Reprinted with permission of Newsweek, Inc.

black women already earn more than the median for all black working men or, for that matter, for all women. And as women in general move up the corporate pyramid, black women, increasingly, are part of the parade. In 1995 women held less than 9 percent of corporate-officer positions in Fortune 500 companies, according to Catalyst, a New York-based organization that promotes the interests of women in business. Last year they held close to 16 percent, a significant step up. Of those 2,140 women, 163 were black-a minuscule proportion, but one that is certain to grow.

These days, few black women are willing to settle for Sula's life. There is a search not only for recognition but for "models of happiness," in the words of Veronica Chambers, author of a new book called "Having It All." But that quest brings with it a host of questions. . . . Is this new black woman finally crashing through the double ceiling of race and gender? Or is she leaping into treacherous waters that will leave her stranded, unfulfilled, childless and alone? Can she thrive if her brother does not, if the black man succumbs, as hundreds of thousands already have, to the hopelessness of prison and the streets? Can she, dare she, thrive without the black man, finding happiness across the racial aisle? Or will she, out of compassion, loneliness or racial loyalty "settle" for men who – educationally, economically, professionally – are several steps beneath her?

Such questions are now being debated because black men and women are, increasingly, following different paths. As choreographer Fatima Robinson put it: "I love brothers. . . . But there is such a gap that I think I may not end up with a black man." Today twenty-five percent of young black males go to college; 35 percent of women do. Only 13.5 percent of young black females are high-school dropouts; more than 17 percent of young black men are. The notion that college was a place to find a man has slowly given way to the conviction that decent, educated black men are rarer, to borrow Shakespeare's words, than pearls in beauteous ladies' eyes.

Daven Jackson, a 25-year-old veterinary student at Alabama's predominantly black Tuskegee University, thinks she understands why. In her high school in Thomasville, Ga., recalls Jackson, "most black males were encouraged to be athletes," not scholars. None made it big as jocks; instead, "over half of the males who graduated with me are in jail." . . . Not just teachers but the entire educational support system now favors girls over boys, argues Monette Evans, a Tuskegee vice president. There is also the powerful drive of the women themselves. "Oftentimes women go into higher education and beyond because they can't depend on anyone else to support them or their children" Evans points out. And whereas boys typically lack focus, girls show up with a sense of purpose. "Females had no excuses about anything"; says Kevin Cook, an administrator at Arizona State University. They arrive with an attitude that quietly announces, "We're here. It's tough. We're black. We're alone."

As they graduate and move into the work world, many black women stay just as tough-minded. . . . "Nobody reaches out to [black women]. . . . And when they reach out, the door gets slammed in their face; says Ella L. J. Bell, a professor at Dartmouth's Tuck School of Business and coauthor of "Our Separate Ways" a study of black and white women in corporations . . .

Still, for significant numbers the atmosphere in corporate America is changing. In a recently released study of corporate women of color, Catalyst found that 57 percent had been promoted between 1998 and 2001. According to that study, 62 percent of black women reported having mentors, up dramatically from three years earlier, when the number was 35 percent.... Corporate types may still not see black women as members of the club, but they "don't feel threatened by us" notes Gwen DeRu, vice president of a black owned consulting firm in Birmingham, Alabama.

In fact ... the most difficult challenge black women face today may lie closer to home.... In bars, colleges and other gathering spots across America, the question is much the same: where are the decent, desirable black men? "When I left high school, I had a boyfriend, but that went down the drain," confides Tametria Brown, 23. As an undergraduate at the University of Virginia, she found "a lot of people dating the same guy.... The dating scene was not good." The marriage scene may be worse. According to the 2000 Census, 47 percent of black women in the 30-to-34 age range have never married, compared with 10 percent of white women...

Gwen McKinney considers herself among the blessed in being married to a black man (a systems engineer) who is unthreatened by her success as a Washington public-relations-firm owner.... McKinney believes her husband's comfort level stems from the fact that they got involved before her business took off. "Most of the time it doesn't work unless those relationships are forged before the woman's ascendancy," she says...

Underappreciated by black men, many black women are looking elsewhere. Connie Rice, a Los Angeles civil-rights attorney and Radcliff graduate, puts it plainly: "If you have to have the same race, your choices are limited." For years, there has been a general assumption that while black men were comfortable dating white women, black women ... generally steered clear of white men. Certainly, statistics show that interracial black-white unions, while relatively rare, have been much more common between black men and white women. But the marriage statistics are shifting.... The dating wall of Jericho is tumbling. In a survey of residents of 21 cities ... 78 percent of black men (average age: 32) had dated interracially at least once, as had 53 percent of black women (average age: 34) ...

Instead of crossing the racial line, others are trying to navigate the currents of interclass romance. Ellen Lewis, 32, a product manager for Oscar Mayer in Phoenix, Ariz., is married to a trucker. With a marketing degree and business experience, Lewis makes more than double her husband's salary. When they began dating, she hid all evidence of her success. "After a while, I could see he could probably handle it." But even now, says Lewis, "it's hard not to sense his resentment and his attitude that black women have it easier." Birmingham banker Malia Fort, who had a child (and is in a long-term relationship) with a laborer, has found the going somewhat smoother-in part because her expectations were brutally realistic. "He doesn't fit into my professional world, but he doesn't have to," she says...

Cassaundra Cain prepared her two daughters (now college-age) early on for the possibility of being alone. A divorced postal worker living in Atlanta, Cain says she "always stressed the Prince Charming thing wasn't our reality." She warned her daughters against getting "caught in what they saw young mainstream girls do.... I tell them they're young black girls – that they may end up on their own and alone." Even for women in "mainstream" white America, says [sociologist Donna] Franklin, hard times may lie ahead. Black women may be the leaders in the trend of marrying less successful men, but white women are surely following. And, argues Franklin, they will reap the same consequences – more domestic tension and higher divorce rates. Professor Bell agrees: "Nothing lies in isolation in a culture this fluid. So what happens to us will happen to them." But what exactly will happen to "us"? Bell concedes that black women, particularly young, black, educated women, are journeying into uncharted waters. "They have a degree of liberty no other group of black women have had.... It'll be interesting to see what they do with it."

Interesting, indeed. There are several competing visions. In the most bleak, more and more black women will lead lives of success but also of isolation, as poorer, less well-prepared black women raise the community's children and perpetuate the existence of the "underclass." Then there is another view... [where] black women are weathering a period of transition, after which they will find a way to balance happiness and success – and perhaps even serve as an inspiration for their sisters across the color line. It is, admittedly, the rosier view; but it is not necessarily less realistic. Given the history of black women on this planet, one would have to be supremely foolish to believe that there is any challenge they cannot overcome.

The Sexist in Me

In the following account, journalist, writer, and activist Kevin Powell described his own attempt to deal with his stereotypes about women that in turn impacted his relationships in an Essence *article in 1992.*

My girlfriend and I had been arguing most of the day. As we were returning from the laundromat, she ran ahead of me to our apartment building. I caught up with her at the front door, dropped the clothes at her feet, went inside and slammed the door behind me. She carried the bundle in, set it down and started back outside. Enraged, I grabbed her by the seat of her shorts and pulled her back into the apartment. We struggled in the kitchen, the dining-area and the bathroom. As we were moving toward the living room, I shoved her into the bathroom door. Her face bruised, she began to cry uncontrollably, and I tried to calm her down as we wrestled on the living-room floor. When she let out a high-pitched yell for help, I jumped to my feet, suddenly aware of what I was doing. Shaking with fear and exhaustion, I watched my girlfriend run barefoot out of our apartment into the street.

I still shudder when I think of that scene one year later. It was my first serious relationship and, notwithstanding my proclamations of "I'm one Black man who's gonna do the right thing," I managed to join the swelling ranks of abusive men with relative ease. Soon after "the incident," accusations of sexism flooded my guilty conscience. Like a lot of men, I tried to pin much of the blame on my now ex-girlfriend. She must have done something to provoke my outburst, I rationalized to myself.

But I couldn't delude myself for too long. I kept thinking of all the women I had ill-treated in some way. Without fully realizing it, I had always taken women for granted, but it wasn't until I committed a violent act that it hit me how deeply I believed women to be inferior to men.

Ashamed of what I had done, I knew that if I didn't deal with my deeply rooted sexism – that desire of man to dominate women – I could not seriously enter into another emotionally intimate relationship with a woman. Psychologically drained, I consulted young women friends my own age, older Black women and men, and any book that dealt with the issue at hand. Everywhere I turned, I found someone who was pointing out the dangers of exhibiting sexism.

For example, one woman friend drew an analogy to racism. If a child is taught from an early age to dislike another child because of his or her race, she said, the former is likely to become a hardened racist by adulthood. The same logic, she offered, applies to sexism.

Keeping in mind my friend's analogy, I recalled my childhood. I evolved as many boys do in this society: Machismo gripped my psyche, and by the time I reached my teen years we "boys" did whatever we felt like doing – which ran the gamut from squeezing girls' buttocks in gym class to "gang-banging" girls in abandoned buildings.

My chauvinistic demeanor merely ripened with age, and even after my political consciousness blossomed in college, I self-righteously continued to rationalize that the real battle was against racism, and if the "sistas" on campus couldn't fall into line, well, then, those women weren't really down with the program anyway.

In retrospect, what happened in my relationship was inevitable. Left unchecked my entire life, my sexist inclinations were building up to a breaking point. Unable to handle the pressures of a serious relationship, I first sought to "control" my girlfriend through verbal tirades and then finally through violence – the highest form of sexism.

The entire experience has been incredibly stressful – including writing about it now. I will never be able to remove the pain I inflicted on my ex-girlfriend, but at least I've taken measures to ensure that it will not happen again.

Acknowledging my inherent sexism was the first step. I then had to recognize that women are not footstools or servants or punching bags, but my equals on every level. And as I've struggled against my own sexism, I've also had to struggle against it when it manifests in my male friends. I can no longer tolerate the use of words like bitch or skeezer to describe women. Silence is acquiescence and acceptance. Moreover, true manhood does not rest on the subjugation of women – verbal or physical – and meaningful relationships between men and women won't exist until we men understand that.

The 2000 Census: Two or More Races Population

Responding specifically to the growing number of biracial (mainly black-white) children in the United States, the Census Bureau created a new category called two or more races for the 2000 Census. Here is a discussion of that category and preliminary information about this population based on the most recent census.

Census 2000 showed that the United States population on April 1, 2000, was 281.4 million. Of the total, 6.8 million people, or 2.4 percent, reported more than one race. Census 2000 asked separate questions on race and Hispanic or Latino origin. Hispanics who reported more than one race are included in the Two or more races population.

This report, part of a series that analyzes population and housing data collected from Census 2000, provides a portrait of the Two or more races population in the United States and discusses its distribution at both the national and subnational levels.... The term "Two or more races" refers to people who chose more than one of the six race categories. These individuals are referred to as the *Two or more races* population, or as the population that reported *more than one race*. Data on race has been collected since the first U.S. decennial census in 1790. Census 2000 was the first decennial census that allowed individuals to self-identify with more than one race.

For Census 2000, the question on race was asked of every individual living in the United States and responses reflect self-identification. Respondents were asked to report the race or races they considered themselves and other members of their households to be. The question on race for Census 2000 was different from the one for the 1990 census in several ways. Most significantly, respondents were given the option of selecting one or more race categories to indicate their racial identities. The Census 2000 question on race included 15 separate response categories and 3 areas where respondents could write in a more specific race.... The six race categories include: White, Black or African American, American Indian and Alaska Native, Asian, Native Hawaiian and Other Pacific Islander, Some other race.

People who responded to the question on race by indicating only one race are referred to as the race *alone* population, or the group who reported *only one* race. For example, respondents who marked only the White category on the census questionnaire would be included in the White *alone* population. Individuals who chose more than one of the six race categories are referred to as the *Two or more races* population, or as the group who reported *more than one race*. For

SOURCE: U.S. Census Bureau, <u>The Two or More Races Population: 2000</u> (Washington, D.C.: Government Printing Office, 2000), 1–9.

example, respondents who reported they were "White *and* Black or African American" or "White *and* American Indian and Alaska Native *and* Asian" would be included in the *Two or more races* category . . .

In the total population, 6.8 million people, or 2.4 percent, reported more than one race. Of the total Two or more races population, the overwhelming majority (93 percent) reported exactly two races. An additional 6 percent reported three races, and 1 percent reported four or more races. . . . Of the total Two or more races population, 40 percent lived in the West, 27 percent lived in the South, 18 percent lived in the Northeast, and 15 percent lived in the Midwest. The West had the largest number and the highest proportion of respondents reporting more than one race in its total population: the Two or more races population comprised 4.3 percent of all respondents in the West, compared with 2.3 percent in the Northeast, 1.8 percent in the South, and 1.6 percent in the Midwest.

The ten states with the largest Two or more races populations in 2000 were California, New York, Texas, Florida, Hawaii, Illinois, New Jersey, Washington, Michigan, and Ohio. Combined, these states represented 64 percent of the total Two or more races population. These states contained 49 percent of the total population. Three states had Two or more races populations greater than one-half million: California was the only state with a Two or more races population greater than one million, followed by New York with 590,000, and Texas with 515,000. These three states accounted for 40 percent of the total Two or more races population.

There were fourteen states where the Two or more races population exceeded the U.S. rate of 2.4 percent, led by the western states of Hawaii (21 percent), followed at a distance by Alaska (5.4 percent), and California (4.7 percent), and the southern state of Oklahoma (4.5 percent). The other ten states included the western states of Arizona, Colorado, Nevada, New Mexico, Oregon, and Washington; the northeastern states of New Jersey, New York, and Rhode Island; and the southern state of Texas. No midwestern state had greater than 2.4 percent of its population reporting more than one race. Four states – California, Hawaii, New York, and Washington – were represented in the top ten states for both number and percent reporting more than one race. There were five states where the Two or more races population represented 1.0 percent or less of the total population: Alabama, Maine, Mississippi, South Carolina, and West Virginia.

Census 2000 showed that, of all places in the United States with populations of 100,000 or more, New York with nearly 400,000, and Los Angeles with nearly 200,000, had the largest Two or more races populations. These places were also the two largest places in the United States. Four other places (Chicago, Houston, San Diego, and Honolulu) had Two or more races populations greater than 50,000 . . .

According to Census 2000, about one in three people in the Two or more races population also reported as Hispanic. About 6 percent of Hispanics reported more than one race, in contrast to 2 percent of non-Hispanics.

The White population, and the Black or African American population had the lowest percentages reporting more than one race. Of the 216.9 million respondents who reported White alone or in combination, 2.5 percent, or 5.5 million, reported White as well as at least one other race. Similarly, of the 36.4 million individuals who reported Black or African American alone or in combination, 4.8 percent, or 1.8 million, reported Black or African American as well as at least one other race.

The Asian population, and the Some other race population had somewhat higher percentages reporting more than one race. Of the 11.9 million individuals who reported Asian alone or in combination, 13.9 percent, or 1.6 million, reported Asian as well as at least one other race. Similarly, of the 18.5 million individuals who reported Some other race alone or in combination, 17.1 percent, or 3.2 million, reported Some other race as well as at least one other race.

The American Indian and Alaska Native population, and the Native Hawaiian and Other Pacific Islander population had the highest percentages reporting more than one race. Of the 4.1 million individuals who reported American Indian and Alaska Native alone or in combination, 39.9 percent, or 1.6 million, reported American Indian and Alaska Native as well as at least one other race. Similarly, of the 874,000 individuals who reported Native Hawaiian and Other Pacific Islander alone or in combination, 54.4 percent, or 476,000, reported Native Hawaiian and Other Pacific Islander as well as at least one other race.

People who reported more than one race were more likely to be under age 18 than those reporting only one race. Of the 6.8 million people in the Two or more races population, 42 percent were under 18. This is higher than the one race population. Of the 274.6 million people who reported only one race, 25 percent were under 18...

All levels of government need information on race to implement and evaluate programs, or enforce laws. Examples include: the Native American Programs Act, the Equal Employment Opportunity Act, the Civil Rights Act, the Voting Rights Act, the Public Health Act, the Healthcare Improvement Act, the Job Partnership Training Act, the Equal Credit Opportunity Act, the Fair Housing Act, and the census Redistricting Data Program. Both public and private organizations use race information to find areas where groups may need special services and to plan and implement education, housing, health, and other programs that address these needs. For example, a school system might use this information to design cultural activities that reflect the diversity in their community. Or a business could use it to select the mix of merchandise it will sell in a new store. Census information also helps identify areas where residents might need services of particular importance to certain racial or ethnic groups, such as screening for diabetes.

Which Side Are You On?

In the following account, Arvli Ward, who is both African American and Japanese American, describes his reaction to the Rodney King uprising in his hometown, Los Angeles, in 1992.

I keep thinking back to a moment that occurred sometime after midnight on the first night of burning and looting. I am standing against a low wall at the edge of a parking lot near Florence and Vermont, watching people stream to and out of a trashed-up supermarket when two men pass me.

"Black power," one of them says in an offhand way.

It strikes me as a remarkable utterance. I am speechless for a moment. "Black power," I finally sputter. In my memory I see the moment punctuated – as if it were a scene out of a movie – by an exploding transformer box that lights up the undersky with a brilliant blue flash before casting the entire area into total darkness.

It was Black Power, wasn't it? This feeling in the soot-filled air. Deep in the African ghetto of Los Angeles where some of the city's poorest live, people are moving casually against property, that concept around which lives are wrapped in this free market world, taking what they please. Authority, in the form of the police, won't show anytime soon; it's clear that some institutions don't apply tonight.

Someone sits a few feet away from me smoking a cigarette and begins to tell it to no one in particular. "Niggas breaking up the slave quarters...looting the goods...overseer can't do a damn thing about it...." From the handful assembled there comes chorus of chuckles, a murmur of agreement.

I thought of the Last Poets and their refrain: "Black day is coming.... Black day is here." I can't deny the exhilaration I felt at that moment. I know I was raised better, but it was a glorious moment. It looked as if the revolution had arrived.

But my mind keeps returning to another moment, this one occurring about twelve hours later. In that moment, I see two faces I recognize as Japanese, though everyone else takes them for Korean. They are the faces of a middle-aged couple in a yellow Cadillac with white interior decorated with crocheted doilies. They are traveling west – out of the ghetto where they may live, perhaps behind the old Crenshaw Square in a manicured duplex – slowing to turn southward on La Cienega, when a bare-chested Crip wearing work gloves and a bandana tied around his face bandit-style, rushes the car and throws a bottle of beer through the driver's side window. The old man takes the exploding window and bottle in the side of the head and neck. He keeps driving, hands clenched at the top of the wheel. His mouth is agape. He spits shards of glass from his lips. His wife cries

SOURCE: Arvli Ward, "Which Side Are You On?" <u>Pacific Ties</u> 16, no. 5 (April 1993), 41–2.

out, takes out her handkerchief and begins to reach up to dab his bloody face. Just then, our eyes seem to meet. Does she recognize me, I wonder, as I recognize her? Her face is so much like my mother's, I imagine, and in her eyes I sense a question. I flinch and look away.

A year later, my memories of the 48 hours I roamed the burning city are dominated by images of love and suffering like these. I have since quit trying to make sense of them, because I can't make the choices necessary. How do you balance Jubilation Day, as the Rasta on 54th called it, with all the Asian ass-kicking you see? Or as James Jenkins, my boyhood friend, used to ask me: "Is you a Jap, or is you a nigga?"

My father was born in rural Georgia to the 15-year-old daughter of a sharecropper. From the little he told me about his early years, I fashioned together a picture that remains as remote to me as literature. There was a farm, just a mean patch of land, an anchor into penury. A childhood without shoes. There was a town, Elberton, whose status as the granite capital of Georgia ensured magnificent monuments to the Confederacy. My father left the farm, moved on to the city, and lived by his wits like many black men in this society. Soon he joined the Marines and shipped out for the Korean War to kill Koreans and Chinese in the name of freedom. Eventually he was stationed in Japan at a base on the beautiful inland sea that faces China and there he met my mother, the displaced daughter of a Kobe shopkeeper. Their courtship was carried out at the Bar Happy, where jazz-loving Japanese women and black servicemen mingled. They married a year later and soon afterwards were disowned by their families. My father died before he could square things with his relatives who continued to believe that it was Georgia anti-miscegenation laws and not their bigotry that kept him away. My mother's rapprochement was finally complete nearly 40 years later, although the elder brother who removed her from the *koseki* – the Japanese family registry that would establish the racial purity of your pedigree – was too senile before his death to notice that she had come back.

My father eventually moved us to Southern California, where I grew up in the racially jumbled milieu of a military town. We were the children of enlisted Marines, the Black, white, Latino, Native American and Samoan poor who came from ghettos, farms, and factory towns to make up the lower ranks. We were crowded into the "Posole," a Chicano barrio and the only neighborhood where nonwhites were free to buy. We were a motley assortment, many of us half something, born at stations in the Philippines, Korea, Guam, Japan and wherever else they sent Marines. We grew up gray girls, black cholos, pop-locking Asians, but Black was the dominant esthetic, absorbing youth of all groups, and I grew up thinking I was Black.

When the 29th of last April arrived, I was already wondering – something I thought I had quit doing long ago–what it meant to be African, what it meant to be Asian. It began when I found myself in an argument on a flight from Washington D.C. to Memphis. Although I was in the practice of denying it, I had been through this many times before. This time it was with a member of the Black Freedom Fighters Coalition, or so his jacket, which was covered in epigrams and names from Black history, said.

A few minutes into our flight, he noticed that I was reading Shelby Steele's *The Content of our Character*. Since he asked, I started to tell him what I thought I understood of the conservative Steele's ideas. I couldn't abide by them, I told him, but I must have sounded like an asshole anyway. "Why do you clutter up your mind with all that stuff?" he asked, his voice dripping with drama like a preacher's.

For the next couple of hours he loomed over me, his large body spilling into my seat, and preached. He asked me what right I had to say I was Black. Yeah, I had black skin, he agreed, but I didn't sound Black, and if he had to guess, my ideas weren't very Black. At a couple of spots in the conversation, he'd pause and ask me: "You Filipino right?" It was meant as an insult, a reminder that what I claimed to be was irrelevant.

"It is people like you that will sell us out when the revolution comes," he said. At one point he challenged me to tell him who the people inscribed on his jacket were: Nat Turner, Bob Marley, Paul Robeson et al. When I proved up to the simple quiz, he looked at his girl and said: "You see what they throw at you?" She smiled knowingly.

What he meant was that I was a "race spy," someone who knew about being Black, but wasn't Black. I was a danger, a potential sellout stuck on succeeding at the expense of real black folks. Would I join the FBI, he asked, if I wasn't already in it?

He had found the button. Could he have known that all my life, I struggled for black acceptance, many times at the expense of my Asian side? Moments like these, long repressed and smoothed over it the making of my personal myth, sprang up. I was kissing his ass – in the same way I had done in these situations since I learned long ago what being half-black and half-Japanese meant – begging him to deem me worthy of being called a brother.

"Every brother ain't a brother," he told me, invoking Chuck D.

After a while, it got nasty. The white folks began looking around.

We landed and I switched seats in Memphis for the rest of the flight back to California. When he found out that I was moving to another seat, he stood up and looked back at me with an expression of utter disappointment and disgust.

But he was right, and it was useless to argue: He was blacker than me.

And he may have been right about even more. I probably was a race spy. And like a spy, I felt no real allegiance to Africa or Japan, especially on the 29th as I watched the events. All I could do was celebrate the love and feel the suffering.

Huey P. Newton on the Gay and Women's Liberation Movements

In the following statement, Huey P. Newton, Supreme Commander of the Black Panther Party, attempts to ally the organization with progressive elements of the Gay Liberation and Women's Liberation Movement.

During the past few years, strong movements have developed among women and homosexuals seeking their liberation. There has been some uncertainty about how to relate to these movements.

Whatever your personal opinion and your insecurities about homosexuality and the various liberation movements among homosexuals and women (and I speak of the homosexuals and women as oppressed groups) we should try to unite with them in a revolutionary fashion...

We must gain security in ourselves and therefore have respect and feelings for all oppressed people. We must not use the racist-type attitudes like the white racists use against people because they are black and poor. Many times the poorest white person is the most racist because he's afraid that he might lose something or discover something that he doesn't have. You're some kind of threat to him. This kind of psychology is in operation when we view [other] oppressed people and we're angry with them because of their particular kind of behavior or their particular kind of deviation from the established norm.

Remember we haven't established a revolutionary value system; we're only in the process of establishing it. I don't remember us ever constituting any value that said that a revolutionary must say offensive things toward homosexuals or that a revolutionary would make sure that women do not speak out against their own particular kind of oppression.

Matter of fact, it's just the opposite, we say that we recognize the woman's right to be free. We haven't said much about the homosexual at all and we must relate to the homosexual movement because it is a real movement. And I know through reading and through my life experience, my observation, that homosexuals are not given freedom and liberty by anyone in this society. Maybe they might be the most oppressed people in the society...

That's not endorsing things in homosexuality that we wouldn't view as revolutionary. But there is nothing to say that a homosexual can not also be a revolutionary.... Maybe a homosexual could be the most revolutionary.

When we have revolutionary conferences, rallies and demonstrations, there should be full participation of the Gay Liberation Movement and the Women's Liberation Movement.... We should never say a whole movement is dishonest when in fact they are trying to be honest; they're just making honest mistakes.

SOURCE: Huey P. Newton on the Gay and Women's Liberation Movements in Gay Flames Pamphlet, No. 7, 1970. Used with permission by The Dr. Huey P. Newton Foundation.

Friends are allowed to make mistakes. The enemy is not allowed to make mistakes because his whole existence is a mistake and we suffer from it. But the Women's Liberation Front and Gay Liberation Front are our friends, they are our potential allies and we need as many allies as possible.

We should be willing to discuss the insecurities that many people have about homosexuality. When I say, "insecurities" I mean the fear that there is some kind of threat to our manhood. I can understand this fear. Because of the long conditioning process that builds insecurity in the American male, homosexuality might produce certain hangups in us. . . . We should be careful about using terms which might turn our friends off. The terms "faggot" and "punk" should be deleted from our vocabulary and especially we should not attach names normally designed for homosexuals to men who are enemies of the people such as Nixon or Mitchell. Homosexuals are not enemies of the people . . .

ALL POWER TO THE PEOPLE!
Huey P. Newton,
SUPREME COMMANDER,
Black Panther Party

Does Your Mama Know About Me?

In the following essay, which appeared originally in 1992, Essex Hemphill protests the discrimination by white gays against gay African American men. But his essay also calls on black gay men to return to the African American community to help confront issues such as AIDS, which afflicts black people regardless of gender orientation.

At the baths, certain bars, in bookstores and cruising zones, Black men were welcome because these constructions of pleasure allowed the races to mutually explore sexual fantasies, and, after all, the Black man engaging in such a construction only needed to whip out a penis of almost any size to obtain the rapt attention withheld from him in other social and political structures of the gay community. These sites of pleasure were more tolerant of Black men because they enhanced the sexual ambiance, but that same tolerance did not always continue once the sun began to rise.

Open fraternizing at a level suggesting companionship or love between the races was not tolerated in the light of day. Terms such as "dinge queen," for white men who prefer Black men, and "snow queen," for Black men who prefer white men, were created by a gay community that obviously could not be trusted to believe its own rhetoric concerning brotherhood, fellowship, and dignity. Only an entire community's silence, complicity, and racial apathy is capable of reinforcing these conditions.

Some of the best minds of my generation would have us believe that AIDS has brought the gay and lesbian community closer and infused it with a more democratic mandate. That is only a partial truth, which further underscores the fact that the gay community still operates from a one-eyed, one gender, one color perception of community that is most likely to recognize blond before Black, but seldom the two together.

Some of the best minds of my generation believe AIDS has made the gay community a more responsible social construction, but what AIDS really manages to do is clearly point out how significant are the cultural and economic differences between us; differences so extreme that Black men suffer a disproportionate number of AIDS deaths in communities with very sophisticated gay health care services.

The best gay minds of my generation believe that we speak as one voice and dream one dream, but we are not monolithic. We are not even respectful of one another's differences...

We are communities engaged in a fragile coexistence if we are anything all. Our most significant coalitions have been created in the realm of sex. What is most clear for Black gay men is this: we have to do for ourselves now and for one another now, what no one has ever done for us. We have to be there for one another and trust less the adhesions of kisses and semen to bind us. Our only sure guarantee of survival is that which we construct from our own self-determination. White gay men may only be able to understand and respond to oppression as it relates to their ability to obtain orgasm without intrusion from the church and state. White gay men are only "other" in society when they choose to come out of the closet. But all Black men are treated as "other" regardless of whether we sleep with men or women – our Black skin automatically marks us as "other."

Look around, brothers. There is rampant killing in our communities. Drug addiction and drug trafficking overwhelm us. The blood of young Black men runs curbside in a steady flow. The bodies of Black infants crave crack, not the warmth of a mother's love. The nation's prisons are reservations and shelters for Black men. An entire generation of Black youths is being destroyed before our eyes. We cannot witness this in silence and apathy and claim our hands are bloodless. We are a wandering tribe that needs to go home before home is gone. We should not continue standing in line to be admitted into spaces that don't want us there. We cannot continue to exist without clinics, political organizations, human services, and cultural institutions that we create to support, sustain, and affirm us.

Our mothers and fathers are waiting for us. Our sisters and brothers are waiting. Our communities are waiting for us to come home. They need our love, our talents and skills, and we need theirs. They may not understand everything about us, but they will remain ignorant, misinformed, and lonely for us, and we for them, for as long as we stay away, hiding in communities that have never really welcomed us or the gifts we bring.

Out of Africa: African Immigration to the United States

Approximately 1.7 million people in the United States claim descent from the 640,000 immigrants who have arrived in the United States from African since 1970. This vignette describes the rapid growth of that population and traces the differences and similarities with Americans of African descent who arrived in the colonial era and with Caribbean immigrants who represent a different wave of immigration.

Over the past 30 years more Africans have come voluntarily to this country than during the entire era of the transatlantic slave trade that transported an estimated half a million men, women, and children to these shores. But this contemporary migration – although larger in strictly numerical terms, and concentrated over a much shorter period-forms only a trickle in the total stream of immigrants to the United States. Nevertheless, small as it is still today, the African community has been steadily and rapidly increasing. Sub-Saharan Africans have recently acquired a high level of visibility in many cities. Close-knit, attached to their cultures, and prompt to seize the educational and professional opportunities of their host country, African immigrants have established themselves as one of the most dynamic and entrepreneurial groups in the United States.

Who are the migrants and why do they come? Immigration from sub-Saharan Africa dates back to the 1860s when men from Cape Verde, the then Portuguese controlled islands off the coast of Senegal, made their way to Massachusetts. They were seamen and most were employed as whalers. Women soon followed, and after the demise of whale hunting, Cape-Verdeans worked mostly in textile mills and cranberry bogs. A small number of African students sent by Christian missions and churches to historically black colleges and universities were also present from the end of the 19th century. The trend continued in the early 20th century. Nnamdi Azikiwe, the first Nigerian president, and Kwame Nkrumah, Ghana's first president, both studied at Lincoln University and pursued graduate studies at the University of Pennsylvania.

Traditionally, Africans had primarily migrated to their former colonial powers-Great Britain, France, and Portugal – and more than a million Africans presently live in Europe. But beginning in the late 1970s, these countries froze immigration due to economic slowdowns. The United States became an option.

At the same time, increasing numbers of students and professionals decided to remain in America due to political and economic problems on the continent.

Concurrently, the mounting debts, sluggish growth, exploding populations and high unemployment at home were pushing many Africans to seek their fortunes elsewhere. In the 1990s, emigration was also spurred by the Structural Adjustment Programs imposed by the International Monetary Fund and the World Bank, which resulted in cuts in education and health services, the discharge of public servants, private sector bankruptcies, and a decrease in middle-class standards of living within African nations. In addition, in 1994 more than a dozen French-speaking countries devalued their currencies by 50 percent, resulting in a restructuring of the public sector, numerous layoffs, more bankruptcies, and fewer prospects for college graduates.

Emigrants were not only pushed out of their countries, they were also pulled to the United States. A number of favorable immigration policies enabled them to make the journey in much greater numbers than before.

Census Department estimates of immigrants, particularly those without documentation, are traditionally unreliable. For example, the 1990 census counted 2,287 Senegalese, even though various studies showed at least 10,000 living in New York City. The 2000 census reports between 511,000 and 746,000 sub-Saharan Africans, with West Africans (36 percent) in the lead, followed by East Africans (24 percent). About 6 percent of the sub-Saharan Africans are South Africans, many of whom are white. A small percentage of East Africans are of Asian origin.

Nationwide, 1.7 million people claim sub-Saharan ancestry. Africans now represent 6 percent of all the immigrants to the United States. It is a recent phenomenon; about 57 percent immigrated between 1990 and 2000. People of sub-Saharan African ancestry now represent almost 5 percent of the African-American community. Those who were actually born in Africa form 1.6 percent of the country's black population. Over the past ten years, this group has increased 134 percent.

Africans are dispersed throughout the country, and in no state are they fewer than 150. New York has the largest African community, followed by California, Texas, and Maryland. However, the District of Columbia, Maryland, and Rhode Island have the highest percentages of Africans in their total populations. With 136,000 officially recorded immigrants, Nigerians are the number-one sub-Saharan African community; Ethiopians (69,500) and Ghanaians (65,600) come far behind.

Although media coverage of African immigrants is most often devoted to the refugees, they represent a minority of the African community. From 1990 to 2001, 101,000 African refugees-10 percent of all refugees who entered the country-were admitted to the United States. More than 40,000 were Somalis, and close to 21,000 came from Ethiopia, while 18,500 arrived from the Sudan.

Africans are highly urban; 95 percent live in a metropolitan area and, like most immigrants, they tend to settle where other countrymen have preceded. A few Senegalese put down roots in New York in the early 1980s; today most Senegalese can still be found there. A large number of Nigerians reside in Texas. Their homeland is a major oil producer and they have experience in that industry. Washington, D.C., the headquarters of the World Bank, the International Monetary Fund, and other international organizations, has attracted large numbers of highly educated Africans.

The Twin Cities, St. Paul and Minneapolis, have America's largest Somali population, estimated at 30,000. Many are refugees relocated directly from camps in East Africa. But the overwhelming majority, attracted by job opportunities, family reunification and educational possibilities, are now coming in a secondary migration from Texas, Virginia, and California.

Because sub-Saharan Africans live in higher-income...areas than other people of African descent, they are largely segregated from African Americans and Caribbeans. Although this trend is somewhat in decline, it still holds true for New York and Atlanta, two cities where Africans are quite numerous.

...Besides their migration experience, the most significant characteristic of the African immigrants is that they are the most educated group in the nation. Almost half have bachelor's degrees or higher compared to 26 percent of native-born Americans. Contrary to popular belief, the most substantial part of African emigration is thus directly linked to the "brain drain," not to poverty. In fact, 98 percent are high school graduates.

Sub-Saharan nations bear the great cost of sending students abroad who will continue their education in the West and may not return home during their most productive years. As renowned Nigerian computer scientist Philippe Emeagwali puts it: "The African education budget is nothing but a supplement to the American education budget. In essence, Africa is giving developmental assistance to the wealthier western nations which makes the rich nations richer and the poor nations poorer."

According to the United Nations Economic Commission for Africa and the International Organization for Migration, 27,000 intellectual Africans left the continent for industrialized nations between 1960 and 1975, while 40,000 followed them from 1975 to 1984. Between 1985 and 1990 the figure skyrocketed to 60,000, and has averaged 20,000 annually ever since.

At least 60 percent of physicians trained in Ghana during the 1980s have left their country, and half of Zimbabwe's social workers trained in the past ten years are now working in Great Britain.... This substantial brain drain is a significant obstacle to development, but African expatriates stress that poor economic conditions and political repression are often responsible for their leaving. They also point out that low salaries, lack of adequate equipment and research facilities, and the need to provide for their extended families are the reasons for their emigration, not individualistic motivations.

Besides professionals who work in the United States, more than 32,000 undergraduate and graduate students from sub-Saharan Africa are enrolled in American universities. They pump more than half a billion dollars into American universities and the general economy each year. As a point of comparison, the total U.S. economic aid to sub-Saharan Africa is slightly more than $1 billion annually.

A significant proportion of African immigrants have "made it" in this country. Besides a few millionaires, 38 percent hold professional and managerial positions. The Africans' average annual incomes are higher than those of the foreign-born population as a whole. More than 45 percent earn between $35,000 and $75,000 a year, and — because of the immigrants' disproportionately high education levels exceed the median income of African Americans and Caribbeans.

The fact remains, however, that the Africans' income levels, high though they may seem, do not mirror their academic achievements. As the most highly educated community in the nation, they should occupy many more top-level professional and managerial positions. There are several reasons for this. Degrees earned overseas are sometimes not readily transferable, so the immigrants must enroll in school once more, holding low-wage jobs to pay for their schooling. "It is at times degrading when you come here and find that all the education you have from home does not mean anything here. It is a shock. We had to start over from nothing," sums up a Sudanese social worker in Philadelphia.

Others, though possessing outstanding qualifications, cannot find adequate employment because of their status as undocumented aliens. Finally, the Africans must confront the same problems as other people of color-racism and job discrimination that result in lower incomes, the employment of overqualified people in lesser positions, and the lack of adequate promotion. Although unemployment is rare among Africans, poverty does exist, particularly among the undocumented who are underpaid and live precarious, stressful lives. But poverty is usually mitigated by solidarity and communal life, as compatriots.

Godwin Ajala at the World Trade Center

Godwin Ajala, one of the thousands who perished in the World Trade Center attack on September 11, 2001, is described in the following article. Ajala, a native of Nigeria, was typical of the African immigrants who have arrived in the United States since 1990.

G odwin Ajala was a striver. Hard work was his ticket to the American Dream. And he strove mightily to reach it – even at the cost of his life. A lawyer in his native Nigeria, Ajala came to the U.S. in 1995, during a time of political unrest in his country. His goal: pass the New York state bar exam and practice law in New York City. It was against great odds. He was a stranger in a strange land with no money. But he rose to the challenge with grit and determination – working odd jobs to pay for his legal studies while supporting his wife and three children in Nigeria.

Ajala eventually found steady work as a Manhattan security guard. But fortune turned to tragedy on Sept. 11 when 33-year-old Ajala became one of

SOURCE: Doug Tsuruoka, "Godwin Ajala, an American Success Story Cut Short," Investor's Business Daily, December 11, 2001, A04. Copyright © Investor's Business Daily, Inc. Reprinted with permission of Investor's Business Daily, Inc.

11 guards, employed by a company called Summit Security Services Inc., who died at the World Trade Center.

Scores of elevator operators, guards, porters, food handlers and other service workers perished in the attack. Like Ajala, huge numbers of them hailed from nations such as Mexico, China and Albania. All could be called American success stories in the making until they were cut down that day.

The son of a retailer from a small town in Eastern Nigeria, Ajala was too poor to attend a U.S. law school. So he found another way to pursue his goal. He sank his salary into prep classes for the bar exam and tried to pass the test on his own. It was the same verve he showed in winning a law degree in Nigeria. Though untrained in U.S. law, Ajala bet his knowledge of Commonwealth Law would help him bridge the gap. After relentless effort, he was close to proving himself right.

By day, Ajala rode elevators and walked floors of the 110-story tower at the Two World Trade Center, helping secure the building and attending to small emergencies. "He worked as a guard from 6 a.m. to 2 p.m. in the afternoon. Then he came back and studied late into the night," said Christopher Onuoha, who shared a modest apartment with Ajala in Queens, N.Y. Outside class, Ajala spent his nights in study, grappling with legal terms and principles. He mastered the vagaries of contract and criminal law, with hours of reading and note taking. When he made errors, he tried to learn from them. Ajala accepted without complaint that he had to pay his dues, despite already having been a lawyer in Nigeria. Ajala flunked the New York bar exam three times, common in a state where the exam's especially tough. But he never gave up. "He was hoping to pass it in February when the Trade Center happened," Onuoha said. "He had nothing. No good dress clothes . . . nothing. But he kept trying."

Still, for all the hardship in Ajala's life, friends recall a caring, spiritual man with a sense of duty to his job. A devout churchgoer, Ajala believed his focus had to be on others before himself. He was quick to extend a helpful hand to friends and strangers – using his experiences as an émigré to encourage them through life's struggles. He was always ready to extend the odd dollar or the meager possession despite his own needs. He made sure he spent less money on himself so he could send money back home.

"He was a generous, caring person, a sociable guy. I miss him a lot – every little thing," Onuoha said. Though Ajala was already sending thousands of dollars home a month to support his wife Victoria, and his three children, he felt duty-bound to help the children of other relatives in Nigeria through college. "He was helping four or five of his relatives' kids through school," said security guard Christopher Iwuanyanwa, a close friend.

Sept. 11 would have been one of Ajala's last days of work before taking a trip to Nigeria to visit his wife and children. The trip would have been a stepping-stone to bringing them to the U.S. – something Ajala looked forward to for years. Ajala's spark inspired his peers. He was elected a steward for the Service Employees International Union Local 32 BJ, which represents 70,000 porters, guards, doormen and other service workers. He put his legal training to good use. Amid tangled union and management politics, Ajala used his skills to unravel legal issues for other union members. "He never supported a measure that would have a bad effect. He had integrity," Iwuanyanwa said.

All those points came to the fore on Sept. 11. Ajala was helping evacuate thousands of people from a street-level security post inside the lobby of Two World Trade Center when the second plane hit the building. It was his moment of truth. "He was on the ground floor. He could easily have run away," Iwuanyanwa said. Ajala didn't run. He came out of the burning tower only once before it fell – to hold the door open for people running out. Then he went back inside to guide more people out of the blazing structure. That was the last time anyone saw Godwin Ajala alive.

Barack Obama's Keynote Address at the Democratic National Convention, 2004

On July 27, 2004 Illinois Senatorial Candidate Barack Obama was propelled onto the national stage when he was chosen to give the keynote speech at the Democratic National Convention assembled in Boston. Obama, then an Illinois State Senator, easily won his campaign the following November and became the fifth African American to sit in the United States Senate. Part of his keynote address appears below. To read this speech in its entirety, please visit TheBlackPast at www.blackpast.org.

On behalf of the great state of Illinois, crossroads of a nation, Land of Lincoln, let me express my deepest gratitude for the privilege of addressing this convention. Tonight is a particular honor for me because – let's face it – my presence on this stage is pretty unlikely. My father was a foreign student, born and raised in a small village in Kenya. He grew up herding goats, went to school in a tin-roof shack. His father – my grandfather – was a cook, a domestic servant to the British.

But my grandfather had larger dreams for his son. Through hard work and perseverance my father got a scholarship to study in a magical place, America, that shone as a beacon of freedom and opportunity to so many who had come before. While studying here, my father met my mother. She was born in a town on the other side of the world, in Kansas. Her father worked on oil rigs and farms through most of the Depression. The day after Pearl Harbor my grandfather signed up for duty; joined Patton's army, marched across Europe. Back home, my grandmother raised their baby and went to work on a bomber assembly line. After the war, they studied on the G.I. Bill, bought a house through F.H.A., and

SOURCE: Vital Speeches of the Day, 70:20 (August 1, 2004), pp. 623–625.

later moved west all the way to Hawaii in search of opportunity. And they, too, had big dreams for their daughter. A common dream, born of two continents.

My parents shared not only an improbable love, they shared an abiding faith in the possibilities of this nation. They would give me an African name, Barack, or "blessed," believing that in a tolerant America your name is no barrier to success. They imagined me going to the best schools in the land, even though they weren't rich, because in a generous America you don't have to be rich to achieve your potential. They are both passed away now. And yet, I know that, on this night, they look down on me with great pride.

I stand here today, grateful for the diversity of my heritage, aware that my parents' dreams live on in my two precious daughters. I stand here knowing that my story is part of the larger American story, that I owe a debt to all of those who came before me, and that, in no other country on earth, is my story even possible.

Tonight, we gather to affirm the greatness of our nation – not because of the height of our skyscrapers, or the power of our military, or the size of our economy. Our pride is based on a very simple premise, summed up in a declaration made over two hundred years ago: "We hold these truths to be self-evident, that all men are created equal. That they are endowed by their Creator with certain inalienable rights. That among these are life, liberty and the pursuit of happiness. . ."

This year, in this election, we are called to reaffirm our values and our commitments, to hold them against a hard reality and see how we are measuring up, to the legacy of our forbearers, and the promise of future generations. And fellow Americans, Democrats, Republicans, Independents – I say to you tonight: we have more work to do. More work to do for the workers I met in Galesburg, Ill., who are losing their union jobs at the Maytag plant that's moving to Mexico, and now are having to compete with their own children for jobs that pay seven bucks an hour. . .

Now don't get me wrong. The people I meet – in small towns and big cities, in diners and office parks – they don't expect government to solve all their problems. They know they have to work hard to get ahead – and they want to. Go into the white collar counties around Chicago, and people will tell you they don't want their tax money wasted, by a welfare agency or by the Pentagon.

Go into any inner city neighborhood, and folks will tell you that government alone can't teach our kids to learn – they know that parents have to teach, that children can't achieve unless we raise their expectations and turn off the television sets and eradicate the slander that says a black youth with a book is acting white. They know those things.

People don't expect government to solve all their problems. But they sense, deep in their bones, that with just a slight change in priorities, we can make sure that every child in America has a decent shot at life, and that the doors of opportunity remain open to all. They know we can do better. And they want that choice. . .

You know, a while back, I met a young man named Shamus [Seamus?] in a V.F.W. Hall in East Moline, Ill. He was a good-looking kid, six two, six three, clear eyed, with an easy smile. He told me he'd joined the Marines, and was heading to Iraq the following week. And as I listened to him explain why he'd enlisted, the absolute faith he had in our country and its leaders, his devotion to duty and service, I thought this young man was all that any of us might hope for in a child. But then I asked myself: Are we serving Shamus as well as he is serving us? I thought of the 900 men and women – sons and daughters, husbands and wives, friends and neighbors, who won't be returning to their own hometowns. I thought of the families I've met who were struggling to get by without a loved one's full income, or whose loved ones had returned with a limb missing or nerves shattered, but who still lacked long-term health benefits because they were Reservists.

When we send our young men and women into harm's way, we have a solemn obligation not to fudge the numbers or shade the truth about why they're going, to care for their families while they're gone, to tend to the soldiers upon their return, and to never ever go to war without enough troops to win the war, secure the peace, and earn the respect of the world.

Now let me be clear. Let me be clear. We have real enemies in the world. These enemies must be found. They must be pursued – and they must be defeated. John Kerry knows this. And just as Lieutenant Kerry did not hesitate to risk his life to protect the men who served with him in Vietnam, President Kerry will not hesitate one moment to use our military might to keep America safe and secure. John Kerry believes in America. And he knows that it's not enough for just some of us to prosper. For alongside our famous individualism, there's another ingredient in the American saga. A belief that we're all connected as one people. If there is a child on the south side of Chicago who can't read, that matters to me, even if it's not my child. If there's a senior citizen somewhere who can't pay for their prescription drugs, and has to choose between medicine and the rent, that makes my life poorer, even if it's not my grandparent. If there's an Arab American family being rounded up without benefit of an attorney or due process, that threatens my civil liberties.

It is that fundamental belief, it is that fundamental belief, I am my brother's keeper, I am my sister's keeper that makes this country work. It's what allows us to pursue our individual dreams and yet still come together as one American family. *E pluribus unum.* Out of many, one.

Now even as we speak, there are those who are preparing to divide us, the spin masters, the negative ad peddlers who embrace the politics of anything goes. Well, I say to them tonight, there is not a liberal America and a conservative America – there is the United States of America. There is not a Black America and a White America and Latino America and Asian America – there's the United States of America.

The pundits, the pundits like to slice-and-dice our country into Red States and Blue States; Red States for Republicans, Blue States for Democrats. But I've got news for them, too. We worship an awesome God in the Blue States, and we don't like federal agents poking around in our libraries in the Red States. We coach Little League in the Blue States and yes, we've got some gay friends in the Red States. There are patriots who opposed the war in Iraq and there are patriots who supported the war in Iraq. . .

I believe that we can give our middle class relief and provide working families with a road to opportunity. I believe we can provide jobs to the jobless, homes to the homeless, and reclaim young people in cities across America from violence and despair. I believe that we have a righteous wind at our backs and that as we stand on the crossroads of history, we can make the right choices, and meet the challenges that face us.

America! Tonight, if you feel the same energy that I do, if you feel the same urgency that I do, if you feel the same passion I do, if you feel the same hopefulness that I do — if we do what we must do, then I have no doubts that all across the country, from Florida to Oregon, from Washington to Maine, the people will rise up in November, and John Kerry will be sworn in as president, and John Edwards will be sworn in as vice president, and this country will reclaim its promise, and out of this long political darkness a brighter day will come.

Thank you very much everybody. God bless you. Thank you. Thank you, and God bless America.

African Americans and Environmental History: A Manifesto

Carl Anthony, an official with the Ford Foundation, former professor of architecture at the University of California-Berkeley and founder of Urban Habitat in 1979, wrote "Reflections on the Purposes and Meanings of African American Environmental History" for the anthology To Love the Wind And Rain. *In the article he described the crucial importance of African Americans to the discourse on the environment, both historically and in the contemporary era. Part of the article appears here.*

∎ ∎ ∎ **M**uch of environmental history has been written out of concerns for the fate of nature in Western culture — the destruction of the forests; the degradation of landscapes; the loss of wolves, bears, cats, and birds; the uprooting of indigenous people. These concerns should and will continue to have force. Yet environmental history from an African American must incorporate an additional theme that is typically overlooked: the importance of inclusion of the stories of African Americans who helped to lay the foundations of the nation, in the face of an atmosphere of hostility and disregard...

The earth is the ground we walk on, the sea and air, the soil that nourishes us, the sphere of mortal life, the third planet in order from the sun, near the center of the Milky Way galaxy. Everything that we do, or aim to do, is governed by our relationship with the earth – to its inspiration and resources, to our consciousness of its relationship to the cosmos, to our affinity with human and other-than-human life. Our knowledge and affinity with the earth, in all of its richness of life and diversity, stretches from the tiniest particles, waves and cells, to its plant forms and ecosystems, its rivers, mountains, and seas, to the majesty of our solar system, galaxies, and outer edges of the universe. The knowledge of the earth, and of our place in its long evolution, can give us a sense of identity and belonging that can act as a corrective to the hubris and pride that have been weapons of our oppressors . . .

What follows from this realization? I began to conduct a little internal audit, a quick survey to think of how this fourteen-billion-year framework could help me to be clearer about my own being. What sort of orientation do I need to have toward these fourteen billion years of life in order to do what I need to be doing in my daily life and my practice?

Around that time I came across a very important book by Thomas Berry, called *The Dream of the Earth*. Berry proposed that, in order to get our bearings in terms of our current ecological crisis, we need a new story about who human beings are in relationship to the story of the earth. Berry outlines the story of the earth and the place of human beings in it. I really liked that. It gave me a starting point for working through these issues.

At the same time, I found I had an uneasy feeling about the book because it didn't appear to include black people at all. There was wonderful talk of Native Americans – the ecumenical spirit, the struggle against patriarchy, etc., were reflected – but where were the black people? In fact, African Americans' experiences were not included in *any* of the environmental literature I could get my hands on about people's relationship to the land. Thoreau, David Brower . . . none of them reflected black people's experience.

How could this be? What was I to do with this?

One day, while reading a Civil War book, I came across a map of North America showing where black people lived on the eve of the Civil War. There is a coastal belt that stretches from the tidewaters of Virginia to the Atlantic coast, to middle Georgia, Alabama, Mississippi, Louisiana, and Texas. Along this particular belt were counties that were 50 to 75 percent black.

At the same time, while reading about the earth's evolution, I found a map of the North American continent as it was shaped fifty million years ago. The continent was the same shape then as it is today, with one exception: the areas where black people lived just prior to the Civil War were underwater . . .

What does all this mean? How does this set of facts illuminate anything of significance? What I concluded was that there is a much bigger story about my relationship to North America than the story I was carrying in my head. The story in my head was that black people were brought here in 1619 by some pirating Dutchmen and then forced to work as slaves for hundreds of years. By no means am I saying that this is not a central part of the story. Yet there is also a much bigger story . . .

As I began to think about the origins of some of my African ancestors, I came to realize what should be obvious to everyone: In some sense, we are all African American. Everyone has African heritage. What happened to that part of the story? What about the first million years of human evolution? The dominant theory of the history of how the human race emerged, in the rainforest and savannah regions of Africa, is a central part of the narrative that needs to be articulated . . .

This reflection on the elements of African American environmental history calls attention to much that has been missing in the conventional story about people and the land in North America. The hidden narrative of race is more than a collection of episodes and facts that have been overlooked. The lesson that comes out of this ensemble of facts has to do with the fragmentation and disruption of personal and community life, and therefore, the quest for wholeness.

African Americans have a long, if not well-understood, relationship to the land in North America. The ancestors of African Americans were uprooted from the land in Africa, transported thousands of miles away, and forced to work the land without remuneration for the benefit of another people. But African Americans survived, and they now live in the cities. . . . The city, in its multiple manifestations, is the largest human invention on the planet. . . . This impulse of species to come together has a deeply rooted biological basis, as evidenced by schools of fish, flocks of birds, etc. We are following a deep-seated trait that is grounded in all of these other species.

The city is also the largest intervention of humans in relationship to the natural world. We shape the cities, and the cities in turn shape us. An inquiry into the character of this relationship necessarily involves an understanding of ecological dependence of urban populations upon the hinterlands for food, building materials, energy, and disposal of wastes.

The connection between the city and the rural environment has always been historically clear. What hasn't been clear is the relationship of this process to the people who lived in those places. You could never live in the cities if the food, the drinking water, the forests that make paper and buildings, the natural resources to produce electricity, weren't coming from somewhere. City building has been based on extracting resources from the surrounding areas, and on exploiting the people who are making these resources available without giving them anything back, without honoring them or their story.

We need a new story about race and place in America. This new story is not only about toxic waste dumps and hazardous materials; it is about the fundamental right of a people to have a relationship with all of creation . . .

All people have their story. Every people comes from a story that is grounded in the evolution of the earth. We all need to come to terms with our own stories, while knowing that we share a common longing and a common struggle: everybody is struggling for a sense of feeling at home on this planet.

In the Eye of the Storm: Race
and Hurricane Katrina

In an article titled "A City of Lies," Rolling Stone *reporter Scott Spencer discussed the aftermath of Hurricane Katrina.*

Is it too soon to suggest that half of what was ever said about New Orleans was a bald-faced lie? Now, with the massive destruction visited upon that fragile, beautiful city, there is a rush to immerse our collective memories of it in a warm bath of nostalgia. Richard Ford, for example, writing in the New York Times, mourns for "our great iconic city, so graceful, livable, insular, self-delighted, eccentric... " It's true: New Orleans is one of those cities about which songs are written, a place that has offered a refuge from the fundamentalist South, a haven to artists, gays and sundry misfits from all over, who found in this permissive port city a place to live, even as the real business of the port – the unloading of slaves, or coffee, or oil – was conducted with ruthless efficiency. Even those New Orleanians who moved north remained enraptured by memories of home. The sound of a steam whistle, the smell of an oncoming rain, the stifling heat of a sticky day was always enough to plunge the New Orleanians I knew into a bout of homesickness.

Surely, a great deal needs to be granted to a city that can inspire such longing, but the epic inequality we saw when the storm tore the Mardi Gras mask off that make-believe city was certainly there all along. When the vast majority of those who are most profoundly afflicted by the storm and its aftermath are African-American; when the city's primary shelter is compared to the hull of a slave ship by Jesse Jackson; when white leaders such as Rep. Richard Baker, a Louisiana Republican, are quoted as saying, "We finally cleaned up public housing in New Orleans. We couldn't do it, but God did," it is impossible to escape the conclusion that – we are once again witnessing a playing out of the deepest and most persistent of all the American tragedies: racism.

Less than two weeks before Katrina, the Associated Press reported a local university experiment meant to determine the attitude that residents in a poor New Orleans neighborhood have toward violence and the police. Seven hundred blank rounds were shot off in a single afternoon, and sure enough there was not one call made for help. In a city where the murder rate was nearly ten times the national average for similar-size cities, and where the police force has earned a reputation not only for being on the take but for rape and murder for hire, citizens in poor neighborhoods were stranded in dire circumstances long before Katrina swept through.

Was New Orleans more racist than other cities? It's a hard thing to measure. But it was a city with a forty percent illiteracy rate, in a state where 50,000 children were absent from school every single day, where 350 kids dropped out every week, never to return. One of my closest companions fled the public schools – and the city itself – at age seventeen. During the next twenty years, we visited her old hometown regularly. In the beginning, despite her words of caution, I was unprepared for the casual racism we encountered. On the streets I saw a population in love with soul food and soul music, with a talent for pleasure and a predilection toward sexual irony; in the drawing rooms, something quite different. On a tour through one graceful home, the lady of the house pointed out a room that had been transformed from "nigger pink" to a more neutral shade, then served us soul food – red beans and rice.

Just as the city had learned to live below sea level and build its stately mansions with the hope that the levees would stave off the forces of nature forever, many of the white people of New Orleans had figured out a way to enjoy black culture while protecting themselves from the people whose history that culture represented. If the African American citizens of New Orleans were frightened, then so were their white neighbors. I hardly met a white [person] who didn't own a gun, who didn't, when venturing out after dark, keep in touch with one another on their cell phones, like astronauts maintaining radio contact with planet Earth.

Catastrophes reveal the nature of not only people but of governments and places. When New York was attacked on September 11th, there was throughout the city a sense of passionate civic pride. Here was a tragedy that cut across class and ethnic lines – bankers and busboys died together, or were saved together – and this democracy created a sense of commonality and equality in the city. Now, four years later, many in New York still look back at 9/11 and its after-math as one of the proudest moments in the city's history. Will the same be said by the people of New Orleans?

Even as we fervently hope for the city's speedy recovery, it's impossible not to wonder how the hucksters, hometown boosters and nostalgia merchants will ever induce anyone to forget the horrifying, shameful images of thousands of stranded African Americans trying to stay alive in a city whose well-off residents had already fled, a city where the likelihood of survival could be accurately predicted by class and race.

When New Orleans is rebuilt, I wonder if its reputation as a place "that care forgot," as Richard Ford ironically put it in his Times piece, can ever be restored now that we've seen the truth. And when the people return, I wonder if some of them will have more trouble than ever looking their neighbors in the eye.